GARLAND
PUBLICATIONS
IN
COMPARATIVE
LITERATURE

JEANNÉE P. SACKEN

"a certain Slant of light"

Aesthetics of
First-Person Narration
in Gide and Cather

GARLAND PUBLISHING, INC.
NEW YORK & LONDON
1985

Library of Congress Cataloging in Publication Data

Sacken, Jeannée P., 1953–
"A certain slant of light."

(Garland publications in comparative literature)
Bibliography: p.
1. First person narrative.   2. Gide, André, 1869–1951
—Technique.   3. Cather, Willa, 1873–1947—Technique.
I. Title.   II. Series.
PN3383.P64S23   1985   809.3'923   84-48361
ISBN 0-8240-6714-2 (alk. paper)

The volumes in this series are printed on
acid-free, 250-year-life paper.

Printed in the United States of America

"a certain Slant of light":
Aesthetics of First-Person Narration
in Gide and Cather

Jeannée P. Sacken
Rochester Institute of Technology

For
C. Hugh Holman

PREFACE

"Why Gide and Cather?" I am frequently asked. Or, by my
colleagues in English departments, "What do Cather and Gide have in
common?" The questions I continue to anticipate, the questions
that more closely concern the present study, usually remain
unposed, perhaps even unformulated by my interlocutors: "Why first-
person narration?" "Why phenomenology and structuralism?" In my
eagerness to discuss narratology, I am sometimes rather flip in my
response to the Gide-Cather question: "Well, actually, they have
very little, if anything, in common." To be more exact, thanks to
the memoirs of her friend and companion, Elizabeth Shepley Sergeant,
we do know that Willa Cather at least possessed a copy of André
Gide's La Porte étroite, a gift from Sergeant herself. Whether or
not she ever read the récit, however, is a question that must go un-
answered. But, although certain similarities and vast differences
in story, plot, character, theme, and setting do emerge during my
readings of these two texts, I do not claim to be writing about Gide

and Cather. I claim instead to be writing about the aesthetic problematic of narration in general and about first-person narrative situations and technique in particular. Hence, I remain unable to provide an acceptable answer to the oft-posed question, "What do Cather and Gide have in common?" In response to the first question, "Why Gide and Cather?", however, I do have an answer, the serious-ness of which is often belied by my initial, unfortunately flip, slip of the tongue.

The answer to this query rests, albeit in a somewhat round-about way, in my discussion of narratology. Why first-person narration? Such an emphasis on first-person narrative situations cannot help but call to mind its third-person counterpart, a semantic misnomer designating both (1) those narrative situations in which an "invisi-ble" narrator refers to all characters by the third-person pronoun "he" or "she," by substantive nominal equivalents, or by proper names (Emma, Charles, etc.); and (2) those narrative situations in which a given character reflects the story's actions and events--that is, the reader "sees" and "experiences" the world of the text through the eyes of the character whose narrative act remains impli-cit. This longstanding opposition of narrative perspectives/points-of-view/voices has generated countless critical typologies that have each sought to categorize literary works, although not necessarily to examine the thematic dimensions and artistic effects either type of narrative situation and technique lend a given text. Depending on the individual type of first-person narrative situa-tion, of course, various different elements and dimensions may be emphasized, whether it be the personality and mediating act of the narrator, the spatial and temporal position at the moment of narra-tion, or the world and characters that are being represented. Whichever aspects are accentuated, their presence constitutes the essential distinctiveness of the first-person narrative situation; their effacement robs the text of its first-person narrational dis-tinctiveness.

First-person narration has undergone considerably fewer changes and variations during the eighteenth, nineteenth, and twentieth centuries than have other narrative techniques. The presented first-person narrator still draws attention to his or her role(s) as both storyteller and character in the text, to the act and nature of storytelling, in short, to the discourse itself. The very presence of storytelling within the story being told forces the reader, in effect, to linger over this second, artistic dimension of the text in an attempt to synthesize these narrational elements and techniques into the overall structure of the artwork. In other words, the very literariness--that which distinguishes the literary from the nonliterary work of art--is emphasized. In addition to issues of the nature of artistic communication, first-person narration in twentieth-century texts, as in its eighteenth- and nineteenth-century manifestations, is particularly appropriate for the literary presentation of such themes as the search for and the evolution of one's self; the self in relation to society; the individual's perception of his or her self; and the moral, existential, and aesthetic dilemmas and conflicts that confront the individual's struggles to define the self. Ultimately, and in this study by way of introduction, the examination of first-person narration opens a forum for the discussion of certain related theoretical issues, including the nature of fiction; the personality of the character; and the artistic, aesthetic, and thematic values generated by narrative technique.

Why structuralism and phenomenology? These two approaches to the perception, cognition, and synthesis of phenomena in life and in art represent two divergent, significant methods for the interpretation of narrative discourse. The structuralist model advanced by Gérard Genette primarily in **Figures** III was molded partly in reference to his linguistic, anthropological, and critical antecedents. Since its publication and translation into English, the model has been propounded by many and amended by several (Seymour Chatman and Mieke

Bal among others). The phenomenological model presented in the following pages is derived by me in large part from the two major works by the Polish philosopher, Roman Ingarden. Unlike Genette's method, admirable for its focused sense of crystalline finiteness, Ingarden's Literary Work of Art and Cognition of the Literary Work of Art examine in a much more general manner, the essential and distinctive nature of the literary work of art as such and the reader's aesthetic (ap)perception of the text. To formulate a phenomenological model useful for the illumination of first-person narrative situations in particular, I have, then, borrowed several key concepts which I employ against the backdrop of Ingarden's more general idea of the literary work of art as an unfolding layered structure. Also unlike Genette, Ingarden remains, for the moment at least, virtually unknown in American circles of literary criticism and theory. Whether it is due to the complexity of his theory or to the impenetrability of his sometimes Germanic sometimes Slavic mode of expression, I hope the present study and the recent work of other scholars will serve to propound what are potentially valuable critical tools. Each of these two models provides the critical reader with textual approaches for the cognition, synthesis, and appreciation of a particular type of narrative situation and its host of related narrative techniques. Some similarities and perhaps even some complementarity between the two models will undoubtedly be observed, particularly in relation to the technique of embedding. For the most part, however, the supporting theoretical foundation as well as the particular concepts and critical methods advanced represent two unique, distinctive approaches.

To return to the original, seemingly innocent question: "Why Gide and Cather?" Gide's L'Immoraliste and Cather's My Ántonia, written in the first two decades of the twentieth century, represent two important traditions in literary history: The French, which has long been recognized; and the American, which has too frequently been undervalued. These two literary works suggest two vi-

sions of the existential, moral, and artistic dilemmas confronted by
the individual in the midst of a modern world that, more often than
not, chooses to lose sight of the individual. And, what is perhaps
of the greatest importance for my immediate objectives, both Gide
and Cather chose to mediate their respective protagonist's search
for and exploration of the "Self" from a first-person narrative perspective and with a first-person voice. Why Gide and Cather? First
and foremost, because the presented worlds of their texts are projected and hence mediated by the evolving self whose very Self is
the object in question. Both Gide and Cather have structured their
stories about the "Self" to reveal the Self as subject and object,
actant and action, signifiant and signifié, seeing and doing, vision
and experience, stasis and dynamic evolution. The Self, seeing and
seen, functions as both the subject of the discourse and the object
of the story. It is Gide and Cather because L'Immoraliste and My
Antonia provide extremely workable and technically dissimilar illu-
strations for the two narrative theories I present and examine; and
because these two theories serve, in turn, to illuminate two texts
that have suffered frequent critically "naive" readings. Ultimately
and quite simply, it is Gide and Cather because their two literary
works of art lie close to my heart.

This study allows me to occupy a coveted position retrospective
to my own numerous readings and interpretations of L'Immoraliste and
My Antonia. I first encountered My Antonia in a seminar early in my
graduate student career. The novel was introduced by a renowned--
and therefore unnamed--professor of American literature who--with a
sympathetic eye to our over-taxed finances--"allowed" us to read
"any Cather novel; they're all the same." Despite such an unfortui-
tous beginning, I discovered, of course, that they are not "all the
same." A subsequent seminar, under the visionary guidance of
C. Hugh Holman, motivated me to come back to My Antonia. A biographical and historical critic himself, Hugh Holman encouraged me

in my love of Willa Cather and nurtured me in my study of narratology and Ingarden. His critical acumen, his demands for his own and my own critical rigor, always his humanity, and, until his death, his willingness to discuss and to advise helped to lay the foundation for both my doctoral dissertation and the present manuscript. For many years, Eugene H. Falk has provided immeasurable help in the formulation and refinement of my ideas, first as a teacher, and subsequently as a dissertation advisor, as a friend, and through his own important work on Ingarden and phenomenology. Edouard Morot-Sir, Diane R. Leonard, Margaret O'Connor, and Joel Black have all read earlier drafts of the present manuscript and have offered valuable suggestions and words of encouragement. My thinking as well as my expression of that thought has benefitted from my students' constant and always welcome questions and ideas and from my participation in and respondents' discussion of my work at several conferences and seminars in recent years.

Most important, my work and my life have been enriched by John Scott Strickland, my most valued critic and most ardent supporter. His faith, love and wonderful cooking--offered unstintingly throughout the writing of this book and his own dissertation--bespeak a devotion and an inspiration that I will cherish always. And, finally, the "troops"--Nat Turner, Rockefeller, Joe Hill, Sophia, and, most recently, Vanzetti and Ántonia--have made this book and this acknowledgement a challenge to write by virtue of their penchant for lap- and draftsitting.

A CRITICAL ASSESSMENT

After reading **Les Nourritures terrestres,** Oscar Wilde tried to exact a promise from its author, André Gide, never to write again from the first-person perspective: "In art, you see, there is no first person."[1] Twenty-three years later, Marcel Proust offered Gide the same advice upon reading the anonymously published **Corydon:** "You can tell anything, but on condition that you never say: I."[2] Of course, neither Gide nor Proust followed this advice, but the motive behind the recommendation is fairly clear: Critical and popular readers have long correlated the presence of the first-person narrator's "I" with an autobiographical intent on the part of the author, frequently identifying the narrator-protagonist as merely a mask to "protect" the disguised author. As Wilde's and Proust's cautionary responses to the implicit and explicit homosexuality in Gide's works imply, the very presence of first-person narration is often believed to authenticate the presented world of the text. Indeed, numerous fictional memoirs and lyrical, confessional, and epistolary novels have attracted a wide readership precisely because of the suggested authenticity and, thus, intimacy, of the presented characters and events. But the narrative situation with its conventionalized "I" narrator that titillatingly alludes to the "authenticity" of the presented world is often unconsciously and naively interpreted by readers as an implicit contract that the work in question is not fiction, but nonfiction. And hence, what such writers as Gide, Proust, Joyce, Camus, and Cather--and before them, writers from Chateaubriand to Dostoevsky--crafted as fiction has often been read and continues to be read as autobiography or as imaginative works that are simultaneously fictional and autobiographical, marked as it were by "an oscillating movement between these two poles."[3] Ultimately, it would seem, that numerous readers--both critically schooled and untrained--have managed to lose sight of the fictive convention of first-person narration with its fictional allusion to reality, choosing instead to transform the narrative situation and its related techniques into an affirmation of real people and real events.

Ultimately, the autobiographical overtones and the implicit suggestions of authenticity that have long been attributed to the first-person perspective give rise to questions of ontic and generic significance: Is the first-person narrator to be defined as an indicator and affirmation of historical reality, and, as such, belonging exclusively to nonfiction with no discernable artistic function? Or, is it a technique of fiction, a technique whose characteristic properties and emergent qualities merit artistic evaluation?

A number of issues demand attention in a study of first-person narration. Not only must we respond to the theoretical opposition to considering the "I" of the first-person narrator-protagonist in relation to other types of narrative situations, we must also investigate the conventionalized narrative code associated with the perspective, a code that differentiates between the spatial, temporal, aspectual, and representational dimensions of first-person narration. In addition, we must explore the major shifts in the popular and critical judgments about the function of the novel in general, and how those different functions have affected the reception accorded first-person narration.

ONE

Although first-person narration has often been construed to be at odds with the basic tenets of fiction, the first-person narrator has been a widely used narrative technique in prose fiction since the rise of the novel in the eighteenth century. The critical assessment of its value has been both positive and negative, the judgments varying with the shifts in popular and critical opinions about the function of the novel and, consequently, the function of novels narrated in the first-person. It is precisely this critical reception of first-person novels and not the technique itself that has undergone considerable fluctuation. For as Michal Glowinski concludes, first-person narration in the novel "has been subject to comparatively slight changes; its structure demonstrates considerable stability and even an inability to undergo radical transformations."[4] By and large, experimentation with the novel's form and narrative technique has occurred in other types of narrative situation--those corresponding to the grammatical categories of third- or even second-person, for example, but not first-person. A survey of European texts allows Glowinski to assert that: "The undoubtable fact is that the first-person novel of the mid-twentieth century has more in common with that of the mid-eighteenth century than the third-person novels of the respective periods."[5]

Evaluation of first-person narrative technique and the novel as a genre has not, however, always been based on either artistic or aesthetic criteria. Indeed, Georges May maintains that in eigh-teenth-century France, a number of critical attacks were leveled against the novel in general because the newly emerging genre appeared to lack both definitive formal principles and an artistic standard: "Le roman [était considéré] un genre artistiquement cor-rompu et corrupteur, parce qu'il ne se conforme à aucune des règles classiques fondées sur le respect du bon sens et du bon goût. . . . Le roman se présentait génériquement comme particulièrement vulnér-able aux coups portés au nom des valeurs esthétiques."[6] In response to this demand for compositional strictures and generic principles, some theorists sought to define the novel's function and by implica-tion establish a set of standards for its evaluation and apprecia-tion. In 1785, Clara Reeve sketched what is a typical definition, juxtaposing the realism of the novel to the improbability of the romance: "The Novel is a picture of real life and manners, and of the times in which it was written. The Romance in lofty and elegant language, describes what never happened nor is likely to happen. The Novel gives a familiar relation of such things as pass everyday before our eyes . . . in so easy and natural a manner . . . as to deceive us into a persuasion that all is real."[7] It is precisely this notion of "realism," argues Ian Watt in The Rise of the Novel, that differentiates eighteenth-century novels from previous fiction. Watt defines realism as not merely the faithful, mimetic portrayal of a wide variety of human experience, but particularly as the manner in which that experience is presented. Because the novel's primary goal since its incipient developmental stages has been con-sidered as conveying the impression of real life, it has frequently been criticized as formless. Watt suggests, however, that: "What is often felt as the formlessness of the novel as compared . . . with tragedy or the ode, probably follows from . . . the poverty of the novel's formal conventions . . . which . . . would seem to be the price it must pay for its realism."[8]

As one of the formal techniques of this newly evolving genre whose overriding compositional principle was that of mimesis, first-person narration enjoyed a measure of critical acclaim. A visible narrator, whose "I" was an explicit part of the text, was perceived by means of allusions to real people, places, and historical events to be establishing a realistic "air" in the fictional, presented world of the text. In short, as Clara Reeve so aptly summarized, the representation of familiar, everyday occurrences by a personal "I"-narrator made it seem as if those occurrences had actually transpired. First-person narration renders the representation of the world of the text "personal" and "intimate" by its very adherence to its mimetic principles. To be believable, probable, and hence persuasive, first-person narration must consistently respect the limits of the spatial, temporal, and aspectual (psychological) dimensions of its perspective and point-of-view. In other words, to achieve the desired realistic effect, the novel had to adopt certain conventions, among them: Allusion to reality; semblance of reality (all characters, actions, and events are of a general, realistic type); and mediation of that pseudo-reality through the perspective of a realistic narrator.

By thus "guaranteeing" the authenticity of the recounted events and personalizing their narration, the first-person novel enhanced the novel's didactic function. Georges May points out that during the eighteenth century, first-person narration fulfilled the widespread reader demand that the novel lend itself to a role of moral edification. In Prévost's Manon Lescaut and Marivaux's Paysan parvenu, the first-person narrative situation provides an air of authenticity and realism; although the events themselves are far from probable, the narrative situations and the various embedded first-person narrators generate an air of realism by virtue of their repeated attestations to the veracity of what they have heard and seen ("strange as it may seem . . .") and by their strict observance of the spatial, temporal, and aspectual parameters of the respective narrative situation. Indeed, suggestions of unbelievability and apparent unreality seem to assure believability and realism when uttered by an "I" (that is, a real and authentic) narrator. By appearing as nonfictional mirrors of socity, such works of fiction served as exempla of behavior to follow or to avoid. With their first-person narrators and first-person letterwriters, a number of epistolary novels--Laclos's Liaisons dangereuses, Diderot's Religeuse, Rousseau's Nouvelle Héloïse, Richardson's Pamela, and Dostoevsky's Poor Folk, to cite just a few examples--also create an illusion of reality that fulfilled a moralizing function. In a preface and/or explanatory footnotes, the first-person editor or authorial-narrator serves to "authenticate" letters which he claims were collected by one of the letterwriters, or perhaps discovered in some old trunk. As in Manon Lescaut with its complexly embedded narrative structure (the duc de Renoncourt, a moral man of quality, encounters the chevalier des Grieux on two separate occasions to hear the latter's tale), the very multiplicity of first-person narrators, who heard the story or found the manuscript that is about to be divulged, generates a certain aura of probability and eventually a certain authenticity. Ultimately, of course, a first-person narrator can and often does redirect his or her focus away from the world of the text to address the readers directly to encourage moral behavior and to condemn immorality, as does the duc de Renoncourt in his introduction to the story of Manon Lescaut and des Grieux. The public

verra, dans la conduite de M. des Grieux, un exemple terrible de la force des passions. J'ai à peindre un jeune aveugle, qui refuse d'être heureux, pour se précipiter volontairement dans les dernières infortunes . . . un caractère ambigu, un mélange de vertus et de vices, un contraste perpétuel de bons sentiments et d'actions mauvaises. Tel est le fond du tableau que je présente. Les personnes de bons

sens ne regarderont point un ouvrage de cette nature comme un
travail inutile. Outre le plaisir d'une lecture agréable, on
y trouvera peu d'événements qui ne puissent servir à l'instruc-
tion des moeurs. . . .[9]

First-person narration has also been an ideal technique for the
inner, psychological realism of lyrical and confessional novels
from the eighteenth through the twentieth centuries. A large
portion of the reading public has craved the private, intimate
adventures of the presented narrator and characters. The
first-person pronoun and the narrative code frequently associated
with it have been conducive to presenting intimate, psychological
portraits of the narrator-protagonists in Rousseau's **Confessions,**
Chateaubriand's **René,** Lermontov's **Hero of Our Time,** Constant's
Adolphe, Nerval's "Sylvie" and "Aurélia," and Hawthorne's
Blithedale Romance and in the twentieth century, Gide's L'Immoraliste and **Porte étroite,** Proust's A la recherche du temps
perdu, Colette's Vagabonde, and Cather's My Ántonia, to name just a
few. Moreover, the autobiographical overtones and implicit suggestions of nonfiction associated with the first-person perspective as
a result of these novels and memoirs have heightened reader
interest, generating popular if not critical approval of the
technique. Even prior to the rise of the novel in the eighteenth
century, affirms Claudio Guillén, authors of the picaresque "novel"
usually chose to relate their picaro's adventures from the first-
first-person perspective in order to reveal not only the actions
and events of the presented world, but to mediate that world
through the picaro's eyes.[10] Even at this fairly rudimentary
stage in the development of first-person narrative technique, then,
mediation of the presented events and characters was considered, at
least by the authors themselves, to be as important as the adventure
story itself. Subsequent critical readers, however, have mislead-

ingly focused on "psychological analyses" of these "pseudo autobio-
graphies."

When assessing the variations in function and hence popularity
of first-person narration, Glowinski cautions us to consider not
only the diachronic frame, but the synchronic one as well:

The functions of a first-person novel do not depend only
upon itself. They are conditioned by the place it occupies
in the totality of the novelistic genre but, primarily, by
its relation to the third-person novel. The first-person
novel had a different meaning and fulfilled different functions in the period preceding the formative stages of the
classic realistic novel, and different ones at the time when
the realistic novel acquired a dominating position, and again
different ones in this, our century, which does not give pre-
ference to any one particular form of narration and subjects
classic models to far-reaching transformations. In the period
preceding Balzac's creations and those of other great realists
the first-person novel was not only the most widely used and
highly approved by the literary taste of those days, but it
was this novel which seems to have been determining the expressive possibilities of the genre in general and social
opinion about it.[11]

What seems to have begun as a literary convention in response to
a need for compositional and aesthetic principles, the first-person
narrative situation as a type remains, for the most part, similar
to its eighteenth-century variations in form, if not in function.
Increasingly, however, what has been a literary convention, understood as a technique of mimesis (the verisimilar representation of
reality), the first-person narrator has been interpreted as consi-

derably more than that. Naively and inaccurately, readers have used the technique to create their own nonfictional sub-text to the fictional text. As Philippe Lejeune suggests in his study of autobiography in France, the proliferation and success during the eighteenth century of novels in the form of memoirs habituated "écrivains et lecteurs à lier l'emploi du récit à la première personne (perspective subjective) à l'histoire de la sensibilité individuelle et à la peinture des moeurs."[12] Although Lejeune recognizes that autobiography is indeed most frequently narrated in the first-person, he cautions against the naive assumption that first-person narration alone constitutes the differentiating factor between autobiography and the autobiographical novel, between nonfiction and fiction. Rather,

> La différence est . . . externe: il faut pour l'établir faire intervenir la connaissance d'éléments extérieurs au texte. Dans l'autobiographie, on suppose qu'il y a identité entre l'auteur d'une part, et le narrateur et le protagoniste d'autre part. C'est-à-dire que le "je" renvoie à l'auteur. Rien dans le texte ne peut le prouver. L'autobiographie est un genre fondé sur la confiance, un genre . . . "fiduciaire", si l'on peut dire. D'où ailleurs, de la part des autobiographes, le souci de bien établir au début de leur texte une sorte de "pacte autobiographique", avec excuses, explications, préalables, déclaration d'intention, tout un rituel destiné à établir une communication directe.[13]

This alliance of first-person narration with autobiography and historical reality has continued to remain prominent in the second half of the twentieth century, so that despite numerous authorial statements to the contrary, many novels continue to be misleadingly

interpreted as autobiography and their first-person narrators continue to be equated with the real author. This critically naive yet
widespread approach to the reading of literary works narrated in the
first-person has received theoretical support from Käte Hamburger in
Die Logik der Dichtung. Hamburger seeks to establish the ontic nature of first-person narration as nonfiction. On the basis of the
"statement system of language" theory, Hamburger contends that the
first-person narrator is not fictive, but that it necessarily posits
itself as a nonfictional reality statement: "The I of the first-
person does not intend to be a lyric I, but a historical one, and
therefore it does not assume the forms of lyric statement. . . .
Like every historical I [, it] is oriented toward the objective
truth of the narrated."[14] What concerns Hamburger is not whether or
to what extent the first-person narrator's story is real or feigned,
but only what form of statement the narrative act assumes. Hamburger defines her concept of statement as a polarized subject-
object linguistic structure; that is, all sentences have as their
correlate the statement of a statement-subject about a statement-
object. She explains that a statement is a reality statement because it has been constituted through a genuine, real statement-
subject. A statement-subject is considered "real," if it has an
identifiable here and now, what is termed an "I-Origo." Thus, any
explicitly presented "I" of a first-person narrator in prose is
ontologically and formally "real" because it has specific temporal
and spatial coordinates which designate the originary point--the
"I-Origo"--occupied by the statement-subject.

Having classified first-person narration as a reality statement
on the basis of its form, Hamburger contrasts it to the "as-reality"
structure that is the primary determinant of fiction. This illusion
or semblance of reality can be realized only in drama or by the
third-person narrative form of epic fiction. Hamburger asserts
that: "Epic fiction is defined solely in that it contains no real
I-Origo, and secondly in that it therefore must contain fictive I-

Origines, [that is,] reference or orientational systems which epistemologically, and hence temporally, have nothing to do with a real I who experiences fiction in any way--in other words with the author or reader. And conversely, precisely this signifies that they are nonreal, fictive."[15]

In Hamburger's system, only the characters of a novel narrated in the third-person convey the illusion of reality; they alone are feeling, thinking, and speaking subjects and hence fictive persons. The mode of the first-person narrator, she argues, cannot engender that illusion. The characters in a first-person narrative are the objects of the narrator's (that is, the statement-subject's), feigned reality statement, and, as such, are always dependent on the narrator's manner of perception and interpretation. They can never achieve the illusion of independent, real existence as in epic fiction. Moreover, a first-person narrator never portrays those characters in a completely objective manner; rather "the narrator's subjective conception enters into his statements in the same logical and epistemological manner as in all reality statements."[16] The first-person narrator does not "engender" the characters and events which he relates; rather, he narrates about those statement-objects in the same manner as in any reality statement. It is in this differentiation of reality statement and fictional narration that Hamburger distinguishes between the generic and ontic status of first-person and third-person narrators, nonfiction and fiction, and between documents of historical reality and novels.

Hamburger is to be applauded for recognizing the significance of narrative perspective in general and first-person narration in particular to the structure of the literary work. She has overextended the range of the abilities of narrative perspective, however, by using the formal linguistic features of first-person and third-person narration to establish the ontic and generic status of literary works. Moreover, by using the linguistic structure of the sentence as the theoretical foundation on which to base her ontic system, Hamburger has in reality shifted the focus away from the mode of existence of the text as a literary work. In addition, she has actually narrowed substantially the range of admissible fictive techniques by asserting that first-person narration is the proper of nonfiction. Finally, by ontically allying this perspective with nonfiction, Hamburger has denied the artistic and aesthetic functions of first-person narration. Although she admits that the first-person narrative statement resides along a continuum between the literary feint and reality, depending on the individual work, she maintains that it can never be considered as a technique of fiction. In Hamburger's system, the properties, emergent qualities, and potential artistic and aesthetic values of first-person narration do not even merit consideration. Ultimately, then, what results from Hamburger's rigid classification of first-person narration as nonfiction is a logic of literature seriously depleted by the failure to evaluate novels narrated in the first-person according to artistic and aesthetic criteria.

My criticism of Hamburger's conclusion that first-person narrative is by virtue of its form an historical reality statement is substantiated by Roman Ingarden's examination of the basic structure and mode of existence of the literary work of art as such.[17] In Ingarden's terms, Hamburger states that quasi-affirmations ("as-reality" statements) occur exclusively in epic fiction, that is, in those works narrated in the third-person. All statements contained in works narrated in the first-person, she argues, are genuine affirmations which make a claim to truth. In contrast to Hamburger's claims linking first-person narration to historical authenticity, Ingarden asserts that the presented world in any literary work is neither real nor ideal. Rather, the ontic nature of any projected world is purely intentional and, therefore, heteronomous because it is composed of the purely intentional correlates (states of affairs) carried by the sentence meanings. Ingarden maintains that every projected state of affairs is necessarily purely intentional; no

statement, whether spoken or written, meant as fiction or nonfiction, is capable of projecting a state of affairs which as projected could be considered as real. In contrast to the concreteness
of reality, every statement and, as a result, every projected state
of affairs is schematic.

The presented world of a text includes only those characters,
things, and occurrences which are presented by the states of affairs
projected by sentences. Because meaning units are the primary
determinant of these presented objects, they differ from real,
autonomous objects in a number of significant ways. For example,
unlike a presented object, a real, concrete object is fully and
absolutely determinate in every detail of each of its properties.
Thus, not only does the voice of a real, storytelling grandfather
have the property of sound, it is determined by a particular pitch
and tone with particular intonations and modulations. Moreover,
when we listen to that storyteller and hear his voice, we apprehend
his many diverse properties as a concrete unity.

In contrast to real objects, a presented object can never attain
a complete and absolute determination because it is determined by
meaning units. When presented in the world of a text, a storyteller
or narrator may well be referred to simply as "I" and "we," and his
voice described in a schematic manner, if at all: "'I was told it
at Orenburg,' I answered" (emphasis added).[18] Although the property of sound is determined as belonging to the narrator, it is determined only generally with no particularization as to the pitch or
tone of his voice. Moreover, such brief mention of a narrator as "I
answered" does not actualize other aspects of the storyteller besides the implied sound. In the following brief quotation from Margaret Atwood's **Surfacing**, the narrator's voice receives some additional qualifying aspects: "When we're back in the car I **say as
though defending myself**, 'Those weren't here before.' Anna's head
swivels around, **my voice must sound odd**" (emphasis added).[19] Although the portrayal of the narrator's voice actualizes aspects of

apparent defensiveness and a certain oddness, many other potential aspects here remain hidden; the reader receives no information as to the pitch and intonation of the speaker's voice, for example. Frequently, moreover, no mention is made of the narrator's physical appearance, height or weight, or personal life, and the narrator's age is often undetermined. Ingarden terms these undetermined elements and dimensions "points of indeterminateness" and asserts that they are necessarily found in every presented object. Since no description, no matter how rich or extensive, could ever exhaust the multitude and particularity of properties belonging to an object, Ingarden explains that presented objects are only schematically (skeletally) determined. Readers, in turn, must apprehend those objects in imagination on the basis of their predetermination by meaning units. In other words, just as no viewer would confuse a painting or a piece of sculpture that depicts a tree--no matter how realistic the portrayal--with a real tree, so no reader should perceive a tree that is verbally projected as a real tree. Barbara Herrnstein Smith suggests that the reason why spectators remain easily able to differentiate between painted or sculpted objects and their real referents but why readers are often unable to distinguish fictive narrators from the real author may well lie with the very media or materials of the respective arts:

The plastic materials that are presumably the media of the visual arts--pigment, stone, metal, and so forth--do not have an expressive function independent of the artworks into which they are fashioned. These materials, moreover, do not in themselves resemble the objects and scenes that they represent. A block of marble is a very different thing from a human figure. The corresponding medium of poetry, however, language, is not a "raw" material, but itself a symbolic system with expressive functions independent of its use in artworks. For this reason, it has been difficult to conceive of language as both the medium of an artwork and also what is represented by it.[20]

The tree that is represented by words may well be of the type of real trees (green leaves, bark-covered branches and trunks), or, as in some expressionist works, it may not (purple leaves, no branches, and a red trunk). However detailed the description of the tree may be and however real the tree may consequently seem to be, the lite-rary representation of that tree is not to be (mis)construed by the reader as a real, completely determined tree, nor is it (in most works of fiction) to be perceived as pointing to a particular, real tree (the one that is growing in my front yard, for example).

The tree that is verbally projected in the presented world of a literary work exists only as a verbal construct in the fictional world of that text. Moreover, each reader and each reading affords the opportunity for a different and unique concretization of that tree. I may well picture that tree, that scene, that character, etc., in a slightly or wholly different manner in my reading at age twenty than at age thirty. And both of my imaginational pictures may differ from those of my husband. Although I must always rely on the text to guide the range of my various concretizations, I may reread the text and thus reconcretize the verbal projections with a new and different insight. I may apperceive "new" details that escaped me or that I ignored for some reason on previous readings. Events, characters, narrators, and in particular first-person character-narrators who "say" I are in their fictiveness no different from this hypothetical tree. Verbally projected, the narrating storyteller who is presented as an explicit or implicit part of the world of the text that he or she, in turn, projects must not be confused with a real storyteller (the author, for example). The narrator portrayed in a literary work cannot do more than represent a **type** of narrating storyteller.

The presented narrator may be of the **type** of **real** storytellers, that is, having a voice (that has sound, a varying pitch and intonation), a corporeal presence (height, weight, and appropriate appendages), a physical appearance (attractive, unattractive), an age (precise: forty-four; or imprecise: middle-aged), a personality (and resultant motivations). (I will discuss the issue of character personality in greater depth later in this chapter.) But a presented storyteller is always schematically determined and hence not determined in a full and complete manner as are all real and concrete storytelling people. As Smith points out, a narrator's utterances constitute **verbal** events within the presented world of the text, events that are equally fictive and that exist on a par with the events and occurrences that the narrator relates: "It is the **act** of reporting events, the **act** of describing persons and referring to places, that is fictive. The novel **represents** the verbal action of a man reporting, describing, and referring."[21] In a production of **Hamlet,** Smith suggests by way of illustration:

we do not watch a queen drinking poison, but the enactment of such an event, which may be said to "occur" only in being thus enacted. But among the acts and events represented on the stage are also verbal ones. As the actor who portrays Claudius leans forward and extends his arms in a gesture of horror and abortive warning, thus representing a man leaning forward and extending his arm, . . . that actor also utters the words, "Gertrude, do not drink," thus representing a man uttering those words.[22]

Even if the author intends the presented narrator to point to an historically real person, as a verbal projection the narrator can be no more than a representation and hence a fictional semblance of that real person.

All characters, objects, and occurrences presented in the world of the text are portrayed through the medium of orientational space. That is, the presented objects and their presented space are exhibited in such a manner that they appear to be perceived from the perspective of the presented or copresented narrating subject's orientational space. The center of spatial orientation--what Husserl refers to as the "zero point of orientation"--is always located within the fictional, presented world of the text and may be that of a given or cogiven narrator or of one or more of the presented characters. Ingarden enumerates several types of narrative situations on the basis of the location of the center of spatial orientation but makes no effort to be exhaustive in his description of possible types of situations.

(1) The "author" can relate the story as an explicitly presented narrating poet in the world of the text; but, as such, he or she remains necessarily distinct from the objectively real author. In such a narrative situation, the center of spatial orientation resides in the "I" of the presented "author"-narrator, and all presented characters, objects, and occurrences are portrayed as if seen, touched, heard, or experienced in some way by that narrator.

(2) On the other hand, the zero point of orientation might be that of an invisible (objective) narrator who belongs only implicitly to the presented world of the text. Ingarden specifies that by virtue of his orientational center, such a narrator is copresented along with the presented world. As long as the center of orientation is that of the invisible narrator, the presentation originates from that point of view, even when the narrator alters his or her position. Thus, the orientational space is still located in the presented world, but it is not centered in any particular character(s) so that all the characters, objects, and occurrences are presented as if perceived from an unspecified, yet determinate

point.

(3) Ingarden suggests several other possible narrative situations arising when the zero point of orientation is centered in the
"I" of a determinately presented character in the world of the text.
The center of spatial orientation would then shift with the character's every move, and all presented objects would be portrayed in
their relation to that character's perception. In this narrative
situation, the narrating act and narrative role of such a character
can remain implicitly cogiven. Or, (4) the character may also function explicitly as the narrator of the story, thereby serving as a
presented first-person narrator-protagonist. Whatever the narrative
form, though, whether "third-person" or "first-person," explicit or
implicit, the narrator is at all times a derived, purely intentional, presented (or copresented) object belonging to the schematically
presented world of the text. By establishing that first-person,
authorial, and character narrators belong to the layer of presented
objects and thus to the purely intentional, fictive world of the
text, we are able to discount Hamburger's claims that such narrators
belong, by definition, exclusively to nonfiction.

Although all projected states of affairs are purely intentional,
Ingarden allows that a speaker or author may in addition mean the
projected purely intentional state of affairs to be understood as
referring to a real, concrete state of affairs. In historical
works, for example, the author intends the presented world to con-
form to reality and means to affirm each statement made with a claim
to truth. To be sure, all literary works of art, including fantasies and fairy tales, contain some adaptation of reality, if only
by virtue of the principle of consistency. In contrast to the
genuine affirmations contained in scientific and scholarly works,
however, the declarative sentences in a literary work of art (a
novel, for example) are only quasi-affirmations whose function consists in lending the objects portrayed a mere semblance of reality.

The function of quasi-affirmations is not to affirm the objective truth of propositions or judgments, because no affirmation in a literary work of art has as its correlate an objective state of affairs. Thus, we can infer that no literary work of art, even those narrated in the first-person, is intended to solicit readers' identification of projected purely intentional objects with autonomous, real ones. Quasi-affirmations are, however, used in order to simulate objective reality in the fictional world of the text. By choosing characteristic, conventionalized features of a certain time period or of a specific group of people, a literary work of art can represent a model of reality. But, it must be emphasized that this represented model is still just a semblance [Schein] of objective reality. Whereas reality is complex, specific, and concrete, the semblance of that world presented by the schematic structure of a literary work of art is marked by cleavages and numerous points of indeterminateness.

To determine whether a purely intentional, presented world is "also intentional," it is useless to look for a first-person instead of a third-person narrator. Ingarden relies on a number of other features to distinguish between scholarly or scientific works and literary works of art such as the types of transitional expressions linking together the sequence of sentences. Logical connections, such as "therefore" and "thus we can conclude," often predominate in scholarly and scientific works and may not normally be found in literary works. Other distinguishing features may include differences in language style, the nature and function of presented objects, the appearance of manifolds of aspects held in readiness, and, particularly, the presence of artistically effective and aesthetically valent qualities. Although literary artistic qualities may appear in scientific and scholarly works, their function is there one of ornamentation which has minimal, if any, connection with the basic function of the work. In the literary works of art with first-person or third-person narration, though, artistically effective qualities and emergent aesthetically valent qualities are essential to the structural coherence and function of the work. To reduce those qualities to a role of mere decoration in a work that is narrated in the first-person would be to ignore the potential richness and satisfaction gained from recognizing the aesthetic function of a literary work of art.

TWO

Contrary to Hamburger, a number of critics do recognize first-person narration as a technique of fiction. Many of them, however, prove narrow in their definition of an artistic standard by which to evaluate the narrative situation of a given literary work of art. The tendency has often been to deal in polarized categories: Invisible (implicit) narrator versus first-person (explicit) narrator; objectivity versus subjectivity; showing versus telling modes of narration. There are two dimensions to the objective-subjective opposition: An objective narrator is implicit in the text and thus does not appear in the presented world, whereas a subjective narrator is explicitly present in the text and also functions as an explicitly presented major or minor character in the imaginary world. As a result, the statements made by these two types of narrators to describe the world of the text also have what has been labeled either an objective or a subjective quality. The statements projected by an implicit narrator appear "objective" because the narrative process is not emphasized. An explicit narrator, however, obviously mediates or filters impressions of the imaginary world, coloring all statements to some degree. Thus, many critics have concluded that an implicit or objective narrator creates and sustains the illusion of genuine life, whereas, they assert, a first-person or subjective narrator fails to engender that sense of real-

ism because the emphasis given to the narrative process and the very
presence of the narrator are obstacles disrupting the intensity of
illusion. The second major problem confronting first-person narration is thus the recurrent critical judgment that the technique is
inartistic or somehow less artistic than other narrative forms because of its subjectivity, its visible narrative apparatus, and the
limitations of the narrative code associated with it.

We can trace the issue of objective versus subjective narrators
and narration to its classical origins in epic poetry. In Book III
of The Republic, Plato reports Socrates's distinction between two
narrative styles for epic poetry: Imitation and simple narration.[23]
Socrates explains that when narrators resemble the presented characters in voice or by gesture, speaking as though some other person,
they are imitating that character and concealing their own role as
narrator. On the other hand, once a narrator relates what a character says, summarizes occurrences between scenes, or explains motivation, the narrator's concealment or imitation ceases, and the style
becomes simple narration. Within this duality, Socrates prizes explicit narration (diegesis or discourse) over the imitation of
reality (mimesis), believing real, direct narrative presentation to
be more valuable than the mimetic representation of reality. In
effect, diegesis constitutes for Socrates the act of storytelling,
whereas mimesis is a degree removed from reality, a mere semblance.
It is Aristotle, who, arriving at the same duality of diegesis and
mimesis, evaluates the imitative--in modern terminology, objective
or dramatic--style as artistically superior to the subjectivity of
simple narration and the presence of the narrator.[24] Each of these
philosophers recognized the same narrative duality, and each valued
a different mode over the other.

Since Antiquity the issue of the artistic and aesthetic value of
the first-person narrative situation in the novel has generated considerable critical debate. As I have already noted, first-person
narration enjoyed much popularity, although not for artistic rea-

sons, during the eighteenth and nineteenth centuries. In contrast to eighteenth and early nineteenth-century acceptance of narrative subjectivity, Gustave Flaubert in 1866 issued his now famous dictum, demanding narrative objectivity for the novel: "Le roman-cier doit dans sa création imiter Dieu dans la sienne, c'est-à-dire faire et se taire."[25] Concurrently and until the end of the nineteenth century, Friedrich Spielhagen also championed the ideal of total objectivity in narration; to be poetic, the novel had to be free of all authorial and narrator intervention. A visible and subjective narrator, he maintained, would destroy the verisimili-tude and the coherence of the created world of the text. Moreover, argued Spielhagen, the narrator's knowledge about the events he re-lates remains at best problematic. Since the narrator must con-stantly have his knowledge of events corroborated and supplemented in some way to offset his lack of omniscience and omnipresence and to engender verisimilitude, Spielhagen found the first-person nar-rative situation disconcertingly and inartistically artificial.[26] Thus, as the novel's avowed function shifted in the mid-nineteenth century to a broader, more realistic re-creation of life, critics and writers alike found fault with the artificiality and the "limi-tations" of the first-person narrative structure. Despite occasion-al practice to the contrary, many considered the first-person narrator's presence to be an intrusion that disrupted the illusion that real life had been created. Moreover, the spatial, temporal, intellectual (focalization), and presentational "limitations" im-posed on the text by the nature of the first-person perspective were felt to diminish the persuasive power of the illusion. Only the om-niscient, omnipresent, and invisible narrator was considered capable of engendering and sustaining the desired illusion of a realistic panorama of life.

In the following descriptive passage from **Madame Bovary**, Flaubert employs an implicit, invisible narrator, positioned outside the ima-ginary world of the text, to relate Emma's and Léon's carriage ride.

The narration is considered objective because the narrator and his narrative apparatus remain invisible.

> Elle revint et alors, sans parti pris ni direction, au
> hasard, elle vagabonda. On la vit à Saint-Pol, à Lescure,
> au mont Gargan, à la Rouge-Mare et place du Gaillard-bois.
> . . . De temps à autre le cocher, sur son siège, jetait
> aux cabarets des regards déséspérés. Il ne comprenait pas
> quelle fureur de la locomotion poussait ces individus à
> ne vouloir point s'arrêter. Il essayait quelquefois, et
> aussitôt il entendait derrière lui partir des exclamations
> de colère. Alors il cinglait de plus belle ses deux rosses
> tout en sueur, mais sans prendre garde aux cahots, accro-
> chant par-ci, par-là, ne s'en souciant, démoralisé, et
> presque pleurant de soif, de fatigue et de tristesse.
>
> Et sur le port, au milieu des camions et des barriques,
> et dans les rues, au coin des bornes, les bourgeois
> ouvraient de grands yeux ébahis devant cette chose si
> extraordinaire en province, une voiture à stores tendus,
> et qui apparaissait ainsi continuellement, plus chose
> qu'un tombeau et ballottée comme un navire.[27]

Since the narrator does not belong as a character to the world presented by the text, the statements he projects to describe the characters and events are not subject to any particular spatial, temporal, or psychological (focalizing) limitations. Omnipre-sent, the narrator is not restricted to a physical body, but is able to describe the movement of the carriage as it rushes aim-lessly through the streets of Rouen. The narrator is also omni-scient in that he portrays the coachman's fatigue and despair as well as the disbelief of the onlookers.

In contrast, the narrator of the following passage from Allen Tate's **The Fathers** functions in a second role as a presented character positioned within that world which he projects. As a first-person narrator, he is subject to certain spatial, temporal, and intellectual limitations:

I was blushing when I heard: "Mercy, child, where you been all this time?" It was Aunt Myra, severe but kind, looking round the end of the house from the upper gallery. "I've looked for you high and low," she said. Jane got up and walked slowly round the house toward the steps, and when Aunt Myra disappeared I knew that she had not been looking for me. I looked about me; the yard was deserted, I could hear only the plunk of an ax in the distance and a calf bawling over the hill in the cupper.[28]

In this scene, narrator-protagonist Lacy Buchan's vision and hearing are restricted to what he can see and hear from his actual location. As a result, he depicts what he sees from a perspective spatially oriented or foreshortened to that location. He cannot see where Jane goes, for the house blocks his view; he knows only that she walks in the direction of the steps. He cannot know what the other characters are thinking; he is only able to relate what they say and how they respond. He ascertains that Aunt Myra is looking for Jane only because she disappears when Jane walks toward the house. He cannot discern his Aunt's motivation for calling Jane. From where Lacy is standing no one is visible after Jane leaves; he cannot see and therefore is unable to describe any of the many other relatives who have come to his home for his mother's funeral.

Nineteenth-century judgments against first-person narration re-

ceived considerable reinforcement from Henry James, who used his
critical prefaces and essays to expound on the artistic value of
what he termed the "mediating consciousness" or "figural" narrator.
This medium is constituted by an undramatized narrative process
whereby the reader seems to view the fictional world through the
eyes of one of the characters. James describes the novel's purpose
and value as dependent on the success of its realistic representation of life; indeed, he writes, "the only reason for the existence
of the novel is that it does attempt to represent life."[29] It is
this correspondence with life that provides the novel with its uni-
fying and cohering force. Because James's ultimate standard of
evaluation is the intensity of illusion achieved by the novel, he
sees the function of narrative perspective as a means to heighten
the overall effect of the illusion of reality. But according to
James, the first-person perspective is a form unsuited either to
creating the illusion of real life or to generating reader identification. A first-person narrator, he asserts, engenders "a form
foredoomed to looseness . . ."--a form from which arises "the
terrible fluidity of self-revelation."[30]

Echoes of James's criticism have resounded throughout the twentieth century with many critics asserting dogmatically the artistic
superiority of objective or figural narrative situations. During
the 1930s, both Ford Madox Ford and Joseph Warren Beach contributed
to the ongoing critical debate concerning the artistic effectiveness
and value of first-person perspective. Each prove in basic agree-
ment with the poetics advanced by James; neither acknowledge the potential artistic value of an explicitly presented narrating persona.
The goal of the novelist, insists Ford, is to immerse the reader so
completely in the world presented by the text that the act of reading is forgotten and the reader believes, "I have been [there]."[31]
To achieve this illusion, Ford asserts that the narrator must remain
invisible and must render objectively, not tell subjectively, the
story. His critical stance undermined by his own literary effort

The Good Soldier, narrated throughout by an explicitly presented first-person character-narrator, Ford concludes nevertheless that the very presence of a narrator creates an obstacle to the illusion that genuine life is being engendered.

In The Twentieth Century Novel, Beach appears at first to be less dogmatic than Ford about an explicit narrative process. For although he welcomes the exit of the authorial and first-person narrative personae as the most impressive aspect of the modern, well-made novel, he tempers his criticism somewhat by recognizing the narrative achievements of Proust and Gide, and by allowing that: "If the the author succeeds in presenting his theme effectively--story, situation, character, states of mind--we shall not quarrel with his personal appearances. . . ."[32] In concluding, however, Beach reiterates the narrator objectivity-subjectivity, artistic-inartistic dogma: "Our main quarrel is with the author who makes his personal appearance a substitute for the artistic presentation of his subject. . . ."[33]

A. A. Mendilow continues the attack on first-person narration in Time and the Novel. We can see Henry James's influence when Mendilow writes: ". . . the merest hint of the author's existence is sufficient to burst the delicate bubble of illusion."[34] Mendilow's criticism of first-person narration, unlike Ford's and Beach's, progresses beyond the imprecision of James's original comment that it "is a form foredoomed to looseness." Mendilow elaborates on the previously vague concept of "illusion of reality" by addressing its spatial and temporal dimensions. Only the novel narrated in the third-person, he suggests, can achieve the illusion of presentness and immediacy, enabling the reader to identify with the here and now of the hero--in Jamesian terminology, the mediating central intelligence--and that of the other characters.

A novel narrated by an authorial or first-person narrator rarely succeeds in conveying the illusion of presentness and immediacy, Mendilow asserts, because the explicitly presented narrating persona and the visible narrative process form an obstacle to reader identification with any of the portrayed characters. Novels narrated in the first-person frequently have two disparate temporal dimensions: The story's events occur in "fictional time," while the narrator records those events retrospectively in "narrative time." As a result of this temporal differential, the story appears to the reader as remote in time, whereas the third-person novel, although also written in the past, is able to generate the illusion that the action is taking place in the reader's here and now by virtue of its implicit narrative time.

In addition to the first-person narrator's temporal distance from the events of the story, Mendilow specifies other obstacles to creating an illusion of reality. Such a narrator cannot present a convincing self-characterization nor can he analyse reliably his own reactions, prejudices, and feelings. Further bounds include what he can believably know and recount about other characters' internal selves and their unvoiced hopes, fears, and feelings. Like Spielhagen before him, Mendilow concludes that a first-person narrator cannot without artificial tricks escape the limiting aspects inherent in its particular narrative stance.[35] Accordingly, for Mendilow, such artificiality and visibility of the narrative process render the issue of artistic value problematic.

Since Aristotle, many critics have described what they consider to be the problems and limitations inherent in the first-person narrative situation. The innate characteristic of fiction, they all claim, is its ability to create an illusion of life, to convey a presentness and an immediacy conducive to reader-character identification. The first-person narrative, they charge, fails to convey the experience of fiction. Hence, the logical conclusion, some assume, is to view this mode of narration as inartistic. Steeped in the Jamesian tradition, many twentieth-century critics and readers embrace as artistically valent only the objectivity, omnipresence, and omniscience of the implicit, invisible, third-person narrative situation.

As early as 1910, Oskar Walzel and Käte Friedemann reacted against this dogmatic promotion of the objective and implicit narrative situation. Unlike those critics who charge that first-person narration is an inartistic technique because it fails to engender the illusion of reality, Walzel and Friedemann assert that the first-person narrative situation does possess artistically effective qualities. Indeed, Walzel even ventures to state that the only genuine narration is that in which the narrator makes himself felt.[36] By asserting the artistic value of the subjectivity and the visible narrative process of the first-person narrator, Walzel and Friedemann are in essence questioning the fundamental assumption that to be considered successful and artistic, a novel must convey an illusion of real life being created. To be sure, throughout the eighteenth and nineteenth centuries, the predominant norm was that the function of the novel meant it to be a realistic recreation of life. In contrast to this widely accepted dictum, however, a number of writers and critics in the twentieth century recognize that the artistic and aesthetic value of the novel need not depend exclusively on the criterion of realism. So long as the generally accepted function of the novel was one of realism, many other dimensions in the novel went unnoticed, including the structural cohesion and artistic effects that different narrative perspectives can generate. All novels are necessarily recounted by a narrator, whether explicitly or only implicitly. But the significance of narrative perspective was not considered in a serious manner until 1921 when Percy Lubbock affirmed that: "The whole intricate question of method, in the craft of fiction, I take to be governed by the question of point of view. . . ."[37] Thus, the very presence of the narrative apparatus and the first-person narrator's explicit presence and subjectivity may well be considered by some critics as a disruption of the illusion of reality. As others have recognized, however, an explicitly presented first-person narrator and a visible narrative process can also function, in effect, to draw readers' attention to various, previously ignored dimensions and artistically effective qualities of the text.

Redirection of critical focus away from the presented objects themselves and their aspects of realism occurred initially in the visual arts. When Wasily Kandinsky first glimpsed Monet's "Haystacks" series, he was struck by "the impression that . . . painting itself comes to the foreground."[38] Gone was art's strict dependence on a realistic portrayal of the referential object; the artist was discovering new subject matter based on his or her own subjective perception of the depicted world. As a result of what Kandinsky described as the "dematerialization" of the presented objects in impressionistic painting, thematic and artistic significance came to be perceived as emerging from the artwork's color, shading, texture, line, and focus--that is, from the artist's apperception of the presented object's essential nature and from the technique used to portray that essence. Characteristic properties and essential qualities previously ignored in favor of realistic representations of the referential object became the focus of impressionism, and subsequently, of abstract, non-objective art as well. Similarly, the very visibility of the narrative apparatus and the first-person narrator's explicit presence and subjectivity can, in effect, function to draw readers' attention to various, previously ignored spatial, temporal, and presentational dimensions and artistically effective elements of the text. Precisely because it is a highly visible technique, first-person narration occupies and can, in fact, prolong our attention, allowing us to linger over our aesthetic perception of an object to appreciate the very artfulness of its presentation--over and above the object itself.[39] Thus, precisely because literary works narrated in the first-person often "fail" to create an intense illusion of reality, readers' attention can be more easily directed not to the presented objects themselves and their aspects of realism, but rather to the artistic and aesthetic values that emerge from the narrative perspective, the narrating persona, and his or her narrating act.

In recent years, a number of critics have attempted to describe the first-person narrative situation and to assess its particular attributes.[40] Although they recognize first-person narration as an artistic alternative to other narrative points-of-view, many critics have not advanced beyond the creation of narrative typology. One of the most widely recognized is that of Norman Friedman. Friedman arranged eight narrative forms in a progression marking the gradual objectification of the narrator and the act of narration:

(1) **Editorial Omniscience.** The tendency . . . in editorial omniscience is away from scene, for it is the author's voice which dominates the material, speaking frequently as "I" or "we." The characteristic mark . . . is the presence of authorial intrusions and generalizations about life, manners, and morals, which may or may not be explicitly related to the story at hand.

(2) **Neutral Omniscience.** The next step toward objectification differs from Editorial Omniscience only in the absence of direct authorial intrusion (the author speaks impersonally in the third person). . . . Regarding characterization, although an omniscient author may have a predilection for scene and consequently may allow his people to speak and act for themselves, his predominant tendency is to describe and explain them to the reader in his own voice.

(3) **"I" as Witness.** The witness-narrator is a character in his own right within the story itself, more or less involved in the action, more or less acquainted with its chief personages, speaking to the reader in the first-person. The witness has no more than ordinary access to the mental states of others.

(4) "I" as Protagonist. With the shift of the narrative burden from a witness to the chief character, who
tells his own story in the first-person, a few more
channels of information are given up and a few more vantage points are lost. The protagonist-narrator, therefore,
is limited almost entirely to his own thoughts, feelings,
and perceptions.

(5) Multiple Selective Omniscience. Here the reader listens to no one; the story comes directly through the minds
of the characters as it leaves its mark there. As a result, the tendency is almost wholly in the direction of
scene, both inside the mind and externally with speech and
action.

(6) Selective Omniscience. Here the reader is limited to
the mind of only one of the characters. Instead, therefore of being allowed a composite of viewing angles, he
is at the fixed center.

(7) The Dramatic Mode. Having eliminated the author, and
then the narrator, we are now ready to dispose of mental
states altogether. The information available to the reader
in the Dramatic Mode is limited largely to what the characters do and say. . . . There is never any direct indication of what they perceive (a character may look out of
the window--an objective act--but what he sees is his own
business). . . .

(8) The Camera. Here the aim is to transmit, without
apparent selection or arrangement, a "slice of life" as
it passes before the recording medium. . . .[41]

With few exceptions, the multitude of studies of first-person
narration has resulted in a proliferation of schematic and inade-
quate definitions. Many critics are content to describe the first-

person narrative situation in a fairly simplistic manner, at most distinguishing only between narrator-as-witness and narrator-as-protagonist. Norman Friedman's frequently cited definition, for example, merely describes the protagonist-narrator's perspective as more circumscribed than that of the witness-narrator. Bertil Romberg's definition of narrative technique in the first-person novel is even more schematic: "By a first-person novel is meant a novel that is narrated all the way along in the first-person by a person who appears in the novel, the narrator."[42]

Such simplistic classification of literary works of art is insufficient to describe the characteristic properties of the first-person narrative situation. As Wayne Booth cautions, "to describe any of . . . [the narrators] . . . with terms like 'first-person' and 'omniscient' tells us nothing about how they differ from each other, or why they succeed while others described in the same terms fail."[43] Gérard Genette supplements Booth's criticism of simplistic typology by emphasizing the need to examine the several constituent elements of any given narrative situation: "It is certainly legitimate to envisage a typology of 'narrative situations' that would take into account the data of both mood and voice; what is not legitimate is to present such a classification under the single category of 'point of view,' or to draw up a list where the two determinations compete with each other on the basis of an obvious confusion."[44]

In his seminal study, **Narrative Situations in the Novel,** Franz Stanzel provides additional critical support for the first-person perspective by establishing a typology of three basic and equally artistic narrative situations: The authorial, the figural, and the first-person. Unlike Mendilow and the numerous other critics who question the artistic effectiveness of first-person narration, Stanzel maintains that the world of the text can be artistically and aesthetically valent when it is presented through the "intellect of [any] sensitive medium which has humanly interesting traits."[45] Stanzel emphasizes the importance of the three different forms of the mediative process and the variety of artistic effects generated by them.

According to Stanzel's typology, the desire for expression and presentation is the sole factor rendering the first-person narrator distinct from the novel's other characters, for the narrator belongs to their world and frequently shares their fate. In first-person narration, the narrator is a presented character standing within the imaginary world of the text and projecting a series of statements about that world or relating the dialogue of other characters. Whereas the third-person narrative situation maintains the separation of the narrator's world from the characters', first-person narration establishes the identity of the two worlds.[46]

Stanzel identifies first-person narration as having both authorial and figural attributes. The authorial narrative situation portrays a dramatized authorial medium having a definitive stance in relation to the story, whereas the figural narrative situation conceals the narrative process. He conceives of all novels in the first-person form as being arranged in a continuous spectrum according to the degree to which the narrative process is visible: "When the narrative process is clearly emphasized and when the narrating and experiencing selves are separated by a recognizable narrative distance, the first person novel approaches the narrative situation of the authorial novel. When the narrative process, narrative distance and narrating self are not portrayed in the text, the first person novel approaches the narrative situation of the figural novel."[47] From this fluctuating relationship between the narrating and experiencing selves in the first-person narrative situation emerges a tension--often ironic--which can play a determinative role in the presentation of the narrative elements. Also inherent in the first-person form, he notes, is a tone of reflection and retrospection through which emerge the important structural and thematic contours of the narrative. Indeed, Stanzel suggests that, "the process of narrative transmission may even form part of the story, mediacy thus being one of the many thematic strands of the narrative. . . ."[48]

The first-person narrator-protagonist generally is reflexive, relating a story in which a younger, innocent self is portrayed through the vision of an explicitly presented, older, more knowledgeable narrating self. For Stanzel, the retrospective nature of the first-person narrative situation necessarily suggests a disparity between the here and now of the narrator telling the story and the here and now of the experiencing protagonist and the narrated events. When the narrative act is emphasized by means of direct, reportlike narration, the narrated events become more distant in time and are seen as having happened in the narrating self's past. Yet, when the narrator-as-protagonist projects a scene in a dramatic mode of presentation, that sense of pastness fades, and the narrated events themselves convey the temporal illusion of being present. This fluctuation of the temporal dimension based on the modes of presentation creates a certain rhythmic tension as the narrative progresses. While Mendilow argues that this temporal differential undermines the intensity of the first-person novel's illusion of reality, Stanzel concludes that the tones of retrospection, reflection, and irony lend this narrative situation order and cohesion.

More recently, Stanzel has come to agree with Genette's demand for narratologists' systematic consideration of the major structural elements which constitute any given narrative situation. Although Stanzel's revised typology differs, sometimes significantly, from Genette's more widely known model, their objective is the same: To explore narrative form (discourse) in its relation to narrative content (**histoire**, story). As Dorrit Cohn astutely observes in her perceptive comparison of the two methods, Stanzel's approach tends to be synthetic whereas Genette's is more strikingly analytic.[49] Both theorists subdivide narrative form into several specific cate-

gories. (I will examine Genette's method in-depth in Chapter Two.)
Stanzel's revised three principal categories of Person, Mode, and
Perspective are, in turn, determined by the binary oppositions of
their distinguishing features: (1) Identity and non-identity of the
fictional characters with the narrator (first-/third-person narration); (2) internal and external perspective (limited point-of-view/
omniscience); and (3) teller-character and reflector-character as
agents of transmission (telling versus showing modes of narrative
presentation). Stanzel concludes his substantially revised model by
noting as he did in his earlier **Narrative Situations in the Novel,**
that: "The structural significance of these basic oppositions
emerges from the observation that a transformation of a narrative
text determined by one pole of one of these oppositions into a
text dominated by its opposite elements usually alters the meaning
of the narrative."[50] Stanzel's revisions and refinement of his
theory of narration follow extensive study of work by Russian and
French structuralists (including Genette) and particularly the work
of Roman Ingarden. He has come to recognize that there can be a degree of flexibility in the narrative code; the first-person narrative situation is not locked into a set of prescriptions. A
writer's decision not to adhere strictly to certain prescribed temporal, spatial, psychological, and narrational dimensions need not
constitute code violations that disrupt the verisimilitude and
consistency of the narrative situation and need not undermine its
artistic and aesthetic value. In addition, on the basis of his
reading of Ingarden's **Literary Work of Art,** Stanzel suggests that
the narrative situation of a novel need not be classified exclusively as first-person, authorial, or figural, but only predominantly as implicit or explicit. Moreover, he recognizes that artistic effect may be achieved by shifting the narrative focus and by
varying the narrative situation.

Like Stanzel's 1955 and 1979 studies, Jean Rousset emphasizes the
structural importance of two temporally distinct personae united in

the first-person narrator-protagonist:

Grâce à la première personne qui unit étroitement le narrateur et le personnage narré, tout le roman bascule donc
pour s'ordonner autour d'un moi central et dominateur . . .
à la fois tout puissant puisqu'il soumet le monde à sa
propre existence, et pourtant limité dans sa vision,
puisqu'il doit renoncer à l'omniscience de l'auteur pour
se borner à sa seule perspective de narrateur inclus dans
l'univers qu'il raconte. Cette perspective intériorise le
roman en le plaçant tout entier sous le regard de ce narrateur qui le réfléchit en lui-même.[51]

According to Rousset's thesis, the first-person point-of-view possesses an innate contradiction: The narrator is at once all-
powerful and yet very limited in perspective spatially, temporally,
and psychologically. By definition, Rousset asserts, the first-
person narrator-protagonist occupies the novel's central position
and arranges the presented world in relation to that privileged
focal point. All other characters--their existence always dependent on the narrator--occupy more or less peripheral positions.

In addition, Rousset reiterates the subjective nature of first-
person narration, suggesting that there are degrees of subjectivity:
Transcendental (abstract) and empirical (concrete). Unlike those
critics who judge subjectivity to be an obstacle to the novel's
ultimate purpose of creating an illusion of life, Rousset, like
Stanzel, values this interior perspective. He also finds this manner of mediation similar to the autobiographical form. He addresses
the issue of autobiography not to question the ontic nature of the
first-person novel as fiction but rather to suggest a means of critical illumination. A novel narrated in the first-person derives

its artistic value and meaning not from the fact of its being fiction or nonfiction, but from its form: "La justification et la cohérence de la forme autobiographique sont là: on rend compte de soi, de son être le plus intime, mais d'un être qui ne peut devenir objet de compte rendu que s'il s'est éloigné dans le temps: tout ensemble proche et différent, sujet et objet du récit."[52] This mode of presentation enables the often mimetically realistic portrayal of a penetrating examination of the narrator-protagonist's intimate self. Such an analysis of consciousness by the narrating self is only possible retrospectively, for as Rousset points out, the intense emotion accompanying the present moment of the experiencing self blinds the narrating character's perception and obscures his or her comprehension: "Réduit à un quasi-mutisme lorsqu'il subit son émotion, le sujet sentant ne pourra se ressaisir pour se dire clairement qu'avec le recul du temps, quand il sera devenu pour lui-même un être du passé."[53]

Rousset asserts that the principle interest of narration is la vérité subjective. The novel presented in the first-person unites inextricably the narrating and experiencing selves; the narrator and and the narrated, the subject and the object are affectively linked, affording the reader an intimate knowledge of both:

Ce privilège a ses limites, mais de ces limites le romancier pourra faire une vertu: tout le récit était suspendu au seul personnage narrateur, qui ne voit le monde qu'en perspective, tel que le découpe son angle visuel, la vérité de son dire sera fragmentaire et douteuse; l'incertitude et la déformation croîtront encore si le personnage est en état de passion. Mais à ce moment, la situation se renverse: c'est la vérité subjective qui fait l'intérêt principal de la narration; c'est lui-même et sa passion que le narrateur révèle, par les limites ou les erreurs de sa vision déformante.[54]

Rousset is cognizant of the limitations of this perspective, but in those limitations and the form it imposes on the novel, he sees potential for considerable artistry and thematic structure.

As both Stanzel and Rousset suggest, then, first-person narration endows a novel or short story with more than a purely external classification and structure. Both critics also seek to resolve some of the problems that have long plagued first-person narration by divorcing it from consideration as a predominantly autobiographical technique, by attempting to evaluate it on the basis of its artistic merits, and by asserting that its characteristic aspects and dimensions actually enhance the meaning of a text by the way they shape and delimit the material.

THREE

In a study of first-person narration, it is helpful to address the complexities and subtleties which foster and enhance the coherence of individual literary works of art. Failure to focus on the fine texture and structural and thematic significance which emerge from first-person narrative situations has resulted in a body of critical literature that has misread and, in a number of instances, denigrated individual texts for their formlessness, lack of cohesion, and their failure to create the illusion of objective reality. We can perhaps better understand what critics have described as the problems and "limitations" of first-person narration by examining its narrative "code," for it is this code that governs the particular characteristics of the narrative situation. The narrative code for first-person narration encompasses the implicit directives in

the text that distinguish the first-person narrator-protagonist from
other types of narrators. Moreover, the code establishes a contract
between author and reader delimiting the latter's expectations
about the spatial, temporal, intellectual (psychological or focalization), and presentational dimensions of the first-person narrative
situation. Adherence by writers to the constituent elements and dimensions of this narrative code serves to create a certain verisimilitude in the narration (the discourse level) of the story and the
presentation of the world of the text. Lack of adherence to the
code (and variations therefrom) can, in turn, undermine the principle of verisimilitude, generating effects that some critics inter-
pret as flaws, failures, or lapses--effects that others believe may
endow the literary work with distinctively unique artistic and
thematic values.

SPATIAL ORIENTATION

As an explicitly presented character within the world of the
text, the first-person narrator has certain specifically defined
spatial dimensions restricting vision and presentation. The range
of perception is necessarily narrower than that of an omnipresent
narrator; the first-person narrator can only "see" and experience
sensorially and thereby portray or describe what is immediately
accessible. Confined to the physical limitations of a body, such a
narrator is unable to see around corners or through walls into adjoining rooms. What is visible is limited to the orientational
space of the first-person narrator, with a resulting foreshortened
and sometimes distorted effect. For example, an involontary
listener to a conversation between his uncle and cousin, the first-
person narrator-protagonist Jérôme in Gide's La Porte étroite is
physically unable to hear his uncle's responses. Much as he strains

to make out his uncle's words, his physical location and his uncle's hushed tones prevent his discerning more than half of the interchange:

Un soir que je m'attardais à lire, étendu sur le gazon à l'ombre d'un des grands hêtres pourpres, séparé de l'allée aux fleurs simplement par la haie de lauriers qui empêchait les regards, point les voix, j'entendais Alissa et mon oncle. Sans doute ils venaient de parler de Robert; mon nom fut alors prononcé par Alissa, et, comme je commençais à distinguer leurs paroles, mon oncle s'écria:

"Oh! lui, il aimera toujours le travail."

. . . J'entendis sa claire voix:

"Papa, est-ce que mon oncle Palissier était un homme remarquable?"

La voix de mon oncle était sourde et voilée; je ne distinguai pas sa réponse. Alissa insista:

"Très remarquable, dis?"

De nouveau trop confuse réponse; puis Alissa de nouveau: "Jérôme est intelligent, n'est-ce pas?"

Comment n'eussé-je pas tendu l'oreille... mais non, je ne pus rien distinguer.[55]

There are, moreover, certain geographical limitations restricting the first-person narrator's movements and the panoramic breadth of occurrences and characters he can present. Lacking omnipresence, a first-person narrator cannot portray simultaneously occurring events, nor can chronologically successive scenes be located at considerable distance from each other. Any events in which the narrator-protagonist does not participate or which are not directly witnessed must have a source, whether a wholly new and different story-

teller, or perhaps a letter, a diary, or a newspaper article. In
Willa Cather's My Ántonia, for example, first-person narrator Jim
Burden listens first to his neighbor Frances Harling and then to the
Widow Steavens recount what has happened to his friend Ántonia while
he has been away from Black Hawk at college.[56]

Critics who consider that only omnipresence is an artistically
effective characteristic charge that the manner of presentation resulting from the first-person narrator's restrictive spatial dimension skews the perspective to an inartistic effect. Moreover, many
critics charge that the inclusion of letters or journals and the intrusion of additional narrators further disrupt the illusion of
reality by increasing the distance between the reader and the imaginary world of the text and by introducing "artificial" techniques
to supplement the narrator's "limited" resources and knowledge.[57]
Such spatial constraints do, however, enhance the first-person narrator's ability to examine intensely and render subjectively the
many aspects that he can apprehend of the characters, objects, and
occurrences of the world being presented. A presentation whose center of spatial orientation is located in a first-person narrator-
protagonist gives rise to artistically effective qualities from
characteristic properties which are different from those of a third-
person presentation of a panoramic recreation of life.

TEMPORAL ORIENTATION

Critics also view the temporal dimension of first-person narration as disrupting the sense of immediacy and presentness necessary
to the illusion created by fiction. A first-person narrator usually
relates a story retrospectively; the narrator must experience or
witness events, then understand and contemplate them, before
fashioning them into a recountable tale. In addition to this retro-

spective nature, the narrator is restricted to a time frame technically beginning with his or her own birth and childhood and ending
with the date of narration. Practically, a first-person narrator
can relate only those incidents that have occurred within his or
her own memory. Any occurrences--other than wellknown historical
facts--before that time, which the narrator may choose to incorporate for background, to explain motivation, or to enrich the
story's texture require another source, for the narrator could not
have experienced or witnessed them. Nor can the narrator recount
events--even of historical importance--that will occur subsequent
to the date of narration, although reference by the first-person
narrator to anticipated occurrences is possible. From his temporal
position as a young character, for example, a first-person
character-narrator like Jim Burden in My Ántonia can prospectively
anticipate certain events. In addition, from his temporally
retrospective position, a first-person narrator may well be aware
of events in his past (in the character's future) and may include
references that foreshadow their occurrence.

Associated with this retrospective nature is the narrator's
memory--the mechanism serving as the repository of all traces and
records of past events, but a mechanism which critics of first-
person narration find problematic. Human memory functions in a pro-
verbially vague and fallible manner, often distorting and repres-
sing. In Time in Literature Hans Meyerhoff points out that relations between remembered events usually are not uniformly and
chronologically ordered; they frequently suggest instead a complex
and confused dynamic order of events. The memory tends to fuse and
confuse things remembered with "things feared and hoped for . . .
[and] . . . facts remembered are constantly modified, reinterpreted,
and relived in light of present exigencies, past fears, future
hopes. . . ."[58] The world of internal experience and memory is not
determined by the objective causality which explains connections between events and affords meaning in the outside world. Although the

objective temporal order represented by dates and records constitutes an aspect of the memory structure, the human memory sequence
is ordered by significant associations which charge remembered
events with value. In contrast to the unidirectional and irrever-
sible objective temporal order of nature, concludes Meyerhoff, the
subjectivity of inner remembered experience exhibits qualities of a
continuous flow and a total intermingling of past, present, and future.

These characteristics of human memory have led some critics to
view analogously the first-person narrator's memory as necessarily
fallible and unreliable.[59] A number of critics suggest, moreover,
that since a first-person narrator relates the story in a retrospective manner, any emotions and experiences concurrent with the events
being narrated color the narrator's perception, thereby "hindering"
the objectivity of presentation. In La Porte étroite, Jérôme's dra-
matization of the early stages of his love for Alissa is overshadow-
ed by his grief at the subsequent tragic outcome. Relating his
youthful fantasies about his future with Alissa, Jérôme interjects
a note of bitterness which cuts short those once hopeful plans:

L'enthousiasme d'Abel disposait du présent et de l'avenir.
Il voyait, racontait déjà nos doubles noces. . . . puis
nous nous lancions dans d'énormes travaux, où nos femmes
devenaient volontiers nos collaboratrices. . . . je pen-
sais m'adonner à . . . [l'étude] . . . de la philosophie
religieuse, dont je projetais d'écrire l'histoire... Mais
que sert de rappeler ici tant d'espoirs?[60]

Elsewhere, Jérôme's love for Alissa leads him to question the accuracy of his memory in recounting conversations: "Sont-ce là pré-
cisément ses paroles? Je ne puis l'affirmer, car je vous le dis,

j'étais si plein de mon amour qu'à peine entendais-je, auprès, quelque autre expression que la sienne."[61] There is also a risk, some
critics assert, that the narrator will jumble events or distort
their linear progression, particularly as the amount of time sepa-
rating the narrated events and the act of narration increases.
Further, some critics question the capacity of the first-person narrator's memory; how could any narrator possibly remember all the
elements and details of the story? A few critics question the capacity and reliability of the narrator's memory to the extent that
they find unjustifiable the inclusion of any dialogue--whether attributed to other characters or to the narrator.[62]

These claims of unreliability and limited memory capacity result
from the mistaken assumption that a first-person narrator-protagonist is based on a real person. Critics have often misjudged the
purely intentional ontic nature of first-person narrators, and have
thus evaluated the memory of that fictional persona as if it were
analogous to the memory of a real person. However, we must neither
suspect that first-person narrators are unreliable nor question
their memory capacity, unless there occurs some explicit manifestation in the text. We should note, moreover, that authorial and
figural narrators as well as first-person narrators make self-conscious references to their own fallibility. A first-person narrator may suggest his consciousness of the possible lack of clarity
and uncertainty of remembered incidents with such phrases as "If I
remember correctly," "As I remember them," and "L'été fuyait si pur,
si lisse que, de ses glissantes journées, ma mémoire aujourd'hui ne
peut presque rien retenir."[63] Or, the first-person narrator may rely on concrete documents as a precaution against a "faulty" memory:
"J'ai gardé toutes ses lettres; mes souvenirs, dorénavant confus,
s'y repèrent. . . ."[64] First-person narrators may, on the other
hand, try to assure the posited reader of the exactitude and cer-
tainty of their own memory: "I can see them now, exactly as they
looked." They might also describe an incident as so vivid that it

defies an imprecise remembrance: "All the years that have passed have not dimmed my memory of that first glorious autumn."[65] Ultimately, though, explicit textual references to the narrator's retrospective position in relation to the events of the story give rise to a certain thematic structure and to qualities of artistic value. Thus, precisely those aspects of the temporal dimension that many critics have judged to be inartistic because of the limitations and constraints they place on the presentation of the world of the text can be evaluated as contributing to the work's artistic and aesthetic value.

INTELLECTUAL (FOCALIZATION) DISTANCE

In addition to temporal and spatial "limitations," many critics consider that the first-person narrator is hindered by existing on the same intellectual level as the other characters. The narrator is not omniscient and cannot know anything gratuitously; anything not directly witnessed or experienced must be attributed to a source. In presenting the other characters, the narrator is limited to an exterior description of their physical appearance and to relating any alteration in that appearance. In The Fathers, for example, Lacy Buchan concentrates his description of his older brother on the latter's face:

There lay Brother Semmes, in his shirt sleeves, on his back, his hands under his head. He did not move. He had the most expressionless face I have ever seen, and he looked up and down with a neutral gaze.   .
   "I'll go down in a minute," he said. He threw one leg over the side of the bed, and out of the deep feathers he

brought himself with a wrench to his feet. He stood, in
his black satin waistcoat, rubbing his arms and swaying a
little to get his balance; he looked older than his twenty-
three years. I was immensely fond of Semmes, and when I
think of the end he came to I remember the long, mask-like
face, which never acquired any of the lines of his ordeal,
the high sloping forehead, the bushy, Scotch black hair,
and the long nose with the Washburn button on the end of it.
He was a humorous-looking fellow without humor; the slight
puff of flesh over each eye gave him a meditative look which
accounted no doubt for his having written at the age of six-
teen some romantic verses which had found their way into the
first issue of the **Washington Star** in 1852. But he hadn't
continued this talent and was now a medical student in
Washington.[66]

Despite Lacy's inability to probe and portray the depths of his
older brother's emotions and thoughts, he is nevertheless able to
provide a considerable amount of information deduced from his physical appearance. Lacy, moreover, displays his own sense of humor
here by suggesting an almost causal relationship between Semmes's
puffy eyes and his ability to compose romantic poetry.

The first-person narrator is free to recount the actions of the
other characters, but any explanation of motivation must originate
in some way from those other characters or from another source. The
narrator is also at liberty to describe changing situations and con-
ditions--financial, interpersonal relationships, and health, for
example--that produce perceptible effects. Moreover, the narrator
is sometimes able to portray or suggest certain mental and emotional
states of other characters by observing gestures, facial expressions, and manners of behavior and speech. By emphasizing his own
anxious feelings of uncertainty in response to characters and inci-

dents, narrator Jérôme in **La Porte** étroite is able to suggest the other characters' state of mind:

> **Le coeur me battait fort** en poussant la barrière du jardin. Juliette aussitôt vint à notre rencontre en courant. Alissa, occupée à la lingerie, ne se hâta pas de descendre. Nous causions avec mon oncle et Miss Ashburton lorsqu'enfin elle entra dans le salon. **Si notre brusque arrivée l'avait trou-blée,** du moins sût-elle n'en rien laisser voir; je pensais à ce que m'avait dit Abel et que c'était précisément pour s'armer contre moi qu'elle était restée si longtemps sans paraître. **L'extrème animation** de Juliette faisait **paraître** encore plus froide sa réserve. **Je sentis** qu'elle désapprou-vait mon retour; du moins **cherchait-elle** à montrer **dans son air** une désapprobation **derrière laquelle** je n'osais chercher une secrète émotion plus vive. Assise assez loin de nous, dans un coin, près d'une fenêtre, **elle paraissait** tout absorbée dans un ouvrage de broderie. . . . **Mon oncle lui-même semblait** particulièrement soucieux. (my emphasis)[67]

Some critics contend that when describing other characters, the first-person narrator must use verbs which specifically designate external events or actions visible from without: Juliette came, Alissa didn't hurry, we chatted. The first-person narrator is not able to use verbs that convey inner experience to describe those around him for he would have no way of knowing what another charac-ter believes, thinks, doubts, or hopes unless that other character verbalizes or in some way acts out those thoughts and emotions.[68] In the preceding passage, however, Jérôme alludes to the emotions and thoughts of the others by couching them in terms of what might be their possible reactions: "Si notre brusque arrivée l'avait troublée," "faisait paraître," and "semblait." He also emphasizes his own perception when describing Alissa's unspoken expression of disapproval: "Je sentais qu'elle désapprouvait." Despite such phraseology, however, critics often charge that the first-person narrator, subject to a restricted exterior perspective, is unable to present other characters adequately.

A number of critics also deem it impossible, strictly speaking, for a first-person narrator to present a complete and objective self-characterization. Restricted to a subjective vision from within when perceiving themselves, first-person narrators tend to portray themselves by means of verbs conveying inner experience. A few critics even contend that in order to adhere closely to the narrative code, first-person narrators cannot observe themselves, as they can others, from an external perspective, participating in an action or in an event. Description of physical appearance would require what critics term artificial devices; the narrator would have to look in a mirror or perhaps in a reflecting pool of water, or introduce another character who could present a more objective, external portrait.[69]

Many critics suggest that the result of the restricted, subjective nature of the first-person narrator produces a lopsided effect. They describe the first-person narrative situation as consisting of flat characters, portrayed only by their actions and with little or no insight on the narrator's part as to their inner selves. These one-dimensional characters stand in sharp contrast to a first-person narrator-protagonist whose characterization often does not proceed beyond the inner self. Yet it is precisely this subjective nature of the first-person narrator-protagonist that fosters what Rousset terms la vérité subjective. When used in lyrical and confessional novels, the first-person narrative situation enhances the creation of a realistic portrait of the narrating protagonist's inner life. Further, the first-person narrator's self-conscious references to his or her own subjectivity and inability to exhibit other characters' thoughts and feelings focus readers' attention on the mode of narration and on its various characteristics, rather than solely on the presented world. With their overt references to the act of narration, such novels as Sterne's **Tristram Shandy** and Diderot's **Jacques le fataliste** manage to exhibit the first-person narrative process and thereby provide readers with a new and often unexpected perception of the presented world, one that is more limited in scope but frequently more penetrating in its probes:

But I was begot and born to misfortunes;--for my poor mother, whether it was wind or water,--or a compound of both,--or neither;--or whether it was simply the mere swell of imagination and fancy in her;--or how far a strong wish and desire to have it so might mislead her judgment;--in short, whether she was deceived or deceiving in this matter, it in no way becomes me to decide.[70]

* * * *

Comme ils en étaient là, ils entendirent à quelque distance derrière eux du bruit et des cris; ils retournèrent la tête, et virent une troupe d'hommes armés de gaules et de fourches qui s'avançaient vers eux à toutes jambes. Vous allez croire que c'étaient les gens de l'auberge, leurs valets et les brigands dont nous avons parlé. Vous allez croire que ces brigands s'étaient imaginé que nos deux voyageurs avaient décampé avec leurs dépouilles. . . . Vous allez croire que cette petite armée tombera sur Jacques et son maître, qu'il y aura une action sanglante, des coups de bâton donnés, des coups de pistolets tirés; et il ne tiendrait qu'à moi que tout cela

n'arrivât; mais adieu la vérité de l'histoire, adieu le
récit des amours de Jacques. Nos deux voyageurs n'étaient
point suivis; j'ignore ce qui se passa dans l'auberge
après leur départ.[71]

* * * *

La voilà remontée, et je vous préviens, lecteur, qu'il
n'est plus en mon pouvoir de la renvoyer.--Pourquoi donc?
--C'est qu'elle se présente avec deux bouteilles de champagne, une dans chaque main, et qu'il est écrit là-haut
que tout orateur qui s'adressera à Jacques avec cet
exorde s'en fera nécessairement écouter.[72]

* * * *

Tout cela est fort beau, ajoutez-vous; mais les amours
de Jacques?--Les amours de Jacques, il n'y a que Jacques
qui les sache; et le voilà tourmenté d'un mal de gorge
qui réduit son maître à sa montre et à sa tabatière;
indigence qui l'afflige autant que vous. --Qu'allons-
nous donc devenir? --Ma foi, je n'en sais rien.[73]

First-person narrators may also abandon these intellectual, temporal, and spatial restraints with a view to disrupting readers'
conventionalized, sometimes almost mechanistic expectations of the
first-person narrative situation. By consciously violating the dimensions of the narrative code, an author may jolt readers into
setting aside their automatized and dulled vision and enable them to
examine the presented world of the text and its artistically effective qualities with a renewed vision.

MODE OF PRESENTATION

In his 1891 essay, "Formen der Erzählung," Otto Ludwig contrasts "true narration"--or, reportlike narration--with scenic or dramatic presentation.[74] Ludwig recognizes that these two modes of narration can each achieve certain unique effects. He finds the panoramic nature of reportlike narration well suited to introduce past material as background, explain character motivation, to present gradual change and development over time, and for any other processes which become meaningful when illuminated by the explicit presence of the first-person narrator's imagination and voice. The use of this narrative mode serves as a reminder of the narrator's retrospective vision of the events being narrated.

The scenic mode of presentation projects characters and events with a dramatic intensity, creating the illusion that the "narrative ceases and a direct light falls upon . . . the . . . people and their doings."[75] Percy Lubbock and Phyllis Bentley assert that these dramatically portrayed scenes mark the structural lines of the story and engender the intensity of the illusion of reality, whereas the survey perspective of reportlike narration functions to prepare for and connect those scenes.[76]

According to Ludwig and Stanzel, the major difference between these two modes of presentation is ultimately the presence or absence of the narrator in the projected world of the text.   When scenic presentation is the predominant mode of narration, the narrator remains invisible. Some critics, therefore, conclude that the first-person narrator--an explicitly presented character whose narrative process is emphasized--necessarily employs the reportlike mode. Rigid alignment of the first-person narrator and reportlike narration, however, denies novels the vividness and structural depth

engendered by scenic presentation. Lubbock points out the structural weakness that the exclusive use of first-person perspective
and reportlike narration entails:

In the tale that is quite openly and nakedly somebody's narrative there is this inherent weakness, that a scene of true
drama is impossible. In true drama nobody **reports** the scene;
it **appears.** . . . When one of the people who took part in it
sets out to report the scene, there is at once a mixture and
a confusion of effects; for his own contribution . . . cannot
have the same crispness or freshness. . . . This weakness may
be well disguised . . . [but] . . . it is always there . . .
and it means that the full and unmixed effect of drama is
denied to the story that is rigidly told from the point of
view of one of the actors.[77]

Although Lubbock aligns first-person perspective strictly with reportlike narration, he departs from previous critical demand for
consistency in narrative point-of-view and applauds the effects
achieved by shifting the perspective and thus the mode of narration. A rigidly adhered to narrative point-of-view, he concludes,
would result in a purely mechanical consistency and a weakly structured, monotonous presentation, lacking in the dramatic highlights
afforded by occasional scenes.

Few novels are mediated solely through one perspective or by one
mode of narration. Virtually all novels consist of a structured sequence of shifts in the narrative point-of-view as well as in the
mode of presentation, with one type usually predominating. Novels
are usually generically classified on the basis of the dominant narrative situation, that is, on the basis of the implicit or explicit
presence of the narrator, the angle of the perspective, and on the

mode of presentation. Stanzel emphasizes the structural importance of the shifting perspectives and modulations in narrative situations: "The shift from first to third or from third to first person is an important part of the intricate machinery introduced to control the perspective of presentation and narrative distance."[78] Narrative forms may shift only occasionally and almost imperceptibly throughout the course of the novel, or there may be tremendous variation from chapter to chapter, scene to scene, and even within sentences. However, we need not assume that "reportlike" or the "telling" mode of narration is tied solely to first-person perspective and that "scenic" or the "showing" mode of presentation can occur only when the narrator is not explicitly present. First-person narrators, too, can and frequently do present scenes and as presented characters participate in those scenes.

FOUR

Phenomenological and structuralist theories provide useful yet sharply distinct suggestions for the study of narration in general. More specifically, the work of French structuralist Gérard Genette and that of Polish phenomenologist Roman Ingarden can prove particularly illuminating as methods of textual analysis for novels, short stories, and récits narrated in the first-person. Their methods represent two distinct approaches to the study of the literary text and, particularly, to the investigation of first-person narration. The narrative theory of Genette is predicated on what he sees as the essentially dual nature of the text. The story is the invariant core composed of a sequence of actions, and it may be envisioned and presented in any of a variety of ways, from any number of perspectives. Action, or the **histoire**, thus exists independently of and, in principle, pre-exists the narrative presentation (**discours**). The structuralist goal is therefore to describe the relationships between the events and the manner of their narrative presentation, that is, the transformation of their "original" order. Ingarden goes beyond this classificatory and descriptive approach to evaluate the artistic effects and the qualities of aesthetic value that emerge from the peculiar properties of what he terms the literary work's four strata. Each method is built on a theoretical foundation and has its own set of terms, thus providing critical readers with a common ground on which to approach the text and a shared vocabulary with which to discuss it. These two methods also direct the focus of interpretation to the texts themselves, rather than to the confining limitations of the code long associated with the first-person perspective; to unascertainable authorial intention; to unverifiable autobiographical data; to strictly personal, emotional reader response; or to an unreconstructable **Zeitgeist**.

In the following chapters, I shall examine relevant portions of first, Genette's work, and second, Ingarden's theory. To illustrate the unique aspects of each method, I have chosen to examine the first-person narrative situation in André Gide's **L'Immoraliste** and Willa Cather's **My Ántonia**. In general terms, both Gide's **récit** and Cather's novel recount the story of a male, first-person narrator-protagonist's self discovery and growth. In more specific terms, the two works illustrate two distinct forms that can structure first-person narrative situations. Whereas **L'Immoraliste** purports to be the first-person narrator-protagonist (Michel's) "oral" confession that is transcribed in a letter by another, anonymous first-person narrator, **My Ántonia** represents the "written" memoirs of the first-person narrator-protagonist (Jim Burden), a completed manuscript that is presented to another, anonymous first-person narrator. Michel's "oral" narration promises a certain immediacy and perhaps an even greater sincerity than Jim Burden's more labored, "written" effort. But, as we shall see, that promised sincerity and sense of spontaneity are undermined by the nature of Michel's studied and self-serving manner of narration. Jim Burden's carefully crafted memoir, on the other hand, manages to impart a certain candid innocence. Each of these texts also serves to illustrate how certain constituent elements of first-person narration (spatial and temporal orientation, for example) may predominate over others. In their retrospective positions as narrators, both Michel and Jim Burden recognize the importance that the past has played and continues to play in their lives and in their narrating acts. Michel struggles to escape the effects of his past immorality, whereas Jim seeks to recover the sensorial and emotional aspects of his past sense of self.

Obviously, each of the critical methods examined here presupposes a theory of character that posits characters and (first-person) narrators as personages. Although Formalists and such structuralists as Vladimir Propp and Claude Brémond view characters strictly as functional products of the plot, other structuralists including Genette, Todorov, and Barthes and, to a greater degree, phenomenologists such as Ingarden recognize the need for an afunctional conception of character. Characters and presented narrators can therefore be depicted and apperceived as portrayals of imaginational beings of the type of real, autonomous beings replete with a personality and mental, physical, and behavioral traits—in short, a "self."[79] Although the structuralist method presented in the following chapter recognizes plot-centered (apsychological) narratives as well as character-centered (psychological) narratives where actions are often "expressions of personality," it is the phenomenological model (presented in the third chapter) alone that outlines a method by which the reader can distinguish the phenomenally perceivable properties or qualifications of the characters and narrators.

Finally, then, reading these two texts with first a structuralist model and second a phenomenological model will enable us to apprehend from two divergent critical points-of-view the manner in which the first-person narrative situation enhances the coherence and meaning of each of these works, works that have frequently been interpreted in autobiographical terms and that have been subjected to charges of flawed, inartistic structures.

A STRUCTURALIST APPROACH

"Il n'y a pas de récit sans narrateur," asserts Tzvetan Todorov in Poétique.[1] Todorov's statement stresses the importance that many French structuralists have placed on the narrator and narrative perspective in regard to the structural configuration and coherence of the novel. Structuralist literary critics such as Todorov, Jean Pouillon, and particularly Gérard Genette view narrative perspective as more than a synonym for "person" or "point-of-view." In Temps et roman, Pouillon proposes emphasizing the narrator's focalization and psychological relationship to the main character(s) as a means of classifying the narrative situation.[2] Todorov and Genette expand on that approach by examining the narrative voice, the narrator's vision (focus or perspective), the types of speech used in narration, and narrative time. For them, a narrative situation thus encompasses what they term the aspectual, modal, and temporal relationships between the narrative content (the story's action or events), the narrative discourse, and the narrating act.[3] Categorization of these elements and sensitivity to their similarities and differences, their hierarchical organization, and their interrelationships allows the critical reader to describe the configuration of an individual text's narrative situation on the micro- and macronarrative levels. Of the various structuralist methods for the study of narration, Genette's is particularly useful for an examination of first-person narrative situations because of his emphasis on textual description and analysis.[4]

Genette distinguishes three mutually dependent components of the narrative situation: The diegesis (story), the narrative discours (discourse), and the narrating act. Although he borrows Saussure's linguistic terms of signifié and signifiant to describe the interrelationship between the diegesis and the discours, a close examination of Genette's theory reveals that his concepts of diegesis and discours actually derive from Viktor Shklovskij's and subsequently from Vladimir Propp's distinction between fabula (story) and sjuzhet (plot).[5] Like Shklovskij's fabula, Genette's diegesis corresponds to the presented world whereas the sjuzhet and the discours refer to the narrative text that projects that presented world. Genette specifies that the diegesis and the discours are necessarily interdependent. The discours can be considered as a narrative only in that it recounts a story. Further, to be recognized as discours, the narrative text must be related by an explicitly or implicitly presented narrating persona. Thus, Genette suggests, the discours exists by virtue of its relationship both to the story and to the narrator and the narrating act.

Genette's distinction between the diegesis and the discours gains significance when amplified by its linguistic context. In his seminal essay, "De la subjectivité dans le langage," Emile Benveniste describes two distinct levels of the speech-act: Story and discourse.[6] These levels refer to an integration of the subject of the speech-act within what is spoken. Benveniste describes the story as the presentation of the phenomena which occurred at a certain moment in time and in a specific place but without any intervention on the part of the speaker in the story. Discourse he defines as any speech-act supposing a speaker and a listener (a *je* therefore automatically posits a *tu*), and in the speaker an intention to influence the listener in some way. All languages, Benveniste points out, possess elements which provide information exclusively about the subject of the speech-act as well as elements which serve exclusively to present the phenomena which have occurred. Both Genette and Todorov stress that it is precisely this distinction between narrative and discourse which provides the opportunity for a better comprehension of narrative "point-if-view." As Todorov explains: "The proportion of the two speech-act levels determines the degree of opacity of the literary language."[7]

For Genette, then, narratology is the examination of the rapports between the story (diegesis), the discourse, and the narrating act. Genette suggests that these rapports, in turn, determine three categories of relationships, which, by way of further analogy between the sentence as a basic linguistic unit and the text, he terms aspect (voice), mood, and time (tense). By aspect Genette means the manner in which the narrator's voice or presence is implicated in the discourse. Mood encompasses the various forms and degrees of the narrative presentation, the narrator's vision and mode of speech. The temporal dimension entails those relationships between the discourse and the story on the basis of the order, duration, and frequency of the events actually presented in the world of the text.

ASPECT (VOICE)

Genette describes narrative aspect or "voice" as a conceptual extension larger than what is represented by "person." In addition, he views the traditional opposition between first-person and third-person narratives as just one facet among others affecting the way in which the narrator and the narrating act are implicated in the discourse. He specifies that the choice of narrator is not between two grammatical forms, or "persons," but between two narrative postures; the story can be related by one of the characters within or by a narrator outside the story.

Genette uses two axes to define the narrator's status: The level of the narrative within the text and the narrator's relationship to the story. He identifies three, hierarchical narrative levels in relation to the story (the diegesis): Extradiegetic, diegetic or intradiegetic, and metadiegetic. The difference in level can be ascertained by noting that any event a narrative recounts is at a diegetic level immediately "higher" than the level of the narrating act that produces this narrative. An examination of the Abbé Prévost's Manon Lescaut thus illustrates that M. de Renoncourt and his act of writing his memoirs are on the extradiegetic level. The narrated events including the presentation of Des Grieux and his act of narration occur on the intradiegetic level. The events related by Des Grieux compose the metadiegetic level. The relationship between the three hierarchical levels of the narrative can be causal, explanatory, thematically contrasting or similar, or the act of narrating itself could function independently as a distraction or complication of the plot.

Genette distinguishes two types of relationship the narrator can have to the story: The narrator who is absent from the story is heterodiegetic, whereas the narrator who is present as a character is homodiegetic. The narrator's presence also has degrees: A narrator can play a secondary role, functioning as a witness, or can have the central role of hero of the narrative. When the narrator as character is the focal point, the narrative can be further specified as autodiegetic. Despite this apparent identity of narrator and character, Genette emphasizes that there are temporal, spatial, intellectual, and experiential distinctions between the narrating "I" and the narrated "I."

MOOD

Genette defines narrative mood as a complex structure, encompassing the posited narrator's perspective as well as mode of narration. The two chief modalities that regulate narrative mood are perspective and distance. The events, characters, and settings of a fictive universe are never presented in and of themselves, but are always mediated by a narrating subject who has a specific vision, or perspective. Variations in perspective and in types of speech result in the narrator appearing to be situated at greater or lesser distances from the narrated events and presented characters.

Narrative perspective reflects the relationship between the subject of the énoncé and the subject of the énonciation, that is respectively, the character or event and the narrator. Any variations in perspective depend on the degree of restrictiveness of the chosen point-of-view, whether it is solely an external observation of characters and events or also an internal analysis. The narrator can tell more or tell less of what he or she tells, providing more or fewer details in a more or less direct manner depending on the codified principles belonging to each particular point-of-view. The quality and quantity of narrative information and its presentation thus depend on the extent and degree of narrator knowledge possible from the particular angle of vision. Narrative information can thus be restricted or expanded according to the capacity of the narrator's or source's knowledge and field of vision. The narrator may, moreover, intend for whatever reasons dictated by the plot to dissimulate facts or to provide false or unreliable information.

Genette presents a three-term typology to categorize the narrator's field of vision. Each term describes a type of narrative vision or focalization, but these terms do not serve to classify types of literary works; in Genette's system, no one type of narrator focalization governs an entire work, only discrete sections of it. Genette identifies "zero focalization" as the least restrictive; since the omniscient narrator is capable of saying more than any given character knows, his vision does not appear to be bounded in any way. "Internal focalization" is more restrictive because the narrator's field of vision is focused as if through the eyes of a character, and thus the narrator recounts only what that given character knows. "External focalization" is also restrictive with the narrator saying less than what the principal character knows.

Genette cautions against confusing focalization and narration particularly in the "first-person" narrative, where the two instances are taken up by the same person. In novels narrated in the first person, focalization may be internal from the point-of-view of the narrator and encompass his or her present information and accumulated experience. In this instance, the narrator knows more than the hero even though the narrator is indeed the hero. Or, focalization may be internal through the restrictive vision of the hero, thereby requiring the narrator to limit him or herself to the information known to the hero at the time of the narrated events. This second mode of focalization is frequently characterized by such modalizing locutions as "perhaps," "undoubtedly," "as if," "seem," and "to appear" that allow the narrator to make certain hypothetical statements without altering the internal focalization.[8] Deviations in focalization often occur without necessarily disrupting the predominant mode. The narrator may, for example, provide more information than is authorized by the given code of focalization (paralepsis), or may divulge considerably less information than is allowable by the code (paralipsis).

With each sentence of the text, the reader gains some knowledge of both the presented events and characters and the narrator from the narrative discourse and the perspective. Genette, Todorov, and Benveniste all attest to this dual subjectivity and objectivity of language in general and particularly in the literary work: "Tout énoncé porte en lui-même des traces de son énonciation, de l'acte ponctuel et personnel de sa production."[9] Benveniste maintains that the speaker or subject of the énonciation is always discernable in the énoncé by virtue of specific linguistic indices of discourse: "L'acte individuel d'appropriation de la langue introduit celui qui parle dans sa parole. . . . La présence du locuteur à son énonciation fait que chaque instance de discours constitue un centre de référence interne."[10] In the act of énonciation, therefore, discourse establishes the speaker's continuous and necessary relation to the world projected by the énoncé as well as to the énonciation. Benveniste contends that personal and demonstrative pronouns are indices of the subject of the énonciation: "Le terme je dénotant l'individu qui profère l'énonciation, le terme tu, l'individu qui y est présent comme allocutaire."[11] The second category of indices-- verbal moods and adverbial modal expressions--conveys the subject's attitude toward the énoncé, attitudes ranging from anger to fear and from uncertainty to joy. The third category of indices involves the paradigmatic structure of verb tenses, determined by their relation to the axial present tense of the moment of énonciation: "De l'énonciation procède l'instauration de la catégorie du présent, et de la catégorie du présent naît la catégorie du temps. Le présent est proprement la source du temps. Il est cette présence au monde que l'acte d'énonciation rend seul possible . . . l'homme ne dispose d'aucun autre moyen de vivre le 'maintenant' et de le faire actuel que de le réaliser par l'insertion du discours dans le monde."[12] Benveniste distinguishes spoken énonciation from written; the latter, he states "se meut sur deux plans: l'écrivain s'énonce en écrivant et, à l'intérieur de son écriture, il fait des individus s'énoncer."[13] Genette and Todorov specify that in the literary work the traces of the énonciation are more or less pronounced depending on the manner in which the narrator presents the story. They note that there are two principal modes of presentation: Mimetic representation where the referential aspect is accented and pure narration where the process of narration (énonciation) is accented.

Within these two general categories, Genette delineates several modes of speech which serve to intensify the illusion of mimetic immediacy or to emphasize the greater distance between the narrator and the presented characters and events. Mimetic representation is marked by imitated or mimetic speech--speech that is fictively reported as it supposedly was uttered by the characters--whereas pure narration is characterized by narrated discourse in which speech and the act of speaking are treated like one event among others. Although mimetic speech seems to depict the events of the fictional world apparently containing no traces of the narrating act of the narrator, Todorov points out that: "Pourtant une lecture plus attentive montrerait que . . . certains éléments ne lui [à l'énoncé] appartiennent pas. Le choix des détails, le ton du narrateur, . . . la construction des phrases . . . nous renvoient au procès de l'énonciation."[14]

Mimetic representation is a direct imitation of character speech and thought which intensifies the illusion of scenic presence and immediacy by minimizing the narrator's presence in the narrative. The mimetic form of speech--both dialogue and inner speech or thought--is a principal means of characterization. Moreover, objectivizing character speech through either a personal, idiosyncratic style (idiolect) or a dialectic, socially imprinted turn of phrase (sociolect) can produce a more intense mimetic effect. Nearly all characters, except perhaps the presented narrator, are marked by some recurrent linguistic or dialect characteristic which serves as a personal marker, describing such aspects as social class and ethnic origin. This effect is intensified by the explicit differentiation between the imitated characters' speech and thought and the narrator's. On a higher level, the continuity and specificity of a personal linguistic style can create such characterizing traits as pedantry, familiarism, officiousness, romanticism, high rhetoric, and decadence. Carried to the extreme, this form of mimetic speech becomes "stylized," creating the effect of a caricature.

In contrast to the illusion of immediacy that is characteristic of mimetic speech, the distinctive features marking narrated speech are condensation and distance between character and reader. Within the category of narrated speech, Genette distinguishes two states of character speech which differ from a direct reproduction of characters' speech and thought. Narrated speech and thought are the most distant and condensed. Instead of presenting the actual dialogue that "occurred," the narrator reports the speech as an event, as we can see in these examples from My Ántonia: "He had come to thank us for the presents, and for all grandmother's kindness to his family," and "We persuaded our guest to stay for supper with us."[15] Transposed speech, or indirect style, is somewhat more mimetic than narrated speech but still does not provide the reader with a sense of fidelity to the words that were "really" uttered. Genette explains that the narrator's presence is still perceptible in the syntax of the sentence narrated in indirect style: "He told us we had a long night drive ahead of us, and had better be on the hike," and "When grandmother was ready to go, I said I would like to stay up there in the garden awhile."[16]

Todorov points out that the context of narrated discourse is necessarily retrospective: "Il a déjà été énoncé ailleurs."[17] This mode of discourse, which includes both narrated and transposed speech emphasizes the mediated nature of narrated language: "Il s'agit d'un témoignage sur le procès d'énonciation des paroles qui suivent."[18] The "subjective" nature of this type of discourse, so called because of the presence of such personal and demonstrative indices as "I," "here," "there," "now," "then," "this," and "that," establishes a relationship between the subject of the énoncé and the subject of the énonciation and "témoigne de la présence de ce dernier dans le discours."[19] The narrator is always present to varying degrees in both narrated and transposed speech, functioning as the source, guarantor, and organizer of the narrative. In addition, the narrator may adopt the role of narrative stylist, commentator, and analyst.

Todorov relies on the concept of énonciation/énoncé to explain the narrator's, particularly the first-person narrator's, relationship to the narrated story. He differentiates between two general categories of narrator on the basis of the degree of their presence in the projected world: "Il y a une limite infranchissable entre le récit où le narrateur voit tout ce que voit son personnage mais n'apparaît pas sur scène, et le récit où un personnage-narrateur dit 'je.' Les confondre serait réduire le langage à zéro."[20] To elucidate this difference, Todorov compares the act of seeing a house and the act of saying, "I see a house." The act of verbalization, he asserts, always remains distinct from the event being related. The énoncé is the object of the speaker's or narrator's énonciation. Thus the "I" of the sentence is not to be confused with the actual subject-speaker of the sentence. In the sentence "Il court," for example, Il is the subject of the énoncé, whereas moi is the subject of the énonciation. Todorov explains that as soon as the subject of the énonciation becomes the subject of the énoncé--as for example, in the sentence, "I see a house"--it is no longer the same subject who verbalizes: "Parler de soi-même signifie ne plus être le même soi-même."[21] The "I" who sees the house is not the same "I" who relates that event. In a first-person narrative situation, therefore, the actual narrator is the subject of the énonciation and not the character designated by "I" in the énoncé: "Le récit à la première personne n'explicite pas l'image de son narrateur, mais au contraire la rend plus implicite encore. Et tout essai d'explication ne peut mener qu'à une dissimulation de plus en plus parfaite du sujet de l'énonciation."[22] Todorov cautions against a complete detachment of the first-person character-narrator from the implicit author-narra-

tor. Nor is the first-person character-narrator on the same level
as the rest of the presented characters:

> Si nous pouvons lire et les répliques des personnages et
> leur description par le narrateur, le personnage-narra-
> teur, lui, n'existe que dans sa parole. Plus exactement,
> le narrateur ne parle pas, comme le font les protagonistes
> du récit, il raconte. Ainsi, loin de fondre en lui le
> héros et le narrateur, celui qui "raconte" le livre a une
> position tout à fait unique, différent aussi bien du per-
> sonnage qu'il aurait été si on l'appelait "il," que du
> narrateur (auteur implicite) qui est un "je" potentiel.[23]

TIME (TENSE)

Genette describes three aspects of the relations between the temporal dimension of the story and the "pseudo-" time of the discourse. He examines (1) the connections between the chronology of
the events in the story and the temporal order of their arrangement
in the discourse; (2) the connections between the duration of those
events in the story in relation to the duration involved in the narration of those events; and (3) the connections of frequency, or the
repetitive (iterative) capacity of the narration in relation to the
story.

Genette begins his analysis of the temporal dimension of a text
by first lettering sections according to their position in the narration and by then numbering those same sections according to their
position in the chronology of the story time. The emerging anachronies (relationships) are marked by contrast, dissonance, or harmony, and are basic to the structure of the text. Genette terms

retrospective anachronies **analepses** and prospective or anticipatory ones **prolepses**. There are several resulting temporal syntactic relationships: Events and sections can be connected by subordination or coordination; and, returns to the original point of narrative orientation can be simple or complex; for example, prolepses can occur within the context of analepses. Anachronies can vary in the distance of their reach into the past or future. Moreover, their duration within the discourse can vary in length. The proliferation of either analepses or prolepses in a text mark the discourse as respectively retrospective (a preponderance of analepses) or as prospective (a preponderance of prolepses). Genette provides detailed examples of each of these syntactic relations on the micronarrative level of A la **recherche du temps perdu** as well as a simplified outline of the main articulations of the text.

The presence of anachronies frequently yields a sort of double narrative within the text--a subtle dialectic of innocent narrative and retrospective, experienced "verification"--that is particularly evident in first-person narration. The dual temporal dimension of order enhances comparison whenever there is a return to a past episode or an advance to a future one. From retrospective comparisons an enlightened viewpoint can emerge, conferring new meaning on the original episode by rendering significant what previously was not so or perhaps by refuting a first interpretation and replacing it with a new one. Genette notes that anticipatory comparisons brought on by temporal prolepsis occur less frequently because of the mimetic tradition built into fiction demanding that a narrator appear to discover the story as he or she tells it despite the sense of predestination that hangs over the main part of the narrative. By virtue of its markedly retrospective nature, concludes Genette, first-person narrative lends itself particularly well to the use of both analepsis and prolepsis. A first-person character-narrator recounting past events may frequently allude to events that occur subsequent to the past action yet still prior to the present act of narrating. Moreover, as we shall see, to the extent that they bring the narrative act into focus, prolepses refer to the level of voice as well as to the temporal level.

The other two aspects of the temporal dimension include duration and frequency. Genette defines duration as the amount of time taken to recount an event on the discourse level in relation to the length of time involved in the event's occurrence on the story level. He sets forth four possible speeds for the narrative presentation: (1) An **ellipsis** implies a chronological gap in narration; (2) a **descriptive pause** suspends time for the sake of description; (3) a **summary**--often in the form of analepsis or prolepsis--functions as background against which scenes stand out and is marked by a sense of acceleration; and (4) a **scene** corresponds most closely in duration on the discourse and story levels. Both the scene and the descriptive pause represent a slowing down of discourse time in contrast to the sense of rapidity of narration generated by the ellipsis and the summary.

The aspect of narrative frequency refers both to the frequency of occurrence and to the repetition of an action, gesture, or event on the story and discourse levels. Placing this aspect in the grammatical context of singular and iterative verb types, Genette explains that many events can occur one or more times, just as the recounting of an occurrence can happen once or be repeated. According to Genette and Todorov, frequency and duration are the two aspects that allow modifications in the temporal pacing to be incorporated into the fabric of narrative discourse. The verb tenses within most languages do not in and of themselves allow for any gentle gradations in speed of narration. Genette therefore emphasizes the relationships between the types of temporal movement, their duration, succession, and interpolation, and the length and frequency of iterative and singular scenes as a means to govern the overall configuration of discourse movement.

* * * *

Genette's structuralist method for the examination of literary texts of the type that have a first-person character-narrator demands more than the simple identification of who the narrator is. Once the narrative voice has been ascertained, critical consideration must proceed to a study of the narrator's vision, mode of presentation, and the text's temporal dimension. When examining the narrator's vision, we should probe the range of his or her perception, the intended and objectively ascertainable accuracy or inaccuracy of narration, and the depth of his or her analytic abilities. The study of the mode of presentation should address the types of speech used, how that speech reflects the narrator's vision, and how speech and vision reflect the first-person character/narrator relationship. Attention to the temporal dimension of the story (diegesis) and the narrative discourse levels should be directed to the aspects of order, duration, and frequency of the events actually presented in the world of the text. Each of these elements--voice, mode, and time--and their aspects gain their significance from being part of a system. Alone they are meaningless. Their significance depends on the context of contrast with other possible replacements as well as the context of the order of linear succession. Finally, these different types of elements must function reciprocally to enhance their similarities and contrasts, their harmony and dissonance.

3:
A PHENOMENOLOGICAL APPROACH

"Ein Erzähler ist in allen Werken der Erzählkunst da, im Epos
wie im Märchen, in der Novelle wie in der Anekdote. Jeder Vater
und jede Mutter weiß, daß sie sich verwandeln mussen, wenn sie
ihren Kindern ein Märchen erzählen." ["A narrator is present in all
literary works, in epics and fairy tales, in novels and short
stories. Every father and mother knows that they must transform
themselves when they tell their children a story."][1] Like Wolfgang
Kayser in "Wer erzählt den Roman?", Roman Ingarden asserts in The
Literary Work of Art that all literary works of art necessarily entail a narrator, one who stands distinct from the actual author.
Whether explicitly presented in the world of the text or invisible,
the narrator and his or her act of narration constitute an essential part of the structure of a literary work. Someone--whether an
authorial narrator, a first-person character-narrator, or perhaps an
invisible, anonymous narrator--must say the sentences that project
the states of affairs determining the fictional world of the text.

Ingarden addresses the issue of narrative perspective within the context of the many-layered structure of the literary work. Thus, to apprehend the complexity and the richness contributed by the first-person narrator and the narrating act to the presentation of the world of the text, we must investigate the first-person perspective as it is grounded in the essential structure of the literary work of art.

According to Ingarden, the structure of the literary work is organic and polyphonic in nature, founded in the uniqueness of the strata and the diversity of their material and functions. He describes the basic structure of the literary work as a formation consisting of four heterogeneous layers or strata: (1) The stratum of linguistic sound formations; (2) the stratum of meaning units; (3) the stratum of presented objects; and (4) the stratum of schematized aspects.[2] Each stratum has its own characteristic material components, and each performs its own particular functions with regard to the other strata and to the work as a whole. The strata thus do not exist in isolation from each other, but are interrelated. Moreover, by virtue of each layer's special properties, there emerge artistically effective elements and qualities of aesthetic value which each stratum contributes to the aesthetic value of the work as a whole. Ingarden specifies, however, that not every element in a literary work of art is artistically effective; that is, not every element helps the reader intuit the aesthetic qualities of the presented world of the text. For example, the layers of the basic structure and the structural order of sequence which distinguish the literary work of art from nonliterary works of art remain artistically neutral in value. It is this neutral skeletal structure that provides the material foundation for potential artistically effective qualities and thus for aesthetic values. Ingarden examines each stratum separately in **The Literary Work of Art** in order to delineate its constitutive moments and to identify its functions. His discussions of the strata of meaning units, schematized aspects, and presented objects prove particularly illuminating for the present study of first-person narration. However important the stratum of sound formations may be to the structure of the literary work as a whole, it is not relevant to the present discussion of first-person narrative situations.

MEANING UNITS

The stratum of meaning units consists of word meanings and their unification into units of higher meaning such as sentences and complexes of sentences. Meaning units play two significant roles in the literary work. First, their particular material properties and qualities enhance the polyphony of the work and contribute to the aesthetic Gestalt and value of the work as a whole. Second, the word meanings and sentence meanings determine the remaining two strata through their function of projecting the presented objects in accordance with their formal and existential structure and their qualitative constitution. In addition, word meanings and sentence meanings contribute to the precise shaping of those objects by presenting and exhibiting them.

Ingarden differentiates between nominal word meanings and verbal meanings. A nominal word meaning projects as its intentional correlate an object of some sort, be it a thing, character, trait, property, process, or circumstance. (As previously stated in Chapter One, an intentional correlate is neither a real, independent object, nor an ideal one, but heteronomous, depending for its existence and subsistence on the meaning intention of the projecting consciousness.) Ingarden cautions that a meaning unit can never mean an object in exactly the way it is meant by direct intentionality. The object projected by a word meaning is only a schema. In contrast to presented objects--which are projected as being static--verbal meanings imply activities which are meant as dynamic unfoldings and happenings.

Word meanings rarely occur in isolation. Particularly in the literary work, they are usually within the context of a sentence or a sentence complex. When word meanings become elements in a sentence, they undergo certain modifications or formal transformations according to the function they perform within the sentence. Although the actual, individual words remain identical to those in isolation, certain structural shifts occur as they connect to form a unit of meaning, depending, for example, on their syntactic function within the sentence.

A sentence transcends the sum of its parts. It constitutes a new unit of meaning with a sound formation and its own purely intentional correlate. The correlate is purely intentional whether or not it is in addition meant to refer to an objective, independent, concrete state of affairs. A state of affairs is projected by a declarative sentence, whereas an interrogative sentence projects as its correlate a problem, and an imperative sentence projects as its correlate a command. Projected by a nominal word meaning, a state of affairs presents or reveals the subject in its relation to the correlates of the rest of the elements in the sentence. Ingarden classifies the modes of presentation of the various types of states of affairs into three categories: (1) States of occurrence ("My dog runs away quickly." "The train arrives on time."); (2) states of existential qualification ("Gold is heavy." "My son does not believe in God."); and (3) states of thus-appearance ("This pear tastes sweet." "This pine cone feels prickly.") In states of occurrence, the subject either actively performs or passively submits to an action. In states of existential qualification, the subject is the carrier of an empirically ascertainable property, but one that we do not immediately and phenomenally apprehend. When it is a question of states of thus-appearance, however, the object is presented as the carrier of one or more phenomenally perceivable properties or qualities. The sentence, "This pear tastes sweet," thus has as its intentional correlate a state of affairs that exhibits the pear as the carrier of the phenomenally perceptible property of "sweetness."

The different modes of presentation of objects through states of affairs are significant in the way they guide the appearance of objects in the literary work. The texture of a literary work is affected by the predominance of any one of the modes of presentation and the apparent lack of the other types. As Ingarden states: "A work can be written so that its text predominantly projects the states of affaires of the thus-appearance of the object and in only a few cases the states of affairs which represent the object in its 'internal,' not directly intuitively apprehendable properties."[3] For example, a prevalence of "concrete" words may enhance the states of affairs' function of exhibiting phenomenal qualifications, while, in contrast, a prevalence of "abstract" words tends to limit the function to a mere presentation. In addition, characters may be presented primarily or solely through the states of affairs of thus-appearance; a character's physical appearance may thereby be determined to a fuller extent than is his or her psychic life which may only be presented indirectly, as in the following characterization from The Professor's House by Cather:

> The crowd was fussing about one fellow, Rodney Blake, who
> had come in from his engine without cleaning up. . . . He'd
> come up town in his greasy overalls and sweaty blue shirt,
> with his face streaked up with smoke. He'd been drinking;
> he smelled of it, and his eyes were out of focus. All the
> other men were clean and freshly shaved, and they were sore
> at Blake--said his hands were so greasy they marked the cards.
> Some of them wanted to put him out of the game, but he was
> a big, heavy-built fellow, and nobody wanted to be the man

to do it. It didn't please them any better when he took
the jack-pot.[4]

Or, a personage's characteristics may be made phenomenally perceptible by displaying them through actions and gestures.[5] In the following passage from **The Professor's House**, first-person narrator Tom
Outland expresses through his actions his concern for the drunken,
card-playing Rodney Blake, afraid lest he be ambushed by one of the
angry losers:

I thought I'd better follow him home. I knew he lodged
with an old Mexican woman, in the yellow quarter, behind the
round-house. . . . He went in, didn't strike a light or make
a stab at undressing, but threw himself just as he was on the
bed, and went to sleep. . . . I struck a match and lit a can-
dle. . . . I took out the clothes and began picking up the
money, and collected the coins that lay in the hollow of the
bed about his hips, and put it all in the grip. Then I blew
out the light and sat down to listen. I trusted all the boys
who were at the Ruby Light that night, except Barney Shea.[6]

Young Tom Outland's gestures also reveal his personal honesty and
integrity and hint at his need for companionship and a sense of
family. Conversely, a character may be presented strictly by means
of psychic occurrences with no directly perceptible presentation of
physical appearance. When Tom learns that Rodney has sold the Indian treasures they had discovered together in an abandoned village
atop a mesa, he describes his emotional reaction, his disbelief,
confusion, and outrage at his friend and at himself, but he does
not depict his own physical appearance:

I had heard all I wanted to hear. I went to the hotel,
got a room, and lay down without undressing to wait for
daylight. Hook was to drive me and my trunk out to the
mesa early the next morning. All I'd been through in Washington was nothing to what I went through that night. I
thought Blake must have lost his mind. I didn't for a minute believe he'd meant to sell me out, but I cursed his
stupidity and presumption. I had never told him just how
I felt about those things we'd dug out together, it was the
kind of thing one doesn't talk about directly. But he must
have known; he couldn't have lived with me all summer and
fall without knowing. And yet, until that night, I had
never known myself that I cared more about them than about
anything else in the world.[7]

There are additional differences between the kinds of thus-apear-
ance; in some cases, for example, the projected states of affairs
may emphasize visual properties: "When I pulled out on top of the
mesa, the rays of sunlight fell slantingly through the little
twisted pinons,--the light was all in between them, as red as a
daylight fire, they fairly swam in it."[8] In others, tonal or
tactile moments may predominate: "Once again I had that glorious
feeling of being on the mesa, in a world above the world. And the
air, my God, what air!--Soft, tingling, gold, hot with an edge of
chill on it, full of the smell of pinons--it was like breathing the
sun, breathing the colour of the sky."[9] In contrast to critics who
link the first-person perspective to reportlike narration, Ingarden
does not envision one particular mode of presentation as the proper
of first-person narration. Indeed, a particular first-person
narrative situation may be stamped by a prevalence of either

states of existential qualification, states of occurrence, or states of thus-appearance; or there may be an intermingling of the various modes of presentation.

The mode of presentation of objects is also affected by the structure of the sentence projecting the corresponding state of affairs as well as by the kinds of connections between states of affairs. As Ingarden notes: "The difference in sentence structure and in the complex of sentences leads primarily to differently constructed individual states of affairs and to a different kind of connection between them."[10] For example, complexly constructed and involuted sentences may project a complex situation composed of a number of partial states of affairs. On the other hand, a series of simple, uncomplicated sentences may project a number of uncomplicated states of affairs, set down in "patchlike manner." These seemingly isolated and self-contained states of affairs may, however, be connected in various explicit or implicit, tightly or loosely knit manners. The different types of connections also affect the compositional structure of the text.

Finally, the manner in which the "narrating" subject belongs to the work on the basis of the particular configuration of the sentences' meaning content gives rise to several significant differences in the mode of presentation. It is characteristic of works written in an impersonal, objective fashion, that the narrator remains anonymous and that the sentences do not perform the manifestation function. Although the narrator in this instance is not projected as a character into the presented world of the text, neither is he or she totally absent; rather, such a narrator is cogiven, standing for the most part invisible behind the sentences he or she utters. In contrast, a first-person narrator is explicitly presented in the projected states of affairs and thereby belongs to the stratum of presented objects. Not only does the first-person narrator project the presented world of the text, he or she is, in turn, projected as a presented character along with the act of narration by a **presentative text.**[11] Unlike the implicit, anonymous narrator, the first-person narrator functions as a highly visible element in the presented world of the text as both narrator and character. His or her presence as narrator and the act of narration are both explicitly and implicitly affirmed in the projected states of affairs. Thus, by virtue of the double projection of the presentative text, we can see extending throughout the entire first-person narrative situation, a complex state of affairs composed of a double layered, "nested," or "boxed" structure. Ingarden points out that the structure of a first-person narrative situation becomes further complicated when "the 'narration' itself becomes a dramatic presentation, . . . --a 'scene,' a situation in which different characters appear, engage in conversation, and thereby, themselves, project new many-layered formations: the speech itself and the twofold stratum . . . of what is meant as such."[12]

PRESENTED OBJECTS

The layer of presented objects consists of the things, characters, properties, traits, occurrences, and situations projected by nominal word meanings or presented by states of affairs. A presented object may not always be directly projected in its objectified self-givenness, but may, in some instances, be indirectly suggested. Character traits, for example, are often exhibited through gestures, behavior, and words rather than being explicitly stated. In addition, Ingarden notes that the same intentional object may be presented or exhibited "in various combinations of properties, states, etc., depending on which manifold presents it."[13] An object may therefore be presented from a variety of perspectives with different perspectival foreshortenings. Because the objects presented in a literary work are derived purely intentional objects projected by states of affairs, they differ from real objects in a number of significant ways.

As discussed in Chapter One, all real objects are absolutely and universally determined in every respect. When a real chair (the one on which I am sitting) is "colored," for example, its color quality is unequivocally determined and can no longer be considered variable. A real chair not only has the property of being colored, its color is determined as a particular shade of that particular color. Thus, although many of the chair's determinations remain hidden from us, when we perceive that real chair, we apprehend a fully determinate, concrete unity.

In contrast, a presented object can never be absolutely and universally determinate in every detail. Since it is projected by meaning units, its form is only a schema which can never be completely determinate. Unlike a real object, a presented object has many properties which are determinate only in a general manner and an infinite number of points that are not determined in any way by the text. Even when a presented object is of the type of "real" objects and projected as if a fully determinate, individual object, it is still a schematic formation with an infinite number of points of indeterminacy; it only simulates a real object.[14] So, for example, although first-person narrator Jim Burden in My Ántonia describes his grandmother in a manner that removes many points of indeterminacy, an infinite number still remain:

She was a spare, tall woman, a little stooped, and she was apt to carry her head thrust forward in an attitude of attention, as if she were looking at something, or listening to something, far away. As I grew older, I came to believe that it was only because she was so often thinking of things that were far away. She was quick-footed and energetic in all her movements. Her voice was high and rather shrill,

and she often spoke with an anxious inflection, for she was
exceedingly desirous that everything should go with due order and decorum. Her laugh, too, was high, and perhaps a
little strident, but there was a lively intelligence in it.
She was then fifty-five years old, a strong woman, of unusual endurance.[15]

Although many of her physical as well as psychic characteristics are
determinate in this seemingly complete description, many more, including the color of her hair and eyes, the type of clothing she is
wearing, and her facial expression all remain indeterminate. Moreover, some of the properties, such as tallness and spareness, which
are determinate as belonging to Jim's grandmother, are determined
only in a general way in this description.

Presented objects that are of the type of "real" objects must be
presented as existing in space and time. The "presented" space in a
literary work is a "unique space which essentially belongs to the
presented 'real' world."[16] Although presented "real" space is not
absolutely limited and finite, it does not have the unlimited and
infinite properties of real, objective space. As Ingarden explains,
when a situation in a novel is presented as occurring in a room and
no mention is made of anything outside that room, the reader still
assumes that there is space beyond the space bounded by the walls
of that particular room. Although the space surrounding that room
is not determined by any corresponding meaning units, the presented
space does not end with the walls because "it is the essence of
space in general not to have any discontinuity."[17] Since space is
by definition continuous, the space outside the walls of the presented room is **copresented**; the space within the presented room thus
constitutes a **segment** of space.

As discussed in Chapter One, the space that is presented along
with the presented characters, objects, and occurrences is deter-

mined by **orientational space.** The location of the center of orientation--what Husserl calls the "zero point of orientation"--for presented space is dependent on the mode of presentation of the states of affairs and thus can vary among the presented worlds of different literary works. If the presentation is such that the narrator does not explicitly belong to the presented world, the center of orientation still is within the presented world although it is not localized in any one of the characters. All objects and occurrences are then presented and exhibited from the point-of-view of this invisible, copresented narrator, and even if this narrator shifts position, the center of orientation remains constant from his perspective. Or, as is the case in a first-person narrative situation, the center of orientation may be located in the "I" of a presented character-narrator, shifting as that character-narrator moves about in the presented world. It is important to note that the center of spatial orientation need not remain fixed continuously in a single character or narrator; a novel may, for example, begin with the center of orientation located in one character or narrator who plays a main role and subsequently may shift to various other major or secondary characters or narrators.

To achieve a semblance of reality in a literary work of art, presented objects must also be portrayed as existing in time. A temporal order within the presented world is established by virtue of the fact that the occurrences in which the characters participate are by nature temporal in their duration and must necessarily be presented as occurring simultaneously or consecutively. As a result, the semblance of temporal phases is achieved.

Ingarden describes the represented time of literary works as an analogue--and strictly an analogue--of concrete, intersubjective and subjective time. Like intersubjective and subjective time, represented time is never homogeneous in its phases; rather, it is "colored" by the nature of the particular events and circumstances associated with it. Because represented time is an analogue of concrete intersubjective and subjective time, it is colored by various tempi, such as rapidity or slowness, which depend on the type of event occurring in the presented world. The **tempi** also depend on what happened "previously" as compared to what is happening "now" in the presented world as well as on the nature of the experience of the presented characters. These colorations of represented time, of course, remain distinct from any colorations of temporal phases that may occur for the reader during reading and from any personal **tempi** that may color the real-life events of the author.

A number of structural differences remind us that represented time is a modified analogue of real time. In real, intersubjective and subjective time, the present moment has a significant ontic advantage over any past or future moments or phases. Each "now-moment" constitutes an actuality, an **in actu esse,** and it is part of the essence of all real objects that they pass through the phase of **in actu esse.** It is by virtue of this vantage point of the "now-moment," that the past and what is part of the past are determined, and likewise the future, that is, the potential present. In contrast, the past, present, and future of represented time are distinguished one from the other strictly on the basis of the order of the presented objects and events; represented present, past, and future temporal moments do not pass through a genuine phase of **in actu esse.** Unlike the real present, the represented present has no preeminence over the represented past or future. Thus, a certain levelling or equalization of all represented temporal moments and phases occurs.

Another difference between real and represented time involves the mode of presentation by means of states of affairs. Ingarden explains that in a literary work time is represented through the presentation of events which fill out the temporal phases. Real time and occurrences are continuous with no gaps, whereas represented time and presented occurrences appear only in isolated moments or phases. What occurs between these isolated events and segments of time remains indeterminate. Although the represented temporal moments and phases are never a unified, continuous flow, as readers we frequently do not notice any gaps. Because real time by its very nature cannot be discontinuous, when considering represented time, we tend to assume that numerous other unknown temporal moments and phases do occur although they are not presented in the text.

Like the center of orientation necessary for portraying presented space, represented time has a zero point of temporal orientation and various temporal perspectives. In real time, the primary zero point of orientation is the present--an orientational center which is in constant displacement and transformation as present moments recede into the past. Although we can "step back" into a particular moment in the past to recollect past events, we can never truly leave the actual present. In contrast, a presented character in a given moment or phase of represented time can leave the present moment and be transposed into the past, for example, when remembering an event or experience, or when recounting an incident to another presented character. Unlike real time, represented past moments and phases can be retrieved and portrayed as if they were vivid, intense present moments.

Depending on the mode of presentation, a novel can have two different points of temporal orientation. Ingarden explains that,

if . . . a series of events is reported as if it were taking place "now"--and in a continuum of such "nows"-- and then, suddenly, an illumination . . . from a "much later" time moment is thrown on what is "just now" taking place, so that it immediately takes on the aspect of something . . . that is being remembered from a much later time moment, then we are dealing with the phenome-- non of a double temporal orientation, one which is only possible in a presented world.[18]

This narrative mode of double temporal perspective is characteristic of first-person narrative situations. Typically, in novels narrated in the first-person, the zero point of temporal orientation "shifts" between the standpoint of the presented narrator's "now-moments" and what are--for the narrator--the retrospectively related "now-moments" experienced by his or her younger self, seen by the reader as a presented character in the world of the text.

Ingarden identifies another mode of presentation of temporal occurrences which is characteristic of all types of narrative situations including, as we shall see, the first-person narrative situations in both L'Immoraliste and My Ántonia. The first-person narrator may provide brief "accounts" of his or her life experiences over long periods of time, summarizing the main lines and only referring to the major events. In the case of a special event or situation of comparatively short duration, however, the narrator may present a scene that is slowly developed in all possible detail, gradually built up phase by phase with a great many aspects and exhibited in its "concrete fullness and its entire concrete course."[19]

Represented time thus achieves appearance in two different ways. It can be compressed so that long stretches of time--weeks, months, years--disappear rapidly and, because of their lack of perceptible concrete coloration, most moments and phases appear as empty intervals. When presented in this manner, time "sinks nearly to the level of an empty schema which merely provides us with an orientation in the temporal order of the indicated events."[20] The time periods of this "informational" mode of narration are always presented by the first-person narrator retrospectively from the standpoint of a "later" time moment as something that has already happened. A temporal distance between the first-person narrator and his or her younger, presented self is thus emphasized. However, a first-person narrator can also exhibit a scene in its concrete fullness as well as in its complete temporal extension, thereby allowing us to grasp its continuity and apprehend the presented phases as they unfold in their exhibited individuality. Although time that is presented in the individuality of its phases can be considered as having occurred in the past, it is exhibited in "characteristic proximity" and so has the vividness and intensity of a presented moment.[21] The center of temporal orientation shifts to that moment in the past that marks the beginning of the presented scene. And, as events occur, it continues to shift with each phase up to the final moment of the scene. Each phase is thus made present. In this case, the temporal distance between the "now-moment" of the first-person narrator and that of his or her younger, presented self becomes invisible. The reader forgets about the narrator's present and, at least temporarily, apprehends the "now-moments" of the younger, presented self (what is actually the narrator's past) as the story's present. Thus, in contrast to Mendilow, Ingarden recognizes that in the first-person narrative situation, time can be exhibited in at least two ways with two different artistic effects: The temporal distance between the narrator's present and the retrospectively related story can be emphasized; or, that distance can be diminished to the point that the "past" events of the story are considered as occurring in the present.

SCHEMATIZED ASPECTS

Ingarden begins his discussion of schematized aspects by examining them first in relation to real objects and, subsequently, in relation to presented objects. When we perceive a real object or occurrence, we apprehend it in particular views or aspects, which are dependent on such factors as the position of the perceiving subject in relation to the object, lighting conditions, and temporal perspective. From each different point-of-view that we perceive a real object, we experience a new and different sensory content, and thus we apprehend a different aspect of one and the same object. The same phenomenally given object appears through a different aspect when it is perceived from various sides and at different angles. Aspects are not identical to the object appearing through them, however, as Ingarden points out in this example: "The perceived red sphere is spherical, but no aspect in which it appears is itself spherical, nor does it contain sphericity in its content. All it contains--if one may put it incorrectly--is a 'red disk,' with, of course, an altogether characteristic reference to sphericity."[22] Although we apprehend the red sphere as a concrete unity, there are always sides that we cannot see during any one act of perception regardless of our center of spatial orientation. All that can be seen at any one time is an aspect, a part of the surface of the red sphere, for example, through which we perceive the red sphere as an absolutely determinate, real object. Because we cannot see the entire surface at once, nor the interior of the sphere, these "hidden sides" are cogiven. We never perceive a single, isolated aspect, but rather a continuous manifold of "flowing and merging aspects," that refer both to the object and to the object's other aspects.[23]

Ingarden asserts that no two perceptions of aspects are identical. Because the act of perception is itself a dynamic experience, not a static one, and because of changing external circumstances as well as variation in the disposition of the perceiving subject, an act of perception can never be exactly duplicated. We must distinguish, therefore, between our concrete, "one-time-only" experience of an aspect and what Ingarden calls a certain idealization, that is, its posited skeletal structure. All concrete aspects have a skeletal structure (schema). It is this unchanging schematic structure that allows us to perceive as essentially identical the "same" aspects of an object which we experience at different times and under different conditions. Because of their schematic structure, Ingarden calls these aspects **schematized aspects.**

In a literary work of art, all objects, even those of the type
of real, fully determinate objects, are presented by states of affairs. In addition, a sequence of states of affairs determines the
aspects of the presented objects by means of the limited number of
selected qualifications they portray as referring to that object.
Most of the explicitly presented determinants are of a general nature (for example, the color red). They usually lack the specificity (the particular shade of red or the particular pitch of a
sound) that would be experienced in the perception of a real object.
Any determinants that are not explicitly presented remain potential.
Presented objects are, therefore, schematic by virtue of the states
of affairs that present the elements of the aspects through which
those objects come to appearance. It is by means of the schematized aspects as they are predetermined by the text that the presented
objects can appear phenomenally in our imagination.

Schematized aspects form the basis for a reader's imaginational
apprehension of a presented object and establish the range within
which the reader may provide additional complementary details and
qualifications to actualize these aspects. To aid the actualization
of schematized aspects, some of the states of affairs must fulfill
the exhibiting function. As previously noted, some states of affairs present the thus-appearance of an object, **exhibiting** it as the
carrier of a phenomenally perceptible property (for example, "My
room is dreary in winter.") In addition, those states of affairs in
which the existential qualification of an object is presented or a
state of occurrence is related may help the reader to constitute the
aspects through which the phenomenally appearing objects can be in-
tuited. As Ingarden explains: "Exhibiting, and in particular, exhibiting the thus-appearance of an object, also brings with it a
holding-in-readiness of the aspect or manifold of aspects belonging
to the presented object."[24] This "holding-in-readiness" of schematized aspects functions to prescribe the direction and scope of the
reader's actualization.

The layer of schematized aspects plays several significant roles in the literary work of art. It is through schematized aspects that presented objects can be made to appear in a way predetermined by the text. Without schematized aspects, Ingarden concludes, presented objects would be empty schemata. It is through the actualization of aspects held-in-readiness that any individuality and vitality of objects (including the first-person character-narrator) can unfold. Moreover, aspects that are held-in-readiness act to bind the reader to the text and to the way it predetermines the aspects and thus the presented objects.

The variety or the similarity of the aspects' content can, in addition, influence the entire character of the work. Ingarden writes that, in principle,

> aspects of every possible content can be held in readiness in a literary work. Thus, in the presentation of one and the same objective situation, visual, acoustic, and tactile aspects can, for example, be employed. The psychic state of a "hero" can be made to appear . . . by means of external aspects of his bodily behavior as well as by internal aspects.[25]

In a given novel or short story, the schematized aspects may all have similar content or they may vary in their content, thereby allowing the objects to appear in a variety of manners almost simultaneously. Displayed from so many sides, the presented world may, as a result, be characterized by qualities of vitality and intensity. Frequently, however, one particular kind of aspect predominates throughout a given literary work. In some texts, for example, the psychic states of presented characters may be portrayed primarily through aspects of their external behavior, whereas in other works, the same purpose may be achieved by "internal" aspects. Texts narrated by a presented first-person character-narrator may be marked by both "internal" and "external" aspects; "internal" aspects may be used to express the narrator's own psychic processes while "external" aspects express the actions or external manifestations of the other characters' psychic processes. There are also literary works in which visual aspects predominate, resulting in a presented world that is "seen"; purely acoustic events or the acoustic elements of events, for example, are eliminated, and events and objects are presented solely in visual terms. Thus, if a man were angrily shouting, we might be shown the appearance of his face and the strain of his facial and neck muscles; we might see how his rage and anger affect his physical appearance rather than "hear" his angry, shrill tones and the curses he utters. In contrast, the world of the text may be presented in acoustic terms; we would then experience the man's raging anger by "hearing" his shouts and might never "see" him.

These different modes of presentation, of course, have a profound effect on the manner of appearance of the presented objects, characters, and occurrences and hence determine the structure and texture of the narrative situation. Ultimately, these various modes of presentation have their basis in the way in which the sentence meanings project the states of affairs. Moreover, the nature of the various predominating aspects provides the work with a characteristic imprint and a particular style that differentiates it from other literary works of art.

* * * *

Each of the strata in the literary work has its own unique material and particular qualities that retain their characteristics while also conditioning the other strata and contributing to the polyphony of the entire work. To grasp the richness of first-person narrative situations in general and here particularly in Cather's My Ántonia and Gide's L'Immoraliste, we must examine close-ly the strata of meaning units, presented objects, and schematized aspects, their properties and the manner in which they function in each of these texts. Especially illuminating will be the effect of the predominance of certain modes of presentation; represented time and space; the effect of the shifting center of temporal and spatial orientation on the mode of narration; and the characterizing im-print that schematized aspects have on the first-person narrator's perspective, his manner of narration, and on the work as a whole.

4:

L'IMMORALISTE:

MASK OF INNOCENCE

André Gide protested repeatedly against the frequently leveled accusation that his récits were really nothing more than disguised self-portraits. Indeed, in the preface to L'Immoraliste, Gide cautions against a strict identification of a fictional narrator-protagonist with the author: "Que si j'avais donné ce livre pour un acte d'accusation contre Michel, je n'aurais guère davantage, car nul ne me sut gré de l'indignation qu'il ressentait contre mon héros; cette indignation, qu'il semblait qu'on la ressentît malgré moi; de Michel elle débordait sur moi-même; pour un peu l'on voulait me confondre avec lui."[1] Following the publication of L'Immoraliste in 1902, Gide sought to counter further the prevailing opinion of the work as his own confession instead of Michel's. In a letter to one of his critics, Gide explained his method of character creation:

Qu'un bourgeon de Michel soit en moi, il va sans dire;
mais il en est ici comme de ces passions opposées dont
parle habilement Pascal, qui se maintiennent en équilibre,
parce que l'on ne peut céder à l'une qu'au détriment de
l'autre. Que de bourgeons nous portons en nous, cher
Scheffer, qui n'écloront jamais que dans nos livres! Ce
sont des "oeils dormants" comme les nomment les botanistes.
Mais si, par volonté, on les supprime tous, sauf un, comme
il croît aussitôt il s'empare de la sève! Pour créer un
héros ma recette est bien simple: Prendre un de ces bourgeons, le mettre en pot--tout seul--on arrive bientôt à un
individu admirable. Conseil: choisir de préférence (s'il
est vrai qu'on puisse choisir) le bourgeon qui vous gêne le
plus. On s'en défait du même coup. C'est peut-être là ce
qu'appelait Aristote: la purgation des passions.[2]

Despite these efforts, L'Immoraliste has often been read as a psychological "case study" of Michel, or of Gide, or of both.

To explicate the récit, critics have tended to hunt for autobiographical data concerning Gide's own sexual idiosyncracies.[3] A number of critics have also examined the nature of the author's marriage with Madeleine Rondeaux to understand the marital relationship between the fictional Michel and Marceline.[4] To be sure, autobiographical elements abound in L'Immoraliste. To name just a few
similarities, both Gide and his protagonist, Michel, traveled
several times to North Africa; both fell ill and on recovering experienced a physical and intellectual rejuvenation and a rebirth of
the senses; both returned to social order and domesticity on estates
in Normandy; both married devoutly religious women; and both had
friendships with renowned homosexuals who professed individualism:

Gide with Oscar Wilde and Michel with Ménalque. Indeed, as Germaine Brée suggests, "autobiographie et roman se côtoient de près."[5] But as Brée also points out, Michel has little in common with Gide either physically or intellectually. For example, there is little indication as to Michel's physical appearance, and he never experiences the religious fervour that is such an essential part of Gide's own adolescence. Moreover, although the récit reflects the author's life in a number of instances, the various events and circumstances are depicted in an order quite dissimilar to their order of occurrence in Gide's own life.

In response, no doubt, to Gide's attempted dissociation from Michel by describing him as only a bud and his own creative act as cathartic, several critics have approached the récit as a means to psychoanalyze the author. Seen as Gide's effort to shed his own egoism and to create a true, objective portrayal of a drama in his life, L'Immoraliste has been judged an artistic and cathartic failure, because, as Thomas Cordle summarizes, "his hero-narrator, Michel, is too much like himself to provide the release, the detachment he sought in a fictional character."[6]

Because of the sympathetic portrayal of Michel and despite the cautionary preface, L'Immoraliste has also been interpreted as a sermon preaching individualism and total liberation from all social constraints. It has thus been viewed as a defense of Michel and as a self-defense of the author.[7] And yet, Gide sought to dissuade his audience from reading the text as a celebration of what he considered immoral, extreme, egocentric behavior by judging his protagonist severely in a letter to the sociologist and economist, Arthur Fontaine:

The special plea would have begun if I had decorated my hero with very noble and sumptuous deeds. But no, I do not think him capable of them. Everything he does that

is not childish is cruel or lamentably vile, and the exaltation of his thought (or of what gradually takes the
place of it) contributes to no real beauty. He **is not**
well; he has become so. He is not free; he is anarchical.[8]

Despite Gide's pleas for attentive reading of the **récit**, few critics
have heeded him. Like the reception L'Immoraliste received upon
publication, much of the current criticism emphasizes the author-
protagonist relationship to the exclusion of any consideration of
narrative technique and its artistic value.[9]

The narrative situation of L'Immoraliste is considerably more
complex than a cursory examination would allow, and it is certainly
not as simple and clear as at least one critic has affirmed.[10] Michel's narration of his life during the previous three years occupies the major portion of the text. He relates his story during the
course of a single evening to the three friends he has called on to
honor an adolescent pact. The story itself is divided into three
parts and entails a series of events and circumstances during Michel's married life that culminate in the death of his wife, Marceline. Now a widower, Michel remains sequestered in an isolated
house in North Africa, pondering the question of his responsibility
for Marceline's death. His life during the three months since her
death and immediately prior to the evening during which he tells
his story has been marked by the very monotony and habituation that
had weighed down on him before his marriage and then during his illness and subsequent quest for liberation. He now passes his days
holding cool, white pebbles in the palm of his hand until they
become warm, whereupon, he explains, "je recommence, alternant les
cailloux, remettant à tremper ceux dont la froideur est tarie."[11]
Michel's act of storytelling functions as a confession and as a plea
to his friends for help and counsel. He leads his posited listeners
through a logically coherent representation of his discovery, fol-

lowing a grave illness, of his "authentic" self, long repressed in
the past by a variety of social, familial, and intellectual restraints and expectations.

By the time he was twenty-five, Michel confides to his friends,
he had experienced very little of life. The son of a renowned
scholar, he has been living so much in his father's shadow and col-
laborating with him so closely that their work has become virtually
indistinguishable. To adhere to his father's dying wish, Michel
marries Marceline, a woman for whom he feels no real affection.
Hence, in death as in life, Michel's father dictates his son's personal and professional goals. During his wedding trip to North
Africa, Michel becomes gravely ill with tuberculosis and is faith-
fully nursed back to health by his new bride. It is this threat of
death and the subsequent observation of healthy, young Arab boys
that awaken in Michel a heretofore unknown love of life and self.
He becomes further dissatisfied with his previous intellectual detachment from life as he discovers the sensuous aspects of his
nature, a side of himself long suppressed by the austerity and the
purely scholarly pursuits of his former life. This first part concludes with the return of Michel and Marceline to Europe; Michel has
recovered his health; his marriage is beginning to prosper; and he
has received an invitation to lecture at the Collège de France.

In the second part, Michel recounts life at La Morinière, the
Normandy estate inherited from his parents, and in Paris, where he
lectures on Athalaric, the young King of the Goths, who chose to
die at age eighteen rather than be a slave to culture or custom.
(The parallel between Michel and the subject of his studies becomes more explicitly manifest throughout the narrative.) At the
outset of part two, Michel and Marceline appear to have established
a tranquil if not harmonious domestic life. The couple has finally
consummated their marriage, and Marceline is pregnant with their
first child. Michel occupies himself at La Morinière with dreams
of becoming a progressive farmer. When Michel and Marceline quit

La Morinière for Paris, however, this sense of order and equilibrium are left behind as well. Life in Paris soon becomes intolerable; Michel grows dissatisfied with the vapid, dull existence his friends lead in the literary salons, and Marceline is physically and emotionally overwhelmed by her duties as a hostess. Michel looks to Ménalque, an "Individualist" known for his unconventional and liberated lifestyle, as the one person who can understand his discontent and yearnings. Ménalque's philosophy of self-sufficiency stands in sharp contrast to Marceline's religious orthodoxy and dependence on the Church, and it is between these two poles that Michel vacillates. As Ménalque's influence on Michel increases, Marceline's inversely declines. This second part ends with a complete disruption of order in their lives, an order which has thus proved temporary. Marceline becomes seriously ill and loses her child, while Michel, who is disenchanted with his teaching career, becomes increasingly estranged from Marceline and rebels against any aspect of his life that requires commitment. With their presence once again at La Morinière, we witness Michel's attempts to sabotage the farming and husbandry on his own property by poaching with several of his less desirable tenants, his perverse delight in hearing tales of the peasants' incest, and his eventual proposal to sell the estate.

In part three, Michel and Marceline travel to Switzerland in the hopes of finding a cure for her illness, which has been diagnosed as tuberculosis. Driven by his irrepressible urge to be free to do something, to fulfill his desires, and to be free to discover his "authentic" self, Michel drags the ailing Marceline away from the healthful climate of Switzerland to Italy and subsequently to North Africa. Although he tries to simulate a loving, compassionate attitude toward his wife, he is aware, as Marceline's illness progresses, that such affection and compassion would demand a profound alteration of his actual feelings. Moreover, Michel has come to abhor the Church and the blind religious devotion and sense of personal commitment which Marceline symbolizes for him. Once in Africa,

Michel rediscovers the Arab boys he previously coveted. Now grown, however, they prove disappointing for him. And so, he spends his time with one former companion, the now corrupt and dissipated Moktir. As Marceline lies dying, abandoned and alone, Michel believes he is exercising his newly-found freedom by sleeping with Moktir's mistress, as the youth looks on passively.

Michel remains in Africa following Marceline's death, exhausted and confused by his freedom and uncertain of his relation to society and of his future. He tells his friends that in the three months since his wife died, he has had a brief affair with an Arab woman. But, he tells them, too, that the woman claims he prefers her younger brother. The counsel he has requested from his friends leaves them, in turn, confused, in light of this confession. They recognize the universality of Michel's story, his longing for emancipation from social and institutionalized constraints, his refusal to admit responsibility for his cruel actions during the death of Marceline and his lack of compassion for her, his inability to live with his freedom, and hence, his submersion into debauchery and dissipation. Despite this recognition, they are incapable of anything more than proposing for Michel a job in the government, a position which would secure him ever more firmly in all that he has struggled to escape.

Michel's confession begins and concludes during that one evening spent on his terrace. Preceding his narrative and serving as a frame is the introductory portion of the letter written by one of Michel's listeners several days after the confession. Directed to the unidentified listener's brother, Monsieur D.R., Président du Conseil, the letter functions as an introduction to his written transcription of Michel's oral confession that he has already heard three days earlier. Although he condemns the dreadful cruelty exhibited by Michel in the evolution of his unrestrained and eventually immoral emancipation, he also seems uncertain as to what he could do to help. Cognizant that Michel is hardly unique in his desires and behavior, the letterwriter is reluctant to condemn him completely. The introductory portion of the letter thus presents Michel and provides a retrospective frame and judgment of Michel's confession before the reader actually reads the transcribed version of the narrative. It also situates Michel's act of storytelling in the solitude of an African plain, a setting that heightens Michel's sense of isolation and confusion. In addition, the letter provides testimony of the devotion of the three friends, who have traveled far to listen to Michel's story and to offer whatever solace and help they can. Finally, the letter functions as a filter, mediating Michel's confession. The friend writing this letter has already listened to Michel's narrative and now, after considerable reflection of what he has heard, is ostensibly retelling that story. Despite the explicit fact that it is the letterwriter, and not Michel, who is writing the story, he makes several efforts to assure his reader that the story is exactly as Michel originally told it: "Je t'adresse donc ce récit, tel que Denis, Daniel et moi l'entendîmes. . ." (p. 12). He also terminates his letter not with the usual formal closing, but with the introduction of Michel as storyteller: "Quand ce fut la nuit, Michel dit: " (p. 13). Indeed, not only is the formal closure for a letter missing, the final punctuation of a colon reinforces the shift in narrative point-of-view to Michel and emphasizes the sense of transition from the introductory frame to Michel's story. Michel addresses his audience directly on occasion throughout his narrative, and the narrating perspective remains with him for most of the rest of the work; the focus shifts back briefly to the letterwriter only once near the conclusion.

Michel thus has two roles in his narrative, functioning as a narrator who retrospectively relates his own three-year-long discovery of his "authentic" self and as the principal character in that story. Throughout his confession, Michel seeks to assure his audience that he is endeavoring to portray himself in an objective and faithful manner: "Souffrez que je parle de moi; je vais vous raconter ma vie, simplement, sans modestie et sans orgueil, plus simplement que si je parlais à moi-même" (p. 15). Michel's effort at sincerity is not limited to his representation of his own behavior and motives. He has been judged by his wife, Marceline, by his friend, Ménalque, and by the Arab youth, Moktir, and he strives to record accurately those judgments also.

Michel's sincerity and his purported intimacy have proved problematic for some critics, however, who describe the oral narrative as sounding like a carefully prepared rhetorical discourse and not like a personal revelation confided to his closest friends. In his dual role as protagonist and narrator, Michel is charged with overplaying his role as narrator to the point of becoming a pompous storyteller and obscuring his role as the story's protagonist.[12] Yet, as Brée hypothesizes, it is precisely Michel's first-person narration that provides the key to Gide's work. For Gide, the only access to understanding the nature of human experience is to formulate it into a coherent, complete, but limited whole.[13] First-person narration, with its limited and relative perspective, provides that inside view of the protagonist's relation to the events and circumstances of the story. Unlike the third-person, omniscient, authorial form, the first-person form enriches the confessional mode of L'Immoraliste; each fact that Michel reports is augmented by the knowledge that he is the sort of character to divulge that information. Not only does the first-person narrative situation enhance the characterization of Michel, it also suggests that the operation of his mind as both protagonist and narrator is essential to our understanding of the text.

A STRUCTURALIST READING

Michel begins his narrative by explaining to his three friends the reason for their visit to his isolated home. This explanation, in turn, signals the purpose behind the narrating act that also functions as his act of confession: "'Je ne veux pas d'autre se-cours que celui-là: vous parler.--Car je suis à tel point de ma vie que je ne peux plus dépasser. . . . --Souffrez que je parle de moi; je vais vous raconter ma vie, simplement, sans modestie et sans orgueil, plus simplement que si je parlais à moi-même" (p. 15). Motivated by his inability to live with his new-found freedom and by uncertainty over his future, Michel undertakes to recount the oc-currences of the previous three years, a confession, he promises, that will be both sincere and complete. The first-person narrative situation of L'Immoraliste is structured as a confession by a series of hierarchical relationships between the various narrative voices, the shifting narrative focus, and on the temporal dimension.

The novel consists of two major parts, the introductory portion of the letter and Michel's confession, which are presented by means of three distinct narrative levels. The unnamed writer of the let-ter, who is also one of Michel's three friends and confessors, and his act of narration through letterwriting function on the extradi-egetic level. This level remains distinct from the characters and events presented in the letter itself, elements that compose the in-tradiegetic level. Michel in his role as a character in the letter and in his role as narrator of his confession, the three friends who comprise his audience, their arduous journey to Michel's isolated house, and Michel's act of storytelling belong to this second, intradiegetic level which is located inside the extradiegetic level. The events and characters belonging to the story (récit) recounted by Michel as his confession and subsequently transcribed by the letterwriter represent the innermost, metadiegetic level. The elements of this narrative level also include Michel as the protagonist of his story and his three listeners as minor characters. Both the unnamed letterwriter and Michel are thus related to the narrative content or story in a number of ways. The letterwriter belongs to each of the three narrative levels, functioning as a narrator in the framing extradiegetic level, as a character in his own story and posited as a listener to Michel's confession on the intradiegetic level, and finally, as a minor character in Michel's story on the metadiegetic level. Michel belongs only to the intradiegetic and metadiegetic levels. He is a presented character in his friend's letter, and he narrates his story in which he is also the protagonist. Michel is thus both a narrating subject and a narrated object; he is the subject of his énonciation and the object of his own énoncé as well as the object of the letterwriter's énoncé. Similarly, the letterwriter is the subject of his énonciation as well as an object of his énoncé and a designated receiver (narrataire) of Michel's énoncé.

The three distinct narrative levels amplify the meaning of the story in various ways. Because Michel's confession about the preceding three years of his life is narrated in the first-person, the story is also considered "autodiegetic." A letter written by one of the friends to whom Michel has already confessed frames Michel's narrative and introduces Michel and his story to the posited reader--that is, the recipient of the letter. The very existence of the letter confirms that Michel's act of narration as well as the events to which he refers during his confession all belong to the past in relation to the first (extradiegetic) narrator's act of letterwriting. In addition to providing a glimpse of Michel's charac-

ter and actions, the introductory portion of the letter also contains an indication of the confusion, anger, and helplessness experienced by the friends in response to the confession they heard
several days earlier: "Le récit qu'il nous fit, le voici. Tu
l'avais demandé; je te l'avais promis; mais à l'instant de l'envoyer, j'hésite encore, et plus je le relis et plus il me paraît affreux. Ah! que vas-tu penser de notre ami? D'ailleurs qu'en
pensé-je moi-même?... Le réprouverons-nous simplement, niant qu'on
puisse tourner à bien des facultés qui se manifestent cruelles?" (p.
10). Undoubtedly, part of the horror experienced by the extradiegetic narrator stems from the realization that Michel's situation is
not unique, that such extreme, individualistic behavior at the expense of other people is increasingly prevalent among mankind:
"Mais il en est plus d'un aujourd'hui, je le crains, qui oserait en
ce récit se reconnaître" (p. 10).

The response on the part of the extradiegetic narrator that is
contained in the introductory portion of the letter occurs three
days after the actual confession and, as he indicates, has received
considerable conscious reflection. Ironically, it is not until the
end of Michel's confession that the extradiegetic letterwriter offers what appears to be an immediate, unreflected reaction to the
story he has just that evening heard. Both sets of reactions play a
role in the overall structure of the text; however, the latter, reflected responses which actually preface the story affect the posited reader's apperception of the story from the outset. Thus, despite the letterwriter's introductory assurances of accuracy in his
efforts to duplicate the story he has heard and despite Michel's
avowal of sincerity when he begins his narration on the intradiegetic level, the very structuring of narrative voices seems to render
the reliability of presentation intentionally problematic. Because
the story has been filtered through several levels of narration,
the objectivity promised by both narrators is colored in advance by
descriptions of the friends' responses. The relationship between

the narrators on the extradiegetic and intradiegetic levels thus functions to probe the nature and existence of sincerity and objectivity in any self-conscious reflection. Moreover, despite the apparent contrast in character and behavior between Michel and his listeners, the frustration and powerlessness felt by each character involved suggest certain similarities of character and behavior present in them all.

The interrelationships among the three extra-, intra-, and metadiegetic narrative levels become more apparent when we examine the temporal order of events in the story as compared to their order of presentation in the discourse. By lettering each major event or situation as it occurs in the discourse and by then numbering each segment according to its chronological position in the story, we can ascertain how the narrators have arranged the events of the story in their presentation. Moreover, the order of events within the story and the discourse can inform us about the temporal position that the narrators themselves occupy in the text.

We can divide the macronarrative structure of L'Immoraliste into fourteen crudely determined segments (A through N) of various lengths. Furthermore, we can identify twelve temporal positions (1 through 12) in the original chronology of events and situations. The first temporal section (A) consists of the letter written by Michel's friend. It is not possible to date the act of letterwriting precisely, but from the indication of 30 July 189_, we can approximate this act of narration as well as the dates of the rest of the story's events. By virtue of the fact that the act of letterwriting must occur after the events which it describes, we can assign this section the final, or twelfth, temporal position (A12). The first episode in the narrative discourse is thus chronologically the last one in the story's order. Further, because the remainder of the narrative segments and Michel in his roles as first-person narrator and character are all introduced in this first segment, they are in a relationship of subordination.

The second section (B) parallels the first in that it, too, introduces a new narrative voice. In this segment, Michel seeks to explain the reasons why he has summoned his friends to his isolated home in North Africa, and why he feels compelled to confess the events of the previous three years of his life. Because it is noted in the letter, we know that this event occurs three days before the act of letterwriting in section A. Similar to the syntactic position of the preceding narrative segment, this segment (B) also is followed by a lengthy subordination, encompassing the eleven (C through M) identified major events and narrative sections that comprise Michel's confession. Anticipating the temporal position of subsequent episodes, this segment is labelled (B11).

The third section (C) represents a considerable shift in the order of the story's events. Michel begins his confession by remembering that three years have elapsed since he and his three friends were last together for his marriage to Marceline. In addition to providing a reference to their reunion, Michel uses this event to explain that at the time of their wedding, he and Marceline were acquainted by virtue of their families' longstanding friendship, but that Michel was hardly in love with his bride. Indeed, the marriage took place only because of Michel's promise to his dying father. Located near the beginning of the story's chronology, this segment is assigned the second temporal position, thus C2. This reminiscence serves to inspire the subsequent brief retrospective summary (D) of Michel's childhood, adolescence, and young adulthood. Because this narrative segment is dependent on the previous one, it stands subordinated to it. Coupled with sketches of his parents' background and character, this section extends some twenty years into the past to Michel's early childhood and, in its range, touches on a number of significant moments during the course of his life. Although this segment spans a considerable amount of time and includes references to numerous events, it functions primarily to provide insight into Michel's character. Throughout his life,

Michel has been occupied solely with intellectual pursuits to the point of ignoring the physical and social aspects of life. Since this section extends further into the past than do any of the others, it stands first in the temporal order of the diegesis (D1).

The nine subsequent narrative sections (E through M) follow, for the most part, in a linear order that mirrors their chronology in the diegesis. In their coordination, each of these sections or events interrelate by virtue of their chronology in the story and their parallel linear order in the narrative discourse. Following the retrospective overview of his background presented in section D, the next section (E) assumes a temporal position that logically and chronologically succeeds the wedding that is depicted in section C2. Labelled, therefore E3, this segment describes Michel's and Marceline's wedding trip throughout northern Africa during the course of which Michel falls ill with tuberculosis. Narrative section F4 follows section E in chronological order to describe Michel's lengthy recuperation. It is during this period that Michel commits himself to regaining his health. He first takes an interest in his own body and physical wellbeing after noticing the sensuality and health exuded by the glistening bodies of the young Arab boys brought by Marceline to entertain her husband. As he begins to regain his strength, Michel explores the gardens and walkways throughout Biskra. After his complete recovery, Michel and Marceline begin their return trip to France, traveling slowly northward through Italy. While en route, Michel seems preoccupied with his newfound health and physique; to rid himself of the vestiges of his exclusively intellectual past, he shaves off his beard, grows his hair long, and spends hours sunbathing. The next section (G), again in a temporal position (5) to match the chronological order of the story, concerns Michel's display of virility by his dramatic rescue of Marceline from a runaway coach. After trashing and binding the coachman, Michel drives Marceline to safety; and it is that night that they consummate their marriage.

The next section (H) follows in linear order and hence occupies the sixth temporal position (H6). This narrative section begins with Michel's and Marceline's arrival at their Normandy estate, La Morinière, and is marked by their apparent happiness. During their stay, Michel is pleased to discover that Marceline is pregnant; and he delights in both the strenuous physical exertion of working the estate's farm by day and the intellectual stimulation of studying his new subject, Athalaric, by night.

The following section (I) occurs in linear order, hence I7, and its syntactic coordination with the preceding section is marked by the contrast of events between the two segments. Living in Paris for Michel's teaching job, neither Michel nor Marceline enjoys the endless series of visitors they must receive and calls they must pay. Michel's lectures are poorly received by all but the renowned individualist and homosexual, Ménalque, and Marceline's strength and health during the late stages of her pregnancy decline seriously. Michel engages in several lengthy philosophical discussions with Ménalque on the topic of individualism. The next section (J) depicts the rapid onset of Marceline's illness and occurs simultaneously with Michel's visits to Ménalque. It is after the second, all-night visit that Michel returns home to find Marceline gravely ill, having delivered a stillborn baby. Because this event occurs simultaneously with those events in section I7, we can assign this section the temporal position of 7^1 (prime).

The eleventh section (K) describes the couple's return to La Morinière, having abandoned Paris as soon as Marceline is well enough to travel. Once again, this section occupies a temporal position (8) that follows chronologically from the previous one, and again, its syntactic coordination to the preceding sections is marked by contrast. Unlike the contentment enjoyed during their autumn stay, their ever increasing discontent is evident throughout their springtime sojourn. Marceline's health and spirits decline steadily, and Michel becomes intrigued, almost possessed, by the opportunity to operate with a group of local poachers to rob his own stock.

The twelfth section (L) occupies the next linear position (9). Although this narrative segment encompasses the entire trip south from Normandy to the final destination of Biskra in Africa, Michel in his role as narrator depicts only a few of their stops in Switzerland and Italy. The journey back to Biskra symbolizes for Michel a return to the original place and moment of his exclusive commitment to his own physical health and pleasures, his rebellion against his previous intellectual pursuits, and his obsessive, ego-centric desire to exert his free will. Conversely, for Marceline, this trip charts her steady advance toward death and her growing awareness of the true nature of her husband's wholly self-oriented character.

The thirteenth section (M) occupies the tenth temporal position and follows in the same linear pattern of the other sections, constituting the subordinated clause that is Michel's confession. With its description of Marceline's death, this section signals the end of Michel's confession and thus the close of this lengthy subordination in which Michel plays the role of both major character and narrator. The final narrative section (N) marks a return to the temporal position (11) occupied by Michel in his role as narrator. Although a number of hours elapse between the beginning and conclusion of Michel's acts of narration and confession, both narrative sections belong to approximately the same temporal position; thus, section N is assigned the position of 11^1 (prime). The return of this narrative section to the eleventh temporal position marks the end of the syntactic subordination of Michel in his role as narrator to the unnamed friend and narrator of the introductory portion of the letter.

The major narrative sections and the order of their temporal positions can be illustrated concretely by the diagram that follows:

A12 [B11 (C2 (D1) E3-F4-G5-H6-I7 (J7^1)-K8-L9-M10) N11^1]

The main articulations of the innermost subordination in the narrative discourse are, for the most part, in a linear order that mirrors the chronology of the diegesis. On the level of the macronarrative structure, Michel, in his role as first-person narrator, is represented only by B11 and N11^1, segments that are outside the boldface parentheses and inside the brackets. Finally, the first-person letterwriting narrator's presence is evidenced by A12, a position outside the brackets. Built on a structure of subordinated analepses, or retrospections, this pattern emphasizes the significance the past has for both narrators and their acts of narration. Although both narrators express concern over Michel's future, it is the events of the past three years and Michel's behavior at that time that dominate the confession which is, in turn, the major portion of the text. Within the actual confession, Michel is prominent in his role as the main character. As the first-person narrator of the confession, however, Michel's presence does not seem to figure into the main articulations of the story he tells.

Although Michel's presence as the narrator of his confession is not very apparent in the macronarrative structure, it becomes highly visible when we examine a typical, brief, but significant event on the micronarrative level. The following narrative segment describes the night after Michel's rescue of Marceline from the runaway coach. In this passage, there are seventeen identifiable shifts in temporal position within the narrative discourse. Each of these shifts is marked in advance by a letter (A through Q). The segments all occur in one of the four different temporal positions which, in this episode, constitute the chronology of the diegesis. By the first temporal position (1) is meant any past event or situation occurring prior to the night being depicted. The second temporal position (2) refers to the events, character gestures, and thoughts occurring on that particular night (cette nuit-là). The third temporal position (3) includes those events or situations that have occurred in the past in relation to the narrator's present moment, but in the future in relation to the night of the second temporal position. The fourth temporal position (4) refers to the present moment of Michel's narrative act and, by extension, to Michel in his role as the narrator of his confession.

(A2) Ce fut cette nuit-là que je possédait Marceline./ (B4) Avez-vous bien compris ou dois-je vous redire que/ (C2) j'étais comme neuf aux choses de l'amour? Peut-être est-ce à sa nouveauté que notre nuit de noces dut sa grâce.../ (D4) Car il me semble, à m'en souvenir aujourd'hui,/ (E2) que cette première nuit fut la seule, tant l'attente et la surprise de l'amour ajoutaient à la volupté de délices,--- tant une seule nuit suffit au plus grand amour pour se dire,/ (F4) et tant mon souvenir s'obstine à me la rappeler uniquement./ (G2) Ce fut un rire d'un moment, où nos âmes se confondirent.../ (H4) Mais je crois qu'il est un point de l'amour unique,/ (I3) et que l'âme plus tard, ah! cherche en vain à dépasser; que l'effort qu'elle fait pour ressusciter son bonheur, l'use; que rien n'empêche le bonheur comme le souvenir du bonheur./ (J4) Hélas! je me souviens de cette nuit.../

(K2) Notre hôtel était hors de la ville, entouré de jardins, de vergers; un très large balcon prolongeait notre
chambre; des branches le frôlaient. L'aube entra librement
par notre croisée grande ouverte. Je me soulevai doucement,
et tendrement je me penchai sur Marceline. Elle dormait;
elle semblait sourire en dormant. Il me sembla, d'être plus
fort, que je la sentais plus délicate, et que sa grâce était
une fragilité. De tumultueuses pensées vinrent tourbillonner
en ma tête. Je songeai qu'elle ne mentait pas, disant que
j'étais tout pour elle; puis aussitôt: "Qu'est-ce que je
fais donc pour sa joie?/ (L1) Presque tout le jour et chaque
jour je l'abandonne; elle attend tout de moi, et moi, je la
délaisse!.../ (M2) ah! pauvre, pauvre Marceline!..." Des
larmes emplirent mes yeux./ (N1) En vain cherchai-je en ma
débilité passé comme une excuse:/ (O2) qu'avais-je affaire
maintenant de soins constants et d'égoïsme? n'étais-je pas
plus fort qu'elle à présent?...

Le sourire avait quitté ses joues; l'aurore, malgré
qu'elle dorât chaque chose, me la fit soudain triste et pâle;
--et peut-être l'approche du matin me disposait-elle à l'angoisse:/ (P3) "Devrai-je un jour, à mon tour, te soigner?
m'inquiéter pour toi, Marceline?"/ (Q2) m'écriai-je au-dedans
de moi. Je frissonnai; et, tout transi d'amour, de pitié,
de tendresse, je posai doucement entre ses yeux fermés le
plus tendre, le plus amoureux et le plus pieux des baisers.
(pp. 73-4)

The pattern of shifting temporal positions can be described concretely by the following diagram:

A2-B4-C2-D4-E2-F4-G2-H4-I3-J4- [K2-L1-M2-N1-O2-P3-Q2]

As the diagram illustrates, the narrative structure in this segment is divided into two main parts, the first consisting of a discussion of love, the second being a depiction of Michel's vision of
the sleeping Marceline just before dawn. Michel's remembrance of
what happened that night includes elements K through Q and is subordinated to the main clause following segment J: "Hélas! je me
souviens de cette nuit...". In the first half of this episode,
noted as A through J, there is a noticeable shifting between temporal positions (2) and (4), that is, (2) the retrospective moment of
that night as experienced by Michel as a presented character on the
metadiegetic level, and (4) the present moment of Michel's act of
narration on the intradiegetic level. With the exception of a single departure from this pattern in I3, the narrative discourse
alternates between the temporal positions of Michel's present moment
as a character and his present moment as narrator.

The episode begins with a narrative segment occupying the second
temporal position--what is the present for Michel as a character
constitutes the past for Michel as narrator--and, in the next sentence immediately shifts to the fourth position when Michel as narrator directs a question to his listeners. The second temporal
position is evident in four of the initial ten narrative segments,
while exactly half of the segments occupy the fourth position. Each
sentence or phrase depicting the actions or thoughts of Michel as a
character is immediately followed by some sort of explanation or re-
joinder on the part of Michel in his present role as narrator. Although Michel does reveal the intellectual as well as the physical
intimacies of his past in temporal position 2, his constant explanatory interjections from temporal position 4 seem to be efforts to
justify those past actions and behavior, and thus, in a way, to seek
vindication for himself.

The predominant temporal positions change in the subordinated analepsis that is constituted by segments K through Q. In the embedded remembrance of what happened that night, the temporal positions of the narrative segments alternate between (2) the moments of that night in the past and either (1) past events occurring prior to the night in question or (3) past events actually occurring after that night. For example, as Michel gazes at the sleeping Marceline in segment K, he reads on her face a new-found happiness with their marriage. But he is also guiltily aware of his continued failure to return that love: "'Qu'est ce que je fais donc pour sa joie?'" His response to this silently posed question entails a shift in temporal position to (1) the past prior to that night because it evokes memories of the numerous occasions on which he has abandoned Marceline while he has gone off in search of amusement. The temporal position shifts back to (2) when the remembrance of those earlier times causes Michel to weep quietly in shame, a shame that is highly ironic in light of his similar behavior throughout Marceline's illness. Further along in the episode, the temporal position shifts from the moment of that night (2) to (3) past events occurring after that night. As Michel studies Marceline's face in segment (O2), he suddenly wonders in (P3) whether their roles will reverse sometime in the future, making it necessary for Michel to care for an ailing wife. The fear inspired by such future uncertainties, in turn, generates a shift in the temporal position of narrative segment (Q) back to that night (2) as Michel bestows a tender, what he describes as "pious," kiss on Marceline's brow. This regular pattern of first analepses and second prolepses suggests an effort on Michel's part to expiate the guilt he becomes aware of while gazing at Marceline that night. Although Michel dwells on the past in the first half of this micronarrative segment through his use of the analeptic shifts, the proleptic shifts in the subordinated second half of the segment reveal his efforts to rid himself of the effects of his past actions and behavior.

Although Michel in his role as character and in his role as a first-person narrator are essentially one and the same personage, there are two relatively distinct personae depicted in the text. As the first-person, autodiegetic narrator, Michel occupies a position that is retrospective to the events and circumstances that he presents in his narrative. The narrator Michel is older than the character Michel by just a few years at the beginning of the narrative and by just a few months at the conclusion. As the older narrator, Michel is more experienced and more knowledgeable because he has had considerable opportunity to reflect on his past actions and behavior. Indeed, as Michel in his role as narrator indicates to his friends at the end of the text, he has done little more since Marceline's death than meditate and wish he could escape the monotony of his thoughts. Despite the complete freedom from all material, social, and personal commitments Michel has gained by Marceline's death and by the proposed sale of La Morinière, all aspects of his life are monotonous: "'J'ai là, voyez, des cailloux blancs que je laisse tremper à l'ombre, puis que je tiens longtemps dans le creux de ma main, jusqu'à ce qu'en soit épuisé la calmante fraîcheur acquise. Alors je recommence, alternant les cailloux, remettant à tremper ceux dont la froideur est tarie. Du temps s'y passe, et vient le soir... Arrachez-moi d'ici; je ne puis le faire moi-même'" (p. 186). As a result of his retrospective position, the older Michel knows more than the younger character Michel who is bound in his experience and knowledge either to past occurrences or to the events in which he is participating. In addition, from his vantage point as narrator, the older Michel is aware of the fate of the other characters and of the outcome of events in which the younger character Michel is participating. Moreover, because the older Michel has greater access to information, he is more capable of discussing the motivation behind his own and other characters' behavior and of analyzing the significance of his own thoughts and the actions and gestures of those around him.

Between the introductory portion of the letter and Michel's confession there is a highly visible shift in focalization. Although
the focalization of both the unnamed letterwriter and Michel is internal, a number of differences in their respective ranges of perception are apparent. While Michel in his role as narrator has a
broader range of perception and a greater ability to analyze his
past behavior than he does as a younger character, he has not yet
achieved a sufficient distance from the events and his emotional response to those events to be able to understand and comment on
their full impact on his life. As a narrator, it is difficult for
Michel to distantiate himself from his own acts of narration and
confession. The explanations that Michel offers as a narrator are
directed only to a limited extent at his actions and thoughts as
they occur on the night of his confession. Instead, he addresses
his commentary and analysis primarily to the actions and thoughts
of the younger character Michel as if seeking to justify or vindi-
cate his past actions. In turn, in his retrospective position,
the unnamed friend and letterwriter stands witness not to the actions of the younger Michel but to the interpretation given them by
the older Michel in his narration of them. Thus, although the letterwriter does not as a narrator have access to the thoughts and intimate behavior of the younger Michel, insights which are reserved
for the older Michel, his position does allow him the opportunity to
provide both an overview of the events depicted by Michel and a response to Michel's act of narration.

Throughout Michel's confession there are also numerous more subtle shifts in focalization. Always subject to the principles
governing internal focalization, the restrictive boundaries of the
field of vision vary according to the shifts in focus between Michel as narrator and Michel as presented character. When the narrative focus is through the eyes of the character Michel, the vision
is even more restricted because he has access to considerably less
information and experience than does Michel as narrator. In addi-

tion to his inability to grasp the full significance of occurrences, the character Michel's vision is stamped by his overwhelming sense of immediacy and by his increasingly ardent desire to escape the repressive inhibitions that have controlled his past life. In contrast, Michel's vision as narrator is defined by its retrospective nature. His vision as narrator is not focused exclusively on the past, however, for he stresses that the reasons for confessing his past behavior stem from his urgent need to escape the anarchical and monotonous freedom of the present and to control his future life. Thus, as the focalization shifts between Michel in his position on the intradiegetic level and Michel in his position on the metadiegetic level, there emerges a constant alternation between Michel's present and past, his actions as a narrator and as a character, his act of narration and the events in which he is participating, and his confession and the behavior that warranted that confession. In brief, the shifts between the internal focalization of these two personae generate a striking juxtaposition of Michel's past immorality and his present need for expiation by confessing. Moreover, it is this continuous juxtaposition of two distinct first-person perspectives, each situated in a distinct temporal position, that emphasizes the novel's narrative structure as a confession.

This pattern of shifting narrative focus is evident from the outset of Michel's confession. Each episode is portrayed at least partially through both Michel's vision as character and as narrator. Thus, each episode is marked by a subtle blending of two narrative foci and two levels of knowledge and experience. Toward the beginning of his story, for example, Michel relates the sudden onset of his tuberculosis and his arrival, near death, at Biskra. He begins the narrative of his slow and lengthy recuperation by direct queries from his focus as narrator to his listeners. (The darker print emphasizes the intradiegetic focalization of Michel in his role as narrator, whereas the lighter print suggests Michel's metadiegetic focalization in his role as character.)

Pourquoi parler des premiers jours? Qu'en reste-t-il?
Leur affreux souvenir est sans voix. Je ne savais plus ni
qui, ni où j'étais. Je revois seulement, au-dessous de mon
lit d'agonie, Marceline, ma femme, ma vie, se pencher. Je
sais que ses soins passionnés, que mon amour seul, me sau-
vèrent. Un jour enfin, comme un marin perdu qui aperçoit la
terre, je sentis qu'une lueur de vie se réveillait; je pus
sourire à Marceline.--Pourquoi raconter tout cela? L'important, c'était que la mort m'eût touché, comme l'on dit, de
son aile. L'important, c'est qu'il devînt pour moi très
étonnant que je vécusse, c'est que le jour devînt pour moi
d'une lumière inespérée. Avant, pensais-je, je ne comprenais
pas que je vivais. Je devais faire de la vie la palpitante découverte. (p. 29)

In this overview of the first weeks of his illness, Michel in his
intradiegetic position as narrator probes the meaning he affixes to
those early days of his marriage and his near encounter with death.
He retrospectively summarizes the entire early period of his illness by mentioning his delirium and hence his lack of consciousness
of the events around him. The narrative focus seems to shift briefly to the bedridden Michel whose limited consciousness and range of
vision enable him to see only Marceline bending over to care for
him. Throughout this time, the level of his understanding is rudimentary; he comprehends only that his life depends on the love and
attention offered him by Marceline. The narrative focus alternates
between the bounded perspective of Michel as character and the reflective nature of Michel as narrator to depict the day on which he
begins to regain his consciousness and strength and first smiles
weakly at Marceline. Within the sentence relating this smile, the

focus shifts briefly from the semi-conscious character to Michel's perspective as narrator. This shift is reflected by the simile that describes Michel's re-emergence into consciousness and life in terms of a lost sailor who has finally sighted land. The focus remains with the narrator as he seeks to explain to his audience the significance of this emergence from death and confusion, this rebirth into life. It is Michel as narrator who describes and analyzes the meaning of this first step of the character's reawakening to life and of the extended exploration of life that follows, events which exceed the parameters of Michel's knowledge as a character. This interweaving of the two foci could suggest, moreover, that even in his present role as narrator, Michel's self-discovery is not yet complete. This hint--through the image of the lost sailor--at Michel's continued lack of consciousness and awareness is reinforced by the image of his monotonous behavior at the conclusion of his confession as he mechanically shifts pebbles from hand to hand.

The first paragraph of this episode functions as a summary overview of the initial stages of Michel's illness and as an anticipatory introduction to the recovery period. Except for a brief shift in the narrative focus to that of the ill, semi-conscious Michel, the focus remains with Michel in his role as narrator as he searches for the meaning behind his illness, his discovery of previously ignored aspects of life, and the decisions he makes as a narrator about what he will relate to his audience. The second paragraph which follows below constitutes a descriptive pause between the narrator's self-examination and explanations to his listeners about his narrative and a subsequent scene between Michel and Marceline:

Le jour vint où je pus me lever. Je fus complètement séduit par notre home. Ce n'était presque qu'une terrasse. Quelle terrasse! Ma chambre et celle de Marceline y donnaient; elle se prolongeait sur des toits. L'on voyait, lorsqu'on avait atteint la partie la plus haute, par-dessus les maisons, des palmiers; par-dessus les palmiers, le désert. L'autre côté de la terrasse touchait aux jardins de la ville; les branches des dernières cassies l'ombrageaient; enfin elle longeait la cour, une petite cour régulière, plantée de six palmiers réguliers, et finissait à l'escalier qui la reliait à la cour. Ma chambre était vaste, aérée; murs blanchis à la chaux, rien aux murs; une petite porte menait à la chambre de Marceline; une grande porte vitrée ouvrait sur la terrasse. (pp.29-30)

The narrator's presence is evident at the outset of this description of Michel's room and the terrace onto which it opens. Such modifiers as "complètement," "Ce n'était presque qu'une terrasse," and "Quelle terrasse" point to the subject of the énonciation, that is, the narrator, in his direct address to his audience. For the actual description of his room and the terrace, the narrative focus shifts to the character's perspective. The focus remains from the character's point-of-view as he walks along the terrace, describing the surrounding houses and gardens, the last of the currant blossoms, and the central courtyard.

The focus shifts briefly back to Michel in his retrospective narrator's role for a summary of his activities as he would lounge day after day on the terrace. The narrator's presence is quite visible in the first two sentences of the following passage by virtue of both his reference to his recent period of solitude and reflection and the iterative nature of the overview: "Là coulèrent des jours sans heures. Que de fois, dans ma solitude, j'ai revu ces lentes journées!..." (p. 30). After the narrator's introductory, iterative reminiscence of long days spent on the terrace, the focus shifts abruptly to the character's point-of-view as he rests in a chair on that terrace:

Marceline est auprès de moi. Elle lit; elle coud; elle é-
crit. Je ne fais rien. Je la regarde. O Marceline!... Je
regarde. Je vois le soleil; je vois l'ombre; je vois la ligne
de l'ombre se déplacer; j'ai si peu à penser, que je l'observe. Je suis encore très faible; je respire mal; tout me
fatigue, même lire; d'ailleurs que lire? Etre, m'occupe
assez. (p. 30)

As in the preceding descriptive passage, the character Michel portrays his immediate surroundings in their relationship to him. He
describes Marceline, for example, as sitting "auprès de moi." The
narrative focus shifts only once during this passage as Michel's cry
"O Marceline!..." interrupts the enumeration of Marceline's activi
ties as she keeps him company on the terrace. The exclamation is so
freighted with emotion inspired by events that occur in the character's future that it would seem to be a cry of anguish uttered by
the narrator in retrospect. This shift in focus is brief, however,
for the character Michel immediately resumes his observations of
the world that he can see from his chair on the terrace. He mea-
sures the passing hours from his stationary position by tracing the
sun's movement across the sky and the corresponding shadows that en-
croach further and further across the terrace.

In the scene that follows this iterative summary, we see one particular day's activities from the character Michel's point-of-view.
As Marceline enters his room one morning, Michel relates that from
his position he can see behind her a young, brown Arab boy, named
Bachir, who stares back at him in silence:

L'enfant, devant la froideur de mon accueil, se déconcerte,

se retourne vers Marceline, et, avec un mouvement de grâce animal et câline, se blottit contre elle, lui prend la main, l'embrasse avec un geste qui découvre ses bras nus. Je remarque qu'il est tout nu sous sa mince gandourah blanche et sous son burnous rapiécé. (p. 31)

It is Michel's first visit from Bachir that is related with the immediacy and detail of a scene. His several subsequent encounters with Bachir are separated one from the other with ellipses--"le lendemain" and "le jour suivant"--and lack the detail and proximity of the first scene. Although the verb tenses change from the present used throughout the preceding scene to the past in the two subsequent visits, the encounters are still related as they are observed and experienced by the metadiegetic character Michel:

Le lendemain Bachir revint. Il s'assit comme l'avant-veille, sortit son couteau, voulut tailler un bois trop dur, et fit si bien qu'il s'enfonça la lame dans le pouce. J'eus un frisson d'horreur; il en rit, montra la coupure brillante et s'amusa de voir couler son sang. Quand il riait, il découvrait des dents très blanches; il lécha plaisamment sa blessure; sa langue était rose comme celle d'un chat. Ah! qu'il se portait bien. C'était là ce dont je m'éprenais en en lui: la santé. La santé de ce petit corps était belle. (p. 32)

The metadiegetic character Michel's close observation of Bachir inspires his preoccupation with his own physical health, his physical pleasures, and his physique.

Following Bachir's third visit, Michel reacts in horror when he

suffers a relapse. After he describes the immediate physical sensation of spitting up the blood clot, and he expresses both fear and
anger in response to this setback in his recovery, the narrative focus shifts to Michel in his role as narrator. From his retrospective and more distantiated position, the narrator is able to explain
the reasons behind the range of emotions experienced by his ill,
younger, metadiegetic self:

    Je fis quelques pas, chancelant. J'étais horriblement
ému. Je tremblais. J'avais peur; j'étais en colère.--
Car jusqu'alors j'avais pensé que, pas à pas, la guérison
allait venir et qu'il ne restait qu'à l'attentre. Cet
accident brutal venait de me rejeter en arrière. Chose
étrange, les premiers crachements ne m'avaient pas fait
tant d'effet; je me souvenais à présent qu'ils m'avaient
laissé presque calme. D'où venait donc ma peur, mon horreur, à présent? C'est que je commençais, hélas! d'aimer
la vie. (p. 33).

That the focus shifts to the intradiegetic narrator is subtly
evident by the "car" in the fifth sentence, signaling an interrup-
tion of the younger, metadiegetic Michel's disturbed response to the
sensation and sight of the clot and the start of the older, intradiegetic Michel's more objective, intellectual analysis of that
emotional reaction. When the intradiegetic narrator pursues his
reflection about the intensity of that response, his presence is
made evident through the remarks he addresses directly to his listeners: "Chose étrange...." There are other indices of the intradiegetic narrator's presence in his énonciation, clues that indicate that the narrative focus is, at least temporarily, through the
eyes of the older Michel: ". . . je me souvenais à présent. . . ."

The question that is posed and the response that is offered also serve to mark the presence of Michel in his intradiegetic role as narrator.

At the conclusion of this intellectual examination on the part of the narrator of the younger, metadiegetic Michel's psyche, the focus returns to that character's point-of-view for a second observation of the clot that caused Michel's display of emotion. It is thus from the younger, metadiegetic Michel's perspective, as he bends over to retrieve the spittle, that the clot is re-examined: "Je revins en arrière, me courbai, retrouvai mon crachat, pris une paille et, soulevant le caillot, le déposai sur mon mouchoir. Je regardai. C'était un vilain sang presque noir, quelque chose de gluant, d'épouvantable. . ." (pp. 33-4).

The interweaving of these two narrative foci is evident throughout L'Immoraliste, and the constant alternation of the intradiegetic narrator's iterative and distantiated mode of presentation with the metadiegetic character's more immediate and intense mode paces the narrative discourse. While the events that occur during the nearly three years of Michel's marriage are depicted from the perspective of the younger, metadiegetic Michel as he experiences them, they are explained or justified from Michel's perspective as the intradiegetic narrator of the story and as a "penitent" seeking expiation for the guilt he feels over Marceline's death.

In his intradiegetic role as narrator, Michel promises his listeners a sincere and complete revelation of his thoughts and actions. It is this assurance of sincerity, uttered at the outset, that establishes a bond of trust between Michel as narrator and his listeners and allows the latter to anticipate a truthful rendition of the events in question. Indeed, near the conclusion of his narrative, as Marceline lies slowly dying, Michel in his intradiegetic role as narrator addresses his listeners more and more frequently in an attempt to persuade them of his profound love for his wife despite his actions to the contrary. Again, the highlighted portions of the following passage indicate the older, intradiegetic Michel's assurances of his love for Marceline and bespeak the considerable thought he has devoted to trying to understand the occurrences during the final days of Marceline's life:

Bien qu'elle se reposât sur moi de tous les soins, ces déplacements précipités la fatiguaient; mais ce qui la fatiguait plus, j'ose bien à présent me l'avouer, c'était la peur de ma pensée.

--Je vois bien, me dit-elle un jour, je comprends bien votre doctrine--car c'est une doctrine à présent. Elle est belle, peut-être,--puis elle ajouta plus bas, tristement: mais elle supprime les faibles.

--C'est ce qu'il faut, répondis-je aussitôt malgré moi.

Alors il me parut sentir, sous l'effroi de ma brutale parole, cet être délicat se replier et frissonner... Ah! peut-être allez-vous penser que je n'aimais pas Marceline. Je jure que je l'aimais passionnément. Jamais elle n'avait été et ne m'avait paru si belle. La maladie avait subtilisé et comme extasié ses traits. Je ne la quittais presque plus, l'entourais de soins continus, protégeais, veillais chaque instant et de ses jours et de ses nuits. Si léger que fût son sommeil, j'exerçai mon sommeil à rester plus léger encore; je la surveillais s'endormir et je m'éveillais le premier. Quand, parfois, la quittant une heure, je voulais marcher seul dans la campagne ou dans les rues, je ne sais quel souci d'amour et la crainte de son ennui me rappelaient vite auprès d'elle; et parfois j'appelais à moi ma volonté, protestais contre cette emprise, me disais: n'est-ce que cela que tu vaux, faux grand homme! et me contraignais à faire durer mon absence; mais je rentrai alors les bras chargés de fleurs, fleurs de jardin précoce ou fleurs de serre... Oui, vous dis-je; je la chérissais

tendrement. Mais comment exprimer ceci... à mesure que
je me respectais moins, je la vénérais davantage;--et qui
dira combien de passions et combien de pensées ennemies
peuvent cohabiter en l'homme?...

Depuis longtemps déjà le mauvais temps avait cessé; la
saison s'avançait; et brusquement les amandiers fleurirent.
--C'était le premier mars. Je descends au matin sur la
place d'Espagne. Les paysans ont dépouillé de ses rameaux
blancs la campagne, et les fleurs d'amandiers chargent les
paniers des vendeurs. Mon ravissement est tel que j'en
achète tout un bouquet. Trois hommes me l'apportent. Je
rentre avec tout ce printemps. Les branches s'accrochent
aux portes, des pétales neigent sur le tapis.. J'en mets
partout, dans tous les vases; j'en blanchis le salon, dont
Marceline pour l'instant, est absente. Déjà je me réjouis
de sa joie... Je n'entends venir. La voici. Elle ouvre la
porte. Elle chancelle... Elle éclate en sanglots.

"Qu'as-tu? ma pauvre Marceline."

Je m'empresse auprès d'elle; la couvre de tendres ca-
resses. Alors, comme pour s'excuser de ses larmes:

"L'odeur de ces fleurs me fait mal", dit-elle...

Et c'était une fine, fine, une discrète odeur de miel...
Sans rien dire, je saisis ces innocentes branches fragiles,
les brise, les emporte, les jette, exaspéré, le sang aux
yeux.--Ah! si déjà ce peu de printemps elle ne le peut plus
supporter!...

Je repense souvent à ces larmes et je crois maintenant
que, déjà se sentant condamnée, c'est du regret d'autres
printemps qu'elle pleurait. --Je pense aussi qu'il est de
fortes joies pour les forts, et de faibles joies pour les
faibles que les fortes joies blesseraient. Elle, un rien
de plaisir la soûlait; un peu d'éclat de plus, et elle
ne c'est ce que j'appelais le repos, et moi je ne voulais
ni ne pouvait me reposer. (pp. 166-69)

Despite his considerable reflection as to the reason for Marceline's tears, however, Michel fails to realize that the grief and sorrow they reveal are not for her own imminent death. Rather, as his listeners and his posited readers can sense, Marceline weeps for Michel's spiritual death and for the callousness he exhibits at the expense of all those around him. Her tears are in recognition of the human sacrifice he readily accepts in order to continue his own, solitary existence, devoid of commitments to any human or to any spiritual being. Not only does the intradiegetic narrator Michel fail to understand Marceline's sorrow even in retrospect, he recounts his gesture of surprising his wife with flowers in an attempt to persuade his listeners of his sincere and actual love for her. Thus, in his intradiegetic role as narrator as well as in his metadiegetic role as character, Michel is unable to recognize his offering of flowers as the empty, meaningless gesture that Marceline and his three friends see it to be. Unlike Marceline, Michel cannot see that the artificial, exaggerated spring he creates in the salon with the numerous branches of almond blossoms reflects both the hollowness of his gesture and the falseness of his love for her. Although the intradiegetic narrator Michel has sworn to be truthful and sincere, he continues to insist that he loves his wife. Indeed, the narrative focus is from the metadiegetic character's point-of--view and not the intradiegetic narrator's when Michel finally admits that his professed love for Marceline has been a deception:

Marceline, exténuée par le voyage, s'est couchée sitôt
arrivée. J'espérais trouver un hôtel un peu plus con-
fortable; notre chambre est affreuse; le sable, le soleil
et les mouches ont tout terni, tout sali, défraîchi.
N'ayant presque rien mangé depuis l'aurore, je fais servir

aussitôt le repas; mais tout paraît mauvais à Marceline et
je ne peux la décider à rien prendre. Nous avons emporté
de quoi faire du thé. Je m'occupe à ces soins dérisoires.
Nous nous contentons, pour dîner, de quelques gâteaux secs
et de ce thé, auquel l'eau salée du pays a donné son goût
détestable.

Par un dernier semblant de vertu, je reste jusqu'au soir
près d'elle. Et soudain je me sens comme à bout de forces
moi-même. O goût de cendres! O lassitude! Tristesse du
surhumain effort! J'ose à peine la regarder; je sais trop
que mes yeux, au lieu de chercher son regard, iront af-
freusement se fixer sur les troux noirs de ses narines;
l'expression de son visage souffrant est atroce. Elle non
plus ne me regarde pas. Je sens, comme si je la touchais,
son angoisse. Elle tousse beaucoup; puis s'endort. Par
moments un frisson brusque la secoue. (pp. 180-81)

Despite his promised sincerity, Michel in his distantiated, intradiegetic role as narrator has masked his true feelings by his constant assurances that he loves Marceline. There is, therefore, an
ironic reversal of roles, when it is the metadiegetic character Michel who declares in a moment of exasperation: "Par un dernier
semblant de vertu. . . ."

The pattern of shifting narrative foci thus becomes increasingly
complex during the course of Michel's confession as the intradiegetic narrator tries to expiate his guilt by persuading his friends
of his love for Marceline. Although the narrator has promised to
recount the truth, he chooses to mask rather than reveal his actual feelings about Marceline to his friends, and it is from the
point-of-view of the metadiegetic character Michel that the truth
is ultimately set forth. Such a deception undermines the intra-

diegetic narrator's original vow of sincerity and renders problematic the bond of trust that Michel has sought to forge between
his friends and himself. This blending of distinct narrative
foci and temporal positions allows us to see the unique structure
of the narrative situation in L'Immoraliste, the major articulations of Michel's growth and development and the reversal of roles
when it is Michel in his metadiegetic role as character and not in
his intradiegetic role as narrator who ultimately confesses.

A PHENOMENOLOGICAL READING

Early in his career, with the publication of Paludes, Gide recognized the importance of both narrative perspective and the characterization of the narrator to the structure and meaning of the text.
He recorded his thoughts abaout this mise en abîme in his 1893 journal: "J'aime assez qu'en une oeuvre d'art, on retrouve ainsi trans-
posé, à l'échelle des personnages, le sujet même de cette oeuvre.
Rien ne l'éclaire mieux et n'établit plus sûrement toutes les proportions de l'ensemble."[14] Characterization is particularly significant in first-person narrative situations because the growth and
development of the narrator-protagonist so often parallels the progression of the story. As a first-person narrator recounting the
story of his own life, Michel projects himself as the central
character in the presented world of his narrative, thereby making
himself and his act of confession the focal point of L'Immoraliste.
The significance of Michel's story is at least partially revealed
through the constant juxtaposition of Michel in his roles as narrator and character and through the evident contrast and shifting
between his respective visions of life. The complexity and extraordinary richness of Michel's character development, the evolution

of his vision, and thus the profound meaning of his narrative, however, become phenomenally apparent through the various types of sentence structure, the predominance of certain types of aspects, and
their impact on the presented world.

The narrative situation of L'Immoraliste is a complexly nested
structure, consisting of narration embedded within narration. As
previously described in the structuralist reading, the novel itself
is actually a letter written by one of Michel's three friends who
has come to hear Michel relate the events of the previous three
years, the circumstances surrounding Marceline's death, and his own
present, solitary, discontented existence outside an isolated North
African village. Divided into two parts, the text opens with the
introductory portion of this letter in which the unnamed friend ap-
prises his brother of the story, more appropriately the confession,
he has just heard. The second and considerably longer part consists
of the letterwriter's transcription of the oral narrative he listened to three days earlier. Although Michel's story is thus technically narrated by the unnamed letterwriter, the zero point of spatial orientation is located in Michel's perspective throughout the
confession. Except for the introductory portion of the letter and
the brief segment at the conclusion of Michel's confession, the aspects through which all the characters, occurrences, and objects
come to appearance are therefore presented as if seen, heard,
touched, or in some way experienced by Michel. It is through
Michel's eyes, for example, that the terrace outside his room in
Biskra is depicted, and it is from his physical position seated on
that terrace, that the shadows from the setting sun can be seen
creeping across the ground. As we have already seen, when Michel
spits up the blood clot following Bachir's third visit, he describes the actual sensation of the clot in his mouth, and subsequently, describes the appearance of the clot as he perceives it.
Michel is also able to describe the emotions of anger and dismay he
feels with the realization that the blood clot signifies a setback

in his recovery. To describe his experience of these emotions, Michel has only to rely on his own inner awareness. In contrast, when he attempts to portray the emotions of other characters, he must depend on his perception and interpretation of their physical behavior. Thus, for example, he relies on Marceline's external manifestation of tears to perceive her unhappiness and frustration when he decorates the salon with almond branches. But then, partially because he does not have access to Marceline's unvoiced thoughts and partially because he is blind to what those tears really signify, he misinterprets the meaning of Marceline's physical display of emotions.

Although the zero point of spatial orientation resides in Michel's point-of-view consistently throughout that part of the novel that constitutes his confession, the presented world of the text is initially depicted from the perspective of the letterwriter and friend. In the introductory portion of the letter and again briefly at the close of Michel's confession, all characters, objects, and occurrences are depicted in their relation to this unnamed first-person narrator. It is from his perspective that the arrival of the three friends is portrayed. He depicts them as exhausted from the heat during their journey, yet exhilirated by the newness of their surroundings. It is also from this unnamed narrator's point-of-view that Michel is judged. His first response to Michel's confession occurs near the end of the novel as Michel completes his narrative. The unnamed narrator relates the silence that blankets the four men and can only hypothesize about the motives that prompted Michel's confession and about Michel's own assessment of his confession on the basis of the tone of his voice and his failure to display any emotions:

Michel resta longtemps silencieux. Nous nous taisions aussi, pris chacun d'un étrange malaise. Il nous semblait

hélas! qu'à nous la raconter, Michel avait rendu son action plus légitime. De ne savoir où la désapprouver, dans
la lente explication qu'il en donna, nous en faisait presque
complices. Nous y étions comme engagés. Il avait achevé
en ce récit sans un tremblement dans la voix, sans qu'une
inflexion ni qu'un geste témoignât qu'une émotion quelconque
le troublât, soit qu'il mît un cynique orgueil à ne pas nous
paraître ému, soit qu'il craignît, par une sorte de pudeur,
de provoquer notre émotion par ses larmes, soit enfin qu'il
ne fût pas ému. Je ne distingue pas en lui, même à présent,
la part d'orgueil, de force, de sécheresse ou de pudeur.
(pp. 184-85)

In this spontaneous reaction to Michel's narrative and to his manner of confession offered before any discussion between the three
listeners could take place, the unnamed narrator attributes his own
response to the two other friends also present with his use of the
plural pronoun "nous," suggesting thereby a certain appropriateness
and universality of such a reaction. The judgment offered by the
unnamed narrator to his brother in the introductory portion of the
letter does not proceed beyond the initial confusion and ambiguity
with which he responded on first hearing the story three days
earlier. Indeed, the narrator conveys his own inner sense of confusion by admitting his hesitency to write at all, by explicitly
questioning his own assessment of the situation, and by stressing
the need to act quickly:

Le récit qu'il nous fit, le voici. Tu l'avais demandé;
je te l'avais promis; mais à l'instant de l'envoyer,
j'hésite encore, et plus je le relis et plus il me paraît
affreux. Ah! que vas-tu penser de notre ami? D'ailleurs

qu'en pensé-je moi-même?... Le réprouverons-nous simplement, niant qu'on puisse tourner à bien des facultés qui se manifestent cruelles?--Mais il en est plus d'un aujourd' hui, je le crains, qui oserait en ce récit se reconnaître. Saura-t-on inventer l'emploi de tant d'intelligence et de force--ou refuser à tout cela droit de cité?

En quoi Michel peut-il servir l'Etat? J'avoue que je l'ignore... Il lui faut une occupation. . . . --Hâte-toi, Michel est dévoué: il l'est encore; il ne le sera bientôt plus qu'à lui-même. (p. 10)

This introductory portion of the letter functions as the "presentative text" for Michel's narrative. Although Michel ostensibly narrates his story, it is the unnamed narrator of the letter who presents Michel in the roles of narrator and principal character of his confession. Thus, while Michel projects states of affairs that describe events and characters during the preceding three years of his life, it is the unnamed friend, functioning as an invisible co-presented narrator, who projects the states of affairs which depict Michel in his role as narrator. For Michel to be an explicit narrator within the presented world of the text, he must be projected by a "presentative text." Similarly, in order to be an explicitly presented element in the world portrayed first in his letter, the unnamed narrator and letterwriter and his act of narration are projected by another, this time invisible, "presentative text."

This "nesting" of narrators and acts of narration results in a narrative situation composed of three distinct perspectives of the events in Michel's confession: That of Michel as a presented character observing and participating in those events during the years of his marriage; that of Michel as a presented first-person narrator recounting and explaining those events and occasionally seeking to justify them; and that of the friend interpreting Michel's version of those events as well as judging the latter's act of narration and confession. Because the characters and occurrences of Michel's confession are filtered both through Michel's memory and interpretation of them and through the friend's understanding and judgment of them, the objectivity and sincerity promised by each narrator at the beginning of his respective act of narration seem intentionally problematic. Indeed, despite the vows of truthfulness uttered by the friend in his letter and by Michel at the outset of his confession, the very nesting of narrative points-of-view suggests that Michel's self-conscious reflection defies objectivity and, to a certain extent, truth. Rather, this nesting of narrative perspectives emphasizes that the examination and interpretation of Michel's behavior, character, and motives are necessarily subjective actions that are dependent on a conscious subject's perceptions. Despite the degree of distantiation achieved through the time lapses between the events' "occurrence" and their narration three years later, it is still Michel--always self-serving and self-justifying--who is confronting his own previous behavior, and it is Michel who selects and arranges the elements of his story to suit his own purposes. From the outset, the nested structure renders the question of Michel's objectivity and sincerity problematic by drawing attention to both the multiple levels of the narrators' mediation and the processes of selection and arrangement of the elements. There is, thus, a fundamental tension between the promises of honesty and the necessary result that a self-serving confession achieves. Established on the basis of first Michel's vow to be bluntly faithful in his narration to what "actually transpired" and supported thereafter by his witness and confessor's corroborative testimony, the nesting of narrative perspectives would appear to provide a firm foundation for moral truthfulness before Michel himself, before his friends, and before God. But, in short, the confesser here controls all to his own egocentric ends in an attempt to win whatever "punishment" or "penance" his friends will meet out--that is, what he actually anticipates will be their aid in extricating him from his present, uncomfortable circumstances. As the nesting of perspectives suggests, Michel's confession is a fabric of surfaces; he promises to unmask himself only to produce another mask. The mirrors here are convex and concave; objects, events, and motives are mediated through several perceptions and are always ultimately filtered through Michel's never objectively mimetic perspective.

The nested structure also emphasizes the several perspectives present within the world of the text, and, thus, the different interpretations offered and judgments pronounced on the presented characters' actions and motives. This labyrinth of narrator mediation and the variety of perspectives are central to the structure of the narrative situation of L'Immoraliste and essential to an understanding of the novel's significance.

We can readily perceive the shifts in narrative vision caused by the relocation of the zero point of spatial orientation from the unnamed letterwriter's perspective to Michel's. A more subtle distinction in vision is apparent throughout Michel's narration as the zero point of temporal orientation shifts continuously between the present moment of Michel in his role as narrator and his present moment as character. The juxtaposition of these two distinct temporal moments and perspectives reveals, in turn, two distinct levels of narration, and ultimately, two parallel, mutually illuminating narratives. From his temporal perspective as the younger character, Michel portrays the evolution of his character, the deterioration of his relationships with the people around him, and finally, the role he plays in Marceline's death. From his temporal perspective as narrator, Michel remembers and interpets his past; he explains the motives behind his confession and struggles to justify and be pardoned for his past actions.

As Michel begins his narrative, the present "now-moment" is that of Michel in his role as storyteller. Having silently gathered his three friends together on the terrace, Michel waits for nightfall to explain the motives behind his confession: "Car je suis à tel point de ma vie que je ne peux plus dépasser. Pourtant ce n'est pas lassitude. Mais je ne comprends plus. J'ai besoin... J'ai besoin de parler, vous dis-je. Savoir se libérer n'est rien; l'ardu, c'est savoir être libre" (p. 15). From his perspective as narrator, Michel also provides a summary overview of his childhood, adolescence, and young adulthood and of the reasons for his marriage to Marceline. Michel offers this background to his character in order to explain and perhaps to justify in advance the dramatic changes he underwent during the nearly three years of his marriage. He confides that, having lost his mother when he was but fifteen, all aspects of his life were devoted to his studies under the tutelage of his father. So single-minded and intense was his dedication to scholarship that, Michel admits, by the time he was twenty, he was fluent in a number of ancient languages but had never experienced life itself. Such an exclusively intellectual vision of life continued until,

j'atteignis vingt-cinq ans, n'ayant presque rien regardé que des ruines ou des livres, et ne connaissant rien de la vie; j'usais dans le travail une ferveur singulière. J'aimais quelques amis (vous en fûtes), mais plutôt l'amitié qu'eux-mêmes, mon dévouement pour eux était grand, mais c'était besoin de noblesse; je chérissais en moi chaque beau sentiment. Au demeurant; j'ignorais mes amis, comme je m'ignorais moi-même. Pas un instant ne me survint l'idée que j'eusse pu mener une existence différente ni qu'on pût vivre différemment. (p. 18)

As Michel points out, he even intellectualized all sentiments and emotions, thus cherishing the abstract concept of friendship, but not the friends themselves.

Michel approached his marriage to Marceline in similarly intellectual terms. Having married to ease his dying father's fears
of leaving his son alone to fend for himself, Michel confesses
that any emotion he felt at the wedding was not out of love for
Marceline but in recognition of the emotion and sentiment expressed
by the wedding guests. As Michel illustrates with these retrospectively recounted vignettes, even at the time of his marriage, he
did not experience for himself the ever-changing phenomena of life
around him. Rather, he studied the static, unchanging past, and he
merely observed the present, reacting to people and events in an indirect manner from his distanced stance. Any emotions he experienced were in response to the emotions displayed by someone else,
and not as a direct response to the situation or occurrence itself.
Thus, Michel can conclude, "j'engageai ma vie sans savoir ce que
pouvait être la vie" (p. 16). Not only has Michel never engaged in
any sort of relationship with other people and never experienced
life itself except in purely intellectual terms, he admits that up
until this point in his life, he has been totally unaware of his
physical self: "Une autre chose que j'ignorais, plus importante
encore peut-être, c'est que j'étais d'une santé très délicate.
Comment l'eussé-je su, ne l'ayant pas mise à l'épreuve?" (p. 19).

Following this retrospectively related summary overview of his
background, the zero point of temporal orientation shifts to Michel's now-moment three years earlier as he begins his honeymoon.
While on the ship from Spain to North Africa, Michel observes Marceline at length and begins to realize that as a wife, she is more
than simply a companion. As the scene of this day on board ship
unfolds, the now-moment is located with the young man, and it is
from this temporal position and perspective that Michel watches
Marceline seated by herself on the bridge of the ship and notices
for the first time his wife's beauty and grace. It is the younger, recently married Michel who approaches Marceline, receives her
tender glance, and bestows a kiss on her eyelids. Unfamiliar with

experiencing his emotions in direct reponse to anything, Michel reacts to this tenderness in an extreme manner: "Nous étions tous
deux seuls sur le pont. Elle tendit son front vers moi; je la
pressai doucement contre moi; elle leva les yeux; je l'embrassai sur
les paupières, et sentis brusquement, à la faveur de mon baiser, une
sorte de pitié nouvelle; elle m'emplit si violemment, que je ne pus
retenir mes larmes" (p. 21). This scene, portrayed from the temporal position of the younger Michel, stands in contrast to the preceding overview of his life before his marriage, the summary presented
from the older narrator's temporal position. In the overview of his
earlier life, the narrator Michel emphasizes his lack of awareness
of his own emotions, his body, and of the people around him. Depicted from the younger character's present moment, the subsequent
scene with the young couple confirms that assessment by portraying
Michel's tentativeness and emotional vulnerability during his first
experience with a person in other than purely intellectual terms.
Further, this indication of the younger Michel's lack of emotional
and sensorial awareness of himself and of the world around him suggests his alienation from humanity in general and thus the initial
fragility of his marital relationship. The impact of Michel's first
consciousness of his emotions and his first inkling of life beyond
the intellectual boundaries he has so long observed gains its
strength both from the shift in the temporal orientation to the
younger man's present and from the juxtaposition of the two portrayals: The narrated background overview and the exhibited interaction between Michel and Marceline in the scene on the ship.

Throughout his narrative, Michel uses his retrospective stance
as narrator not only to explain and justify his past actions, but
also on occasion to reaffirm the attitudes and the philosophical
stance he had adopted when he was younger. As Michel's recovery
from his illness progresses, for example, Marceline stresses the
importance of one's faith in God to regaining strength and health.
Michel, however, rejects Marceline's suggestion to seek spiritual

help, insisting that his recuperation is strictly a matter of his physical recovery. Following the young character Michel's denial of his need for spiritual assistance, the center of temporal orientation shifts to the narrator's retrospective position:

Je vais parler longuement de mon corps. Je vais en parler tant, qu'il vous semblera tout d'abord que j'oublie la part de l'esprit. Ma négligence, en ce récit, est volontaire; elle était réelle là-bas. Je n'avais pas de force assez pour entretenir double vie; l'esprit et le reste, pensais-je, j'y songerai plus tard, quand j'irai mieux. (p. 38)

This change in temporal orientation to the older narrator's present moment allows him to reassert the younger man's rejection of the religious, spiritual, and psychic aspects of life in favor of the physical. Thus, in the present moment of his role as narrator, Michel parallels his previous decision by embracing the physical and sensorial side of life and by denying the spiritual. Ironically, although his act of confession is itself a spiritual and intellectual process, Michel in his role as narrator chooses to probe neither the implications of his past denial of God nor the significance of his present reaffirmation of that denial.

From his temporal position as narrator, Michel also endeavors to explain his act of narration to his listeners. As a self-conscious storyteller, Michel discusses the purpose of his narrating act, revealing the reasons why he emphasizes certain occurrences in his narrative and why he exhibits them only through certain aspects. Immediately following the scene in which his collapse from tuberculosis is depicted, for example, Michel explains to his audience that he is delving into the early days of his marriage specifically because it was during this period of time that he first glimpsed the vitality and diversity life has to offer:

Pourquoi parler des premiers jours? Qu'en reste-t-il?
Leur affreux souvenir est sans voix. Je ne savais plus ni
qui, ni où j'étais. . . . Pourquoi raconter tout cela?
L'important, c'était que la mort m'eût touché. . . . L'important, c'est qu'il devînt pour moi très étonnant que je
vécusse, c'est que le jour devînt pour moi d'une lumière
inespérée. Avant, pensais-je, je ne comprenais pas que je
vivais. Je devais faire de la vie la palpitante découverte.
(p. 29)

As Michel progresses in his narrative, he explains that because
his primary interest after this reprieve from death was his physical experience of life, he will, in turn, address the issues of his
physical health and sensorial awakening almost exclusively. Each
event and circumstance is, therefore, mentioned or depicted as it
relates either to the younger character's rejection of his repressive, intellectual past life or to his obsessive devotion to his
health and his sensorial exploration of life:

Je ne parlerai pas de chaque étape du voyage. Cer-
taines n'ont laissé qu'un souvenir confus; ma santé, tantôt meilleure et tantôt pire, chancelait encore au vent
froid, s'inquiétait de l'ombre d'un nuage, et mon état
nerveux amenait des troubles fréquents; mais mes poumons
du moins se guérissaient. Chaque rechute était moins
longue et moins sérieuse; son attaque était aussi vive,
mais mon corps devenait contre elle mieux armé. (p. 58)

As this passage indicates, for example, the return journey from Biskra to France is remembered, and therefore, portrayed, not in terms
of the cities visited, but on the basis of the stage it represented
in his recovery.

An examination of Michel in his temporal position as narrator reveals not only his efforts to describe and explain the evolution of
his character, but also the complexities and the motives behind his
confession. Michel asserts to his friends that he is confessing his
past actions out of frustration over the monotony of his present
life and out of fear of being unable to envision any other mode of
existence in the future. He asserts that he recognizes his guilt in
Marceline's death and, on occasion, seems to exhibit some pain and
anguish over having dragged her from Switzerland to her death in
Biskra.   Yet Michel ultimately admits that his confession and his
efforts to expiate any guilt he might feel over Marceline's death
proceed not from a spiritual need to have his sins forgiven, but
rather out of a desire to gain his friends' assistance to escape his
stultifying life in North Africa and to be reintegrated into a more
comfortable and pleasurable social environment:

Ce qui m'effraie c'est, je l'avoue, que je suis encore très
jeune. Il me semble parfois que ma vraie vie n'a pas encore commencé. Arrachez-moi d'ici à présent, et donnez-
moi des raisons d'être. Moi, je ne sais plus en trouver.
Je me suis délivré, c'est possible; mais qu'importe? Je
souffre de cette liberté sans emploi. Ce n'est pas, croyez-
moi, que je suis fatigué de mon crime, s'il vous plaît de
l'appeler ainsi,--mais je dois me prouver à moi-même que je
n'ai pas outrepassé mon droit. (p. 185)

Thus, although Michel voluntarily confesses his cruelty in abandoning the ailing and weakened Marceline to a lonely death, he does not
deviate from his egotistical behavior either during his confession
or even at the end as he awaits his friends' response and judgment.
Moreover, Michel has not invested his friends with the right and responsibility to impose on him either his act of confession or any
penance, the performance of which would assure him the forgiveness
of his sins. Indeed, Michel in his temporal position as narrator
does not seek from his friends any sort of moral or spiritual assistance, but rather rescue from what he senses to be his physical purgatory.

To achieve this end, Michel in his role as narrator frequently
tries to justify and thus win pardon for his past egocentric behavior. Hence, for example, a brief temporal shift in perspective occurs when the zero point of temporal orientation is initially located in the younger character's present moment in the scene depicting the onset of Michel's illness. The rocky coach ride, Marceline's deep sleep, Michel's continuous coughing-up of blood, and his
decision to hide the telltale stained scarf from his wife are all
exhibited as they are occurring through the perspective of the
younger character Michel. Upon their arrival at the hotel the next
morning, Michel becomes irritated and distraught when, despite his
own silence, Marceline fails to deduce what happened during the
course of the preceding night. When Michel finally tells Marceline
that he has spit up blood, he is, in turn, vexed that Marceline
faints in response: "Je m'élançai vers elle avec une sorte de rage:
'Marceline! Marceline!--Allons bon! qu'ai-je fait! Ne suffisait-
il pas que moi je sois malade!--Mais j'étais, je l'ai dit, très
faible; peu s'en fallut que je ne me trouvasse mal à mon tour" (p.
26). The temporal perspective shifts briefly from the present moment of Michel as he egotistically rages at the unconscious Marce-

line. In his temporal position as narrator, Michel seeks to explain, and thereby to justify, to his listeners such obsessively
egotistical behavior by attributing it to his general physical
frailty and his current weakened state.

The narrator Michel's retrospective attempts to justify his
cruelly self-centered actions, and thus to have such behavior understood by his three friends, reach a crescendo of pathos near the end
of the narrative during Marceline's and Michel's rapid, breakneck
journey through Italy. A frail and exhausted Marceline sadly confronts her husband over his philosophy of life:

"Je vois bien, me dit-elle un jour, je comprends bien
votre doctrine--car c'est une doctrine à présent. Elle est
belle, peut-être,--puis elle ajouta plus bas, tristement:
mais elle supprime les faibles.
--C'est ce qu'il faut, répondis-je aussitôt malgré moi.
Alors il me parut sentir, sous l'effroi de ma brutale
parole, cet être délicat se replier et frissonner... Ah!
peut-être allez-vous penser que je n'aimais pas Marceline.
Je jure que je l'aimais passionnément. Jamais elle n'avait
été et ne m'avait paru si belle. La maladie avait subtilisé
et comme extasié ses traits. (pp. 166-67)

As soon as Michel sees Marceline's horrified and resigned shudder in
response to this thoughtlessly cruel retort, the center of temporal
orientation shifts to the narrator's perspective, and he hastens to
convince his listeners of his actual and profound love for his wife
long after his actions and words exhibited from the character's temporal orientation have revealed his true feelings of frustration,
annoyance, hostility, and even indifference. The impossibility of
Michel's love for Marceline is apparent as a result of the emptiness

of his gestures and tokens of love. The tears shed over the sleeping Marceline, the "pious" kiss bestowed on her brow, the armfuls of almond branches, and the long hours spent by her side until he gains the freedom to roam the streets when she has fallen asleep all bespeak the same effort on Michel's part in his temporal position as both character and narrator to appear to love his wife. But as if to support his assertion and thereby to persuade his companions of his passionate love, Michel describes Marceline's beauty and the exquisite effects her illness has had on her physical appearance. This declaration of love and devotion rings false, however, in part because it is founded on Michel's physical, not emotional or spiritual, attraction to Marceline. Indeed, Michel in his temporal orientation as character finally admits his love was but a sham when in Touggourt he confesses: "Par un dernier semblant de vertu" (p. 181).

Paradoxically, Michel ultimately tries to extricate himself from any sense of guilt in Marceline's death by asserting that he was not in control of his own actions. Although Michel in his temporal position as the younger character has constantly attempted to assert his free will with no thought as to the consequences for himself or for the other people around him, he uses his retrospective stance as narrator to suggest that he was at that time totally incapable of being the master of himself or his actions:

Par quelle aberration, quel aveuglement obstiné, quelle volontaire folie, me persuadai-je, et surtout tâchai-je de lui persuader qu'il lui fallait plus de lumière encore et de chaleur, invoquai-je le souvenir de ma convalescence à Biskra... L'air s'était attiédi pourtant; la baie de Palerme est clémente et Marceline s'y plaisait. Là, peut-être, elle aurait... Mais étais-je maître de choisir mon vouloir? de décider de mon désir? (p. 171)

Thus, Michel in his temporal orientation as narrator employs a variety of methods in his attempts to gain his friends' assistance. Not only does he try to explain his actions and extreme character change as the result of his repressed background and not only does he hollowly try to persuade his listeners of his real love for Marceline, Michel finally attempts to explain his behavior by denying any responsibility for his actions. Like the character Michel's empty gestures of love toward Marceline, the narrator Michel's act of confession is itself but an empty gesture, composed of false assurances of his love for Marceline, denials of responsibility for his actions, and frequent attempts to justify his behavior. Founded on an explicitly stated motive of self-interest and survival through escape from the monotony of his life, Michel undertakes and indeed parodies the ritualized gestures of confession in order to gain his friends' help and thus a return to life.

The two distinct zero points of temporal orientation and the shifts between the two respective present now-moments allow us to distinguish two unique points-of-view within Michel's narrative. Like the characters, objects, and occurrences belonging to the presented world that Michel portrays, Michel himself as a character and as a first-person narrator is a schematically presented personage who comes to appearance through a few selected, readied aspects. An examination of those aspects through which Michel and the presented world come to appearance will, therefore, enable us to trace his development in his temporally distinct roles as character and narrator.

As we have already seen, Michel describes his vision of life prior to his marriage and illness at the beginning of his narrative. To review briefly, Michel relates that since adolescence his outlook on life and his relationship to the people and the world around him has been an exclusively intellectual one. At the time of his marriage, he had experienced virtually no other aspects of life beyond his scholarly pursuits, even to the point of intellectualizing his emotions. Indeed, Michel continues to cultivate his narrow, purely intellectual vision of life when he marries Marceline and, in fact, determines the itinerary of his wedding trip to include some ancient ruins he desires to visit for his studies. As he gradually regains consciousness following the initial stage of his illness, Michel begins to explore the surrounding environment through those aspects immediately accessible to him. Incapacitated and therefore confined to his chair on the hotel terrace, Michel relies solely on his power of observation in order to relate to the outside world. From his position on the terrace, Michel describes in a very schematic manner what he can see. He watches Marceline's activities, and he observes the passage of time on the basis of the lengthening shadows that he can see. When Marceline brings the young Arab boy, Bachir, to his room to amuse him and to offer some human companionship, Michel observes the boy, but does not interact with him. During the first visit, Michel watches the boy become increasingly disconcerted in the face of his coldly silent reception. As Bachir silently carves a whistle, the scene comes to appearance in a solely visual manner. Besides Marceline's initial laughing introduction of Bachir at the beginning of the scene, the only other sound comes when she gently admonishes the boy to play quietly. Other than these two instances of sound, the scene and the characters are portrayed as they are seen through the eyes of Michel in his temporal position as a young and ailing character:

Au bout d'un peu de temps, je ne suis plus gêné par sa
présence. Je le regarde; il semble avoir oublié qu'il
est là. Ses pieds sont nus; ses chevilles sont charmantes,
et les attaches de ses poignets. Il manie son mauvais couteau avec une amusante adresse. . . . Ses cheveux rasés à

la manière arabe; il porte une pauvre chéchia qui n'a qu'un
trou à la place du gland. La gandourah, un peu tombée,
découvre sa mignonne épaule. J'ai le besoin de la toucher.
(p. 31)

Although his observation of Bachir's golden skin is powerful enough
to inspire the desire to touch the boy, Michel only continues to ad-
mire his beauty from a distance. Indeed, the only physical contact
in this scene is that which Michel watches when Bachir, fearful of
Michel, presses himself against Marceline and kisses her hand.

During Bachir's second visit, Michel again watches as the boy
cuts himself while carving. Michel shudders as he watches the blade
penetrate into Bachir's thumb and mentions in passing that the boy
responds to his wound by laughing. Yet even Michel's portrayal of
Bachir's laughter is in visual terms. Rather than depict the sound
or even his own response to the sound, Michel describes the whiteness of the boy's teeth and the pink of his tongue which become visible when he laughs: "Quand il riait, il découvrait des dents
très blanches; il lécha plaisamment sa blessure; sa langue était
rose comme celle d'un chat. Ah! qu'il se portait bien. C'était
là ce dont je m'éprenais en lui: la santé. La santé de ce petit
corps était belle" (p. 32). As he watches the brilliant red blood
run down Bachir's thumb, witnesses the boy's laughter in response to
the older man's shudder, and watches him sensuously lick up the
blood, Michel in his temporal orientation as a character is overcome by the ease of movement of the youth seated in front of him and
by his own, unexpected passion to possess a similarly healthy physique. Indeed, this realization on the part of the character Michel works to fire his commitment to his own physical health, physical pleasures, and, in short, what subsequently becomes a commitment to himself to the exclusion of all others around him.

Bachir's third visit does not come to appearance strictly in
terms of its visual aspects. Wishing to play with the older man,

Bachir initiates physical contact between the two by grabbing Michel's arm and forcing him to participate, not merely watch. After such emphasis on the visual aspects of Michel's perception of Bachir, the boy's touch seems to Michel all the more dramatic and powerful. Similarly, when Michel collapses, exhausted from the game and from his brief physical contact with Bachir, the boy's subsequent one-word inquiry chimes even more beautifully because it is the first real sound in a series of scenes built of visual aspects: "Bachir, un peu troublé, me regardait. 'Malade?' dit-il gentiment; le timbre de sa voix était exquis" (p. 33).

Following his relapse, Michel shifts the focus of his observation from the outside world to himself. Having seen and coveted Bachir's physical strength, agility, and beauty, Michel in his temporal position as character seeks to discover the inner sensations and rhythms of his own body. Thus, when he undertakes an activity, he portrays not what he observes from his temporal position as a character, but rather the effect that such physical exertion has on him:

Pour un rien j'étais en sueur et pour un rien je prenais froid . . . souvent, dès le matin, un sentiment d'affreuse lassitude, et je restais, alors, prostré dans un fauteuil, indifférent à tout, égoïste, m'occupant très uniquement à tâcher de bien respirer. Je respirais péniblement, avec méthode, soigneusement; mes expirations se faisaient avec deux saccades, que ma volonté surtendue ne pouvait complètement retenir; longtemps après encore, je ne les évitais qu'à force d'attention. (p. 38)

As he gains sufficient strength to venture outside to the public gardens with Marceline, Michel turns his perception outward again, not only to see the surrounding natural beauty, but also to experience its sounds, to feel it, to smell it, and even to taste it.

Walking along the garden pathways, Michel in his temporal orientation as character exalts in his new-found sensory awareness of nature. The myriad sights, sounds, and sensations create a veritable
explosion of life. By abandoning all objective measure of time and
by recognizing the sensorial aspects of his world rather than observing it in strictly analytic terms, Michel succeeds in expanding
his mode of perception beyond the previously parochial confines of
his purely intellectual vision. Not only does Michel divorce himself from an arithmetic measure of the length of his stay in the
garden, he also closes his eyes and lets himself hear and feel the
surrounding whirlwind of life:

> Combien de temps nous y restâmes? je ne sais plus;--
> qu'importait l'heure? Marceline était près de moi; je
> m'étendais, posai sur ses genoux ma tête. Le chant de
> flûte coulait encore, cessait par instants, reprenait;
> le bruit de l'eau... Par instants une chèvre bêlait.
> Je fermai les yeux; je sentis se poser sur mon front la
> main fraîche de Marceline; je sentais le soleil ardent
> doucement tamisé par les palmes; je ne pensais à rien;
> qu'importait la pensée? je sentais extraordinairement.
> . . . (p. 49)

With his eyes shut to the visual aspects of the garden, Michel in
his temporal position as character allows himself for the first time
to listen to the wind rustling through the uppermost branches of the
palm trees and to feel the warmth of the sun's rays. Previously, he
had watched the sun's movement as it created elongated shadows on
the terrace, and on his approach to the garden, he had relied on his
eyes to see the effects of the wind as it blew the branches to one
side: "Des souffles légers s'élevèrent; toutes les palmes s'agi-

tèrent et nous vîmes les palmiers les plus hauts s'incliner" (p. 48).

Michel's brush with death has inspired him to expand his sensorial awareness of the world around him, and hence, to celebrate all the physical aspects of his life. His near-death experience has also awakened him to his own emotions and, at least temporarily, to his need for relationships with the people around him. No longer does he merely observe the reactions of other people from a safe analytic distance. Now conscious of his own feelings, he directly experiences for himself (from his temporal position as a character) the pleasure and the pain, the contentment and the anxiety, the intrigue and the monotony of his life. Although Michel has been able to tear down some of the repressive barriers of his intellectual, parochical past that hindered his awareness and experience of life, he still remains isolated from humanity. For while he experiences and participates in life instead of merely observing it, he is still unable to recognize and comprehend the emotions of other people.

During Marceline's and Michel's first stay at La Morinière, he does cultivate a friendship with the estate manager's son, Charles, and enjoys the time the two spend together. As Michel helps Charles repair a pond, the two men engage in a minimum of conversation. Yet, by working in unison they are able to sense a certain affinity and closeness between them, so that, by the end of the day, Michel in his temporal orientation as character discovers: ". . . que je tutoyais Charles, sans bien savoir quand j'avais commencé. Cette action commune nous en avait appris plus l'un sur l'autre que l'aurait pu le faire une longue conversation" (p. 88). Whereas this friendship allows him to feel closer to Charles, it also initiates the process of his gradual alienation from Marceline and all that she has come to represent for him. Hence, when Marceline fails to stop by the pond to watch Michel at work, he realizes that he does not regret her absence. Indeed, he secretly rejoices, sensing that his wife's presence would have jeopardized the beginning of his new friendship. Although Michel and Charles spend considerable time together that fall, exploring the different farms on the estate and deciphering the management of the grounds, their friendship proves to be shortlived. The relationship Michel begins with Charles in the autumn does not survive his equally shortlived friendship with Ménalque in Paris during the winter months. Moreover, Michel's increasing intimacy with Ménalque parallels the decline of his affection for Marceline. In his search for his authentic self, Michel seems unable to appreciate or even tolerate other people's aspirations, morals, and lifestyles when they run counter to his own. Michel's vision of life and his behavior are in the end determined solely on the basis of his own particular desires. As Michel himself acknowledges, in a world based solely on the cultivation of physical pleasures, it is only the physically healthy and the cunning opportunists who can survive. Those people, including Marceline, Bocage, and Charles, who cannot accept Michel's vision of life, cannot long remain a part of his life.

The deterioration of his relationship with Marceline is due in large part to the lengthy visits and conversations he has with Ménalque, discussions in which Michel discovers his disenchantment with the responsibilities and commitments demanded by his present life and his desire to exert himself and his free will. But despite Michel's recognition of his true desires and emotions, in short, what he terms his "authentic" self, he still remains as isolated from humanity as when he was previously sequestered by his strictly intellectual vision of life. Just as he previously devoted himself wholly to intellectual pursuits for the sake of scholarship alone, he now revels obsessively in the experience of his emotions to the point of poaching his own lands to enjoy his own cunning behavior and roaming the docks at midnight in Italy to feel the pleasure of asserting his free will. Michel's actions are themselves devoid of meaning; they merely signify what he believes is the exertion of his free will. Thus, although Michel experiences and participates in

life directly, he fails to grasp the real significance of his actions, and, perhaps most important, he fails in his efforts to
develop relationships with the people around him.

Although Michel believes he is aware of his emotions, he remains
unable to comprehend the reality of other people's emotions. When
on their wedding trip he alerts Marceline to his illness, he is out-
raged that she displays her shock by fainting: "'Ne suffisait-il
pas que moi je sois malade?'" (p. 26). Such an egotistical response
indicates that Michel denies the appropriateness of Marceline's
reaction of pain. Subsequently, Michel's response to Marceline's
tears at the sight of the almond blossoms is equally egotistical:

Sans rien dire, je saisis ces innocentes branches fragiles,
les brise, les emporte, les jette, exaspéré, le sang aux
yeux.
--Ah! si déjà ce peu de printemps elle ne peut le plus supporter!...
Je repense souvent à ces larmes et je crois maintenant que,
se sentant condamnée, c'est du regret d'autres printemps qu'
elle pleurait. (p. 168)

Because he has never learned to empathize with the people around
him, and because he has never fully comprehended the significance of
his own emotions, Michel can only guess and guess incorrectly at the
reason behind Marceline's fainting and her tears. His egotism is
such that he is able to convince even himself during subsequent moments of reflection of other causes for Marceline's responses; in
his mind, his philosophy of life and empty gestures could not have
been the cause of Marceline's sorrow.

Thus, in his quest to discover his real, his authentic self, Michel leaves one with the impression that he merely vacillates from

one narrowly-bounded view of life to another just as narrow. After
the initial veritable burst of his sensory perception during his recovery, Michel's development and awakening stagnate because he
merely repeats his previous pattern of behavior and interaction. He
develops only his physical self and his sense of individuality. As
before, he devotes himself to the cultivation of only one aspect of
his life, and he continues to ignore, for the most part, the people
around him. By advocating that only the strong can survive and that
the weak must perish, Michel, in turn, discovers following Marceline's death that his own life has no meaning. His activities, his
thoughts, and his life all resemble the monotonous and meaningless
shifting of pebbles from hand to hand. In his temporal position as
narrator, therefore, Michel has not really grown beyond the boundaries that restricted his life in the temporal position as a younger character. For although he has exerted his will and gained his
freedom, he admits that he still does not know how to live; and,
thus, he does not know himself.

Near the end of his confession, Michel wishes that the very
structure of the sentences in his narrative could convey the process
of his self-discovery, his cultivation--indeed, his celebration--of
those aspects of life that he perceives sensorially, and, ultimately, his retrospective attempt as a narrator to understand and inter-
pret all that has happened:

Il fait chaud. Il fait beau. Tout est splendide. Ah! je
voudrais qu'en chaque phrase, ici, toute une moisson de
volupté se distille... En vain chercherais-je à présent
à imposer à mon récit plus d'ordre qu'il n'y en eut dans
ma vie. Assez longtemps j'ai cherché de vous dire comment
je devins qui je suis. Ah! désembarrasser mon espsrit de
cette insupportable logique!... Je ne sens rien que de
noble en moi. (p. 174)

As an examination of the various types of sentence structure reveals, the ordering of words and the structuring of sentences amplify Michel's development in his temporal positions as both a character and a narrator, and, thus, the significance of the text.

Other critics have studied the importance of Gide's sentence structure and style to the meaning of the text. Indeed, Georges Kassaï postulates that the essence of the plot in L'Immoraliste can be reduced to the binary structure present in many sentences throughout the récit. Kassaï suggests that the dynamic quality of Gide's work resides in the consistent juxtaposition of opposing ideas and concepts on the story level--Michel's illness and health, the present and the past, appearance and reality--with a similar binary arrangement of antagonistic or complementary semantic elements on the sentence level. Thus, Kassaï concludes that, "la forme de la phrase amplifie les mouvements de l'intrigue."[15] Although Kassaï observes the correspondence between the sentence structure and the movement of the structure of the story, he does not examine the variation in types of sentence structure when the narrative focus alternates between Michel's point-of-view as the older, analytic narrator and as the younger character who is participating in the events. He also fails to study how the structure of the sentences enhances the portrayal of Michel's character development and the changes in his vision of life.

The binary structure that Kassaï identifies is evident on the semantic level of the sentences uttered from Michel's perspective in his temporal position as narrator. In the following passage, for example, Michel emphasizes the dichotomy between past and present, his illness and his recuperation, his previous, narrowly analytic vision of life and his present life governed only by instinct:

Depuis le début de mon mal, j'avais vécu sans examen, sans loi, m'appliquant simplement à vivre, comme l'animal ou l'enfant. Moins absorbé par le mal à présent, ma vie redevenait certaine et consciente. Après cette longue agonie, j'avais cru renaître le même et rattacher bientôt mon présent au passé. . . . (p. 58)

If we delve past the explicit semantic duality of past and present, though, we can see the complexity of Michel's character development as it is revealed on the syntactic level. The following passage repeats the semantic juxtaposition of past and present, but its repetitive, periodic structure also suggests Michel's ever increasing disenchantment not only with his own previous, intellectual approach to life but also with the communal past, his own personal and society's historical heritage and culture:

L'histoire du passé prenait maintenant à mes yeux cette immobilité, cette fixité terrifiante des ombres nocturnes dans la petite cour de Biskra, l'immobilité de la mort. (p. 59)

Michel first equates history, the communal sense of the past with "immobilité," and hence a halt to society's evolution. He expands on this concept of social stagnation by exploring the meaning of of "immobilité" on a personal level. His reference to the nighttime shadows that fill the hotel courtyard generates the sense of Michel's own terror in the face of his previous career as a scholar of ancient civilization, his former strictly analytic vision of the

life around him as well as the fear for his life that he experienced as a result of his close brush with death in Biskra. The structure of the sentence builds to a dramatic crescendo with the third
and final clause. As Michel probes his reasons for rejecting his
previous cultivation of the past, he associates the immobility
and rigidity of history, his own personal past, and his narrowly-
bounded vision of life with death itself. Although Michel is here
asserting his rejection of his sequestered and stultifying past, the
structure of the sentence belies any effort on Michel's part to expand beyond the strictures of his vision of life. The emphatic
movement of the clauses reveals a progression from the concept of
community to that of individualism. Thus, the structure of the
gradual examination of "immobilité" does not suggest Michel's rejection of all restrictions and boundaries on his view of life.
Rather, it indicates that Michel merely substitutes one bounded vision of life for another. The sentence structure mirrors his eventual adoption of the philosophy of individualism--an equally restrictive approach to life--that Michel cultivates.

The variation in sentence structure throughout the course of Michel's narrative emphasizes the changes he undergoes during his recovery, as he substitutes a sensorial perception of life for his
previous intellectual vision, and ultimately, as he seeks repeatedly
to exert his free will in an attempt to prove his existence. For
example, when Michel is first able to venture onto the terrace outside his hotel room in Biskra, he engages in no other activity than
to sit and observe Marceline and the immediate world around him:

Marceline est auprès de moi. Elle lit; elle coud; elle
écrit. Je ne fais rien. Je la regarde. O Marceline!...
Je regarde. Je vois le soleil; je vois l'ombre; je vois
la ligne de l'ombre se déplacer; j'ai si peu à penser, que
je l'observe. (p. 30)

The simple structure of the sentences and the individual clauses with their repeated subject-verb word order emphasizes the almost childlike innocence of the world vision that is being projected. Michel himself states that he is not thinking--participating in his usual intellectualized manner of relating to the world--but merely watching the occurrences. The simple structure of the phrases with their mere cataloguing of activities conveys the simplicity of the observer's activity as well as the newness for Michel of observing without analyzing or intellectualizing what he sees. In addition, the frequency with which "je" begins the sentences and clauses emphasizes the significance that Michel's sense of self comes to have in his life after his awakening from this deathlike illness.

The sentence structure increases in complexity when Michel, having regained sufficient strength, is able to walk with Marceline to a public garden. Again, Michel does not intellectualize the phenomena which he perceives around him; during this period of observation, however, he expands his range of perception to enable him to feel and hear as well as see the phenomena:

(1) J'oubliais ma fatigue et ma gêne. (2) Je marchais dans une sorte d'extase, d'allégresse silencieuse, d'exaltation des sens et de la chair. (3) A ce moment, des souffles légers s'élevèrent; toutes les palmes s'agitèrent et nous vîmes les palmiers les plus hauts s'incliner;--puis l'air entier redevint calme, et j'entendis distinctement, derrière le mur, un chant de flûte. (p. 48)

Michel's celebration of the senses is reflected in the expansion of the second sentence by the three prepositional phrases describing the crescendo of his perception and emotions as he walks. The third sentence does not adhere to the subject (**je**)-verb pattern that orders the two previous sentences. Beginning each major section of this lengthy and complex sentence with adverbial locutions of time suggests two distinct moments in time for Michel, moments rendered meaningful by the simple, yet significant, sensorial experiences he associates with them. There are several clauses within each half of this sentence, and each clause projects an aspect of the world that Michel is perceiving and exhibiting in a sensorial manner. Unlike the mere catalogue of activities that Michel presents as he sits on the terrace, this piling up of clauses and hence of aspects creates what amounts to an expansive sensorial experience. During the first moment, Michel can sense the light breeze and see how it also bends the tree branches. During the second moment, as the rustle of the wind in the branches subsides, he can discern the music from a flute as it wafts from behind the wall.

The sentence expansion that reflects Michel's character development is also evident in instances when he insists on exerting his free will to no one's real benefit and to Marceline's decided detriment. In the following passage, Michel battles his conscience as he tries to convince both Marceline and himself that despite her illness he must keep his engagement with Ménalque. The first main clause and the state of affairs it projects are further developed in a number of the subsequent sentences by a series of modifying nouns, prepositional phrases, verbal and adjectival clauses:

Cependant le soir vint que j'avais promis à Ménalque; et malgré mon ennui d'abandonner toute une nuit d'hiver Marceline, je lui fis accepter de mon mieux **la solennité du rendez-vous, la gravité de ma promesse.** Marceline allait un peu mieux ce soir-là, et pourtant j'étais inquiet; une garde me remplaça près d'elle. Mais, sitôt dans la rue,

mon inquiétude prit une force nouvelle; je la repoussai, lut-
tai contre elle, m'irritant contre moi de ne pas mieux m'en
libérer. Je parvins ainsi peu à peu à un état de surtension,
d'exaltation singulière, très différente et très proche à
la fois de l'inquiétude douloureuse qui l'avait fait naître,
mais plus proche encore du bonheur. Il était tard; je marchais à grands pas; la neige commença de tomber en abondance;
j'étais heureux de respirer enfin un air plus vif, de lutter
contre le froid, heureux contre le vent, la nuit, la neige;
je savourais mon énergie. (p. 123)

At the beginning of this passage, Michel tries to use the repetition
of such nominal phrases as "la solennité" and "la gravité" to
aggrandize the importance of his appointment with Ménalque and
thereby both fuel his reasons for going and justify his need to
abandon Marceline. But Michel does not succeed in completely convincing even himself, and thus, once out of his apartment, he discovers that he must again quell his anxiety over abandoning his sick
wife. With the repetition of the verbal and participial phrases, we
can sense the gradual progression of Michel's attempts to overcome
the prickings of his conscience. As he manages to stifle any worries he has for Marceline, he senses a surging of his emotions. The
expansion of this sentence and the amplification of the corresponding state of affairs enable Michel to transform his sense of anxiety and tension into happiness and, ultimately, into exaltation. The
invigorating sense of happiness that Michel feels as he succeeds in
liberating himself from any concern over Marceline is emphasized in
the final sentence of this passage. The imperfect verb tense in
each of the five clauses in this sentence suggests the simultaneity
of all the depicted aspects in this state of affairs. The lateness
of the hour, the cold and the falling snow further invigorate Michel
as he strides away from his worries, responsibilities, and his con-

science. Finally, the repetition of the first-person pronoun je and the repeated indications of such emotions and actions as **heureux** and **savourais** conclude Michel's exertion of his will and his departure with the focus on his sense of self and individualism and on his belief that the strength of his rights and desires pre-empts the rights and desires of other people.

Michel's ever expanding sense of egocentricity pervades his narrative, emerging through the constant juxtaposition of the two distinct zero points of temporal orientation, through the aspects that present and exhibit his character, and through the structure of the sentences that project the narrative situation. The duality of temporal perspectives within Michel's confession reveals that there are actually two narratives as well as two levels of narration. Not only does Michel recount the story of his actions during the course of his marriage, he also reveals his narrating act and thereby lays bare the process and motives of his confession. The two narratives parallel each other and prove to be mutually illuminating. Michel is the focal point in each of his narratives, and, in each, he struggles to discover his authentic self. Yet, Michel also demonstrates in each narrative that he is unable to find his unified self. Isolated as he is from a sense of community with the rest of humanity and driven to pursue his own egocentric philosophy of life, Michel can only vacillate between the fragmented extremes of his self. The aspects that exhibit Michel's character development reveal that while his vision of life changes, it does not evolve into a cohesive, balanced vision. He merely substitutes one egocentric view of life for another. He remains unable to unify those divergent visions of life into a cohesive whole because, as he demonstrates repeatedly by his actions and his narration, he cannot comprehend the value of the life around him, the community with its history, its present, and its future, and the lives and emotions of other individuals. The expansion and periodicity of the sentence structure also emphasize, often to dramatic effect, Michel's sense of individualism and his alienation from the community and from any comprehension of the value of human life. By confessing and thus confronting his own past, Michel hopes to win his friends' help in escaping the monotonous existence he has led since Marceline's death and to expiate the guilt he feels over her death.

Michel's sense of guilt seems to be twofold: In his temporal position as character, he reflects on his previous self-centered behavior that results in what he considers to be a fairly benign abandonment of Marceline, whereas in his temporal position as narrator, he realizes that it was his own subsequent, obsessed, egotistical behavior that drove Marceline to her death. His tears in response to having abandoned Marceline in the past and his pious kiss in anticipation of having to care for her in the future both figure symbolically in Michel's confession. With their religious overtones the tears and the kiss are significant gestures within the ritual of confession. In light of Michel's perspective as a character, these gestures suggest the beginning of his seemingly sincere love for Marceline. In light of his subsequent behavior in his temporal position as character and the more complete knowledge of events that he possesses in his position as narrator, however, the kiss and the tears are merely empty gestures which mask Michel's true feelings for his wife and himself. Thus, as Michel's narrative reveals, his confession itself is but a ritualized and thus deceptive, even meaningless, gesture. By merely following and thereby parodying the highly ritualized procedure, Michel can acquit himself without ever realizing the significance of his actions and without having to come to value fully the human life he sacrificed.

The binary structure of Michel's temporal perspectives establishes two complexly balanced, symmetrical narrative situations in which Michel fails repeatedly to know his true self. The symmetry of Michel's temporal perspectives is complemented by the narrative point-of-view of his unnamed friend who serves as witness to his confession. The explicitly stated role of this narrating persona is to function as a judge of Michel's actions and his confession. Implicitly, however, when he recounts Michel's narrative to his brother, this unnamed friend reveals himself incapable of sitting in moral judgment on another individual whose actions and guilt are so prevalent among all humankind. Unable to condemn Michel, this friend can only try to help him be reintegrated into society, an action he undertakes through his own narration. Together, the narratives and perspectives of the unnamed friend and Michel create a cohesively structured, complementary narrative situation which through its three individual and distinct visions is raised to a level of universality.

5:

MY ANTONIA:

LISTENING TO THE PAST

While writing My Ántonia, Willa Cather described her work in progress to Elizabeth Shepley Sergeant by placing an old Sicilian apothecary jar in the middle of an antique table and announcing: "'I
want my new heroine to be like this--like a rare object in the
middle of a table, which one may examine from all sides.'"[1] At
first glance this anecdote implies that Cather intended Ántonia Shimerda and the surrounding Nebraska frontier to be the focus of My
Ántonia. Yet the anecdote also suggests the importance of narrative
perspective and focalization within the novel, thereby emphasizing
the significant role played by first-person narrator Jim Burden.
Indeed, a number of Cather's novels, including My Ántonia, A Lost
Lady, One of Ours, The Professor's House, and My Mortal Enemy, represent variation and a certain experimentation in the types of narrators and narrative perspectives used. In My Ántonia and her suc-
ceeding novels, Cather alternates between first-person character-

narrators, authorial narrators, and the Jamesian centrally placed mediating consciousness. Although her experiments may not be con- sidered as innovative as those of such contemporaries as Marcel Proust, Ford Madox Ford, James Joyce, John Dos Passos, and e. e. cummings, Cather did achieve unique artistic and aesthetic effects not only by the manner in which her various narrators shape the material of the novels but also by the structural shifting of the narrative temporal and spatial centers of orientation and by the em- bedded narrative voices.

Since its publication in 1918, considerable criticism has been devoted to the question of what My Ántonia is actually about: Ne- braska and the West, Willa Cather's life experience, the character Ántonia, or the first-person character-narrator Jim Burden. When her fourth book appeared, Cather thought she was publishing a novel quite different in subject matter and form from the western and sen- timental kinds then in vogue. Although she had followed the advice of Sarah Orne Jewett by relying on the knowledge of her Nebraska background in the creation of My Ántonia, Cather did not believe that she was writing in the vein of such popular western books as The Virginian.[2] Reviewers writing for such journals as Outlook, Bookman, and North American Review, however, generally greeted Cather's third novel as an excellent "guidebook" to Nebraska. As a regional western novel, it was noted particularly for the histori- cal value of "its minute and colorful depiction of life on Nebraska prairies and in the Nebraska towns about 1885."[3] Maxwell Geismar read My Ántonia as a chronicle of the frontier settlers which Cather carried forward to "the framework of early western town life and the merchants and farmers, the commercial travelers, the eccentrics, and outcasts of what was almost a society of outcasts."[4] Bernice Slote also recognizes this dimension in the novel: ". . . the order of the book takes us from the kind of country Willa Cather first knew in the Nebraska of the 1880's--unsettled, young, rough . . . to the first small communities, like Black Hawk to cities and universities. . .".[5]   There is thus a tendency to view Ántonia's life as an allegory for the frontier experience and for the West itself. Having suffered during her confrontation with the harsh land, Ántonia comes to represent all that is triumphant, vigorous, and beautiful in a region where so many have given in to repression and defeat.[6] Some critics have described My Ántonia as the fictional counterpart to Frederick Jackson Turner's thesis that everything vitally democratic in American life has evolved from the western frontier experience.   Depicting Cather as a product of the time of Turner's greatest acceptance, they discover in My Ántonia a tension between East and West and conclude that Cather envisioned the West as a place of unending vastness and hope, a poetic dream.[7]

In contrast to such timebound interpretations, H. L. Mencken recognizes Cather's fourth novel as much more complex than its western prairie setting first indicates: "Beneath the swathings of balder-dash, the tawdry stuff of Middle Western Kultur, she discovers human beings embattled against fate and the gods, and into her picture of their dull struggle she gets a spirit that is genuinely heroic, and a pathos that is genuinely moving."[8]   Carl van Doren commends Cather's artistry and the strength of her ability to "look past casual surfaces to the passionate center of her characters."[9]

Critics appear to be divided, however, on the issue of whether Ántonia's story or Jim Burden's story is the focus of the novel. Adhering to Jim's assertion in the "Introduction" that the manuscript he has composed consists solely of the memories and thoughts evoked by Ántonia's name, a number of critics have approached the novel as being Ántonia's story. They have, in turn, found it flawed. René Rapin questions Ántonia's lengthy disappearance from the novel; excluded completely from Book III, she appears only briefly in Book IV.[10]   David Daiches criticizes the lack of a consistent focus, charging that narrator Jim Burden's sensibility takes control and that his development overshadows Ántonia's.[11]   Finally, E. K.

Brown senses that the novel is fundamentally flawed by the masculine narrative point-of-view. The relationship between Ántonia and Jim is one of emptiness rather than the one of love which, he asserts, readers could logically expect.[12] Several other critics suggest that the novel involves the two parallel stories of Jim and Ántonia, two innocent, exiled orphans whose happiness and sense of self come from the land.[13] Still other critics have explained the structure of the novel as one of opposition between Jim and Ántonia. The richness and fecundity of Ántonia's family life stand sharply juxtaposed to the sterility of Jim's childless marriage.[14] And David Stouck notes that the value of Ántonia's strength and creativity are mediated by the memories and feelings of a man who is a failure of sorts in his personal life.[15]

Almost from the time of its composition, Jim Burden's roles as character and narrator have elicited critical attention. Cather herself once stated in an interview that she had intended Jim Burden to be at once fascinated with Ántonia as only a man could be and yet remain relatively detached, an appreciative but passive observer.[16] A few critics have puzzled over the nature of his relationship to Ántonia, however, seeing Jim not merely as a secondary character and witness to Ántonia's life, but cast as the focal point of the novel. In this light, he has been interpreted as an image maker, creating of Ántonia's ultimate agrarian success and domestic bliss a poignant and personal symbol.[17] He has also been described as a man so discouraged by the disappointments and unhappiness of his present life hinted at in the "Introduction" that he retreats to his romanticized, idyllic memories of childhood and adolescence.[18]

Because he is a first-person narrator, Jim Burden is often considered to be a narrative mask for Willa Cather, allowing the inclusion of a considerable number of autobiographical elements without risking the author's personal involvement.[19] Indeed, Brown goes so far as to conclude that My Ántonia is not a novel at all but Cather's memoirs: "She always showed impatience at the complaint that My Ántonia is not precisely a novel. Why should it be? She had never said it was. In this book she was gathering her memories of some persons and places dear to her, and as she was a writer of stories, the memories had taken a narrative form."[20]   In rebuttal, Eudora Welty argues that no novel should be judged as autobiographical on the basis of its first-person narration. Jim Burden remains a created character, she asserts; he cannot be equated with his creator: "It's not the voice of Willa Cather but the voice of Jim Burden, a character, telling [the story]. That is the character, just as if it were a stage and he were a character on the stage--he's that much of a creation."[21]

To comprehend the structural coherence of My Ántonia, we cannot ignore the function of Jim Burden's narrative perspective. More than just a technical device, his point-of-view and mode of narration invest the work with meaning and unity. The depiction of his sensory perception and the spectrum of his memory shape the material, lending the novel a significance more complex than the series of unconnected anecdotes and memories that Jim suggests it is. A great deal of the novel's complexity and its dramatic tension derive from the "Introduction" in which the unnamed narrator relates an encounter with Jim Burden on a train ride through Iowa.[22]   During the trip, the two reminisce about their childhood spent on the Nebraska prairie, frequently couching their memories in terms of their Bohemian friend, Ántonia. Months later, Jim delivers to the narrator of the "Introduction" a written version of "all that [Ántonia's] name recalls to me"--the manuscript that is My Ántonia. Contrary to van Doren's assertion that "the introduction to My Ántonia is largely superfluous," we see that it is precisely the "Introduction" which frames Jim's text and establishes the temporal, spatial, and intellectual contrasts between the world and characters presented in the "Introduction" and the world and characters presented in Jim's manuscript.[23]

Cather made a number of slight but significant revisions in the second edition of the novel. In the first edition of My Ántonia, both Jim and the narrator of the "Introduction" agree to record their memories of their childhood friend. When they meet again the following winter, the narrator, identified only as a woman, has jotted down just a few notes, whereas Jim has completed a manuscript. After reading it, the narrator foregoes her own version and presents the reader with Jim's. This decision establishes a tension which influences the reading of Jim's entire manuscript: How different would the novel have been if written from a woman's point-of-view?[24] The 1926 revision of the "Introduction" reorients the reader's question, however, by leaving the introductory narrator's sex unidentified. Moreover, Jim is presented as already at work on his manuscript when he encounters his childhood friend on the train, thereby implying that his artistic creation stems from a more deeply seeded and personal impulse than the earlier version with its "conversation as the inspirational force" would allow. This second version of the "Introduction" thus suggests a greater intimacy between Jim and the world he presents in his text. Cather also removed from the 1926 edition of the "Introduction" many of the satirical aspects in the portrait of Jim's wife which in the 1918 "Introduction" called into question Jim's ability to judge women, thereby undermining the romanticized portrait of Ántonia in his narrative. The more abbreviated characterization of Mrs. Burden in the second version functions to depict some of the unhappy and less successful aspects of Jim's personal life. This briefly sketched portrayal of his unfulfilled personal life, in turn, contrasts, with the picture of his childhood, adolescence, and young manhood which he presents in his text--a juxtaposition of past and present, at times poignant, that is sustained throughout the novel.

Jim in the role of narrator begins his story by recounting his arrival on the Nebraska prairie. Orphaned at the age of ten, young Jim travels with Jake Marpole, a former hand from his parents' Virginia farm, to Nebraska to live with his grandparents. It is during this train ride that Jim first hears of the fourteen-year-old Bohemian girl, Ántonia Shimerda, and her immigrant family who take up residence near his grandparents' farm. The cavelike, sod hovel in which the Shimerdas spend their first year stands in sharp contrast to the Burdens' fine, large house. The single coat shared by all the members of the Shimerda family during their first winter further emphasizes their poverty. Despite their difference in age, Jim and Ántonia spend much of their time together that first autumn, playing and exploring the prairie that is new to them both. Jim helps Ántonia with her English, and together they listen to Russian Pavel's tale of throwing the bride to the wolves. Following Mr. Shimerda's suicide, Jim spends considerably less time with Ántonia who must devote all her energy to working the farm with her brother, Ambrosch.

In the second book, Jim relates his grandparents' move into the town of Black Hawk. Because Jim is thirteen, his grandparents decide that he needs the formal schooling available only in town. Ántonia subsequently moves to town also, becoming a hired girl first for the neighboring family, the Harlings, and sometime later, for the miserly merchant, Wick Cutter, and his wife. Jim narrates the events of his life during the several years spent in Black Hawk, describing the dancing tent that is set up one summer, picnics and a berry-picking expedition with Ántonia and some of the other hired girls. As part of his sexual awakening, he experiences erotic dreams and fantasies involving one of those hired girls, the enchanting and sensual Lena Lingard. The summer before he leaves town to enroll at the University of Nebraska in Lincoln, Jim spends studying trigonometry and Virgil. Just prior to his departure he takes the frightened Ántonia's place in her bed at the Cutter house and suffers a severe beating when Wick Cutter sneaks in that night in an attempt to rape Ántonia.

In the third book, Jim recounts his memories of his freshman year in Lincoln studying Virgil's **Georgics** with his young teacher, Gaston Cleric. During the spring of his sophomore year of intellectual discovery, Jim once again encounters Lena Lingard. It is through Lena that he learns of Ántonia's engagement to the railroad worker, Larry Donovan. Jim spends a carefree spring with Lena, his first love, and together they discover the cultural life of Lincoln. In June of that year, Lena encourages him to break off their affair in order to follow his mentor to Harvard where a fresh academic start awaits him.

Jim devotes book four to describing his reunion with Ántonia during the summer before entering Harvard Law School. Frances Harling catches him up on what has happened to the three hired girls with whom he has been friends: Lena has become a smart businesswoman in Lincoln; Tiny Soderball has gone West to seek her fortune; and Ántonia is working on her brother Ambrosch's farm and raising her baby daughter. It is from the Widow Steavens, living in the Burdens' old farmhouse, that Jim learns the details of Ántonia's fate. Seduced by Larry Donovan, Ántonia returned to work for her brother and bear her beloved daughter out-of-wedlock. While visiting with Ántonia before his return East, Jim realizes the significance she has in his life. In her he recognizes the beauty and strength of sustained friendship and the importance of close human relationships.

Book five depicts Jim's return to the Nebraska prairie of his youth and another visit to Ántonia after a twenty-year lapse. Afraid to discover what the years have done to Ántonia, Jim has avoided seeing her during the intervening years. But encouraged by Lena, Jim, now in his early forties, pays a surprise visit to Ántonia Cuzak, her husband, and her brood of children. He finds Ántonia grizzled and worn from hard work, but hardly diminished in the strength and vigor of her personality. After enjoying several quiet days with his childhood friend and her family, rekindling fond memories of the past, Jim sets out on his journey home with the promise of a return in the near future. Jim's subsequent, disappointing day spent in Black Hawk contrasts sharply with his idyllic and nostalgic stay at Ántonia's. The inhabitants are all strangers incapable of inspiring that remembrance of the past that he and Ántonia have achieved together.

Jim alone is present throughout the novel. The structural cohesion of My Ántonia does not, however, depend solely on Jim's continuous presence as a character in the "Introduction" and then in the world depicted in his manuscript. Equally important are his relationship to the story as narrator and his vision and perspective as he presents the other characters and the events in My Ántonia. The nature of Jim's memory thus plays a key role in the presentation of the world of the text. Jim's act of remembrance shapes the material and enhances the meaning by creating a dramatic tension. The significance of Jim's relation to the story as narrator and his presentation as a character in the story can be illustrated to two different effects with the aid of the structuralist and phenomenological methods.

A STRUCTURALIST READING

The narrative situation of My Ántonia is structured by the hierarchical relationships between the various narrative voices, temporal moments, perspectives, and modes of speech. Structurally, My Ántonia consists of five books framed by an "Introduction" and presented by means of three distinct narrative levels. The narrator and act of narrating within the "Introduction" function on the extradiegetic level, a level beyond the events recounted and characters presented in this section. The train ride, the conversation between the unnamed narrator and Jim Burden about their childhood memories, Jim's visit to the narrator's apartment several months later, Jim Burden as character and writer, and his narrating act which is implied by the presence of his manuscript all belong to a second narrative level, the intradiegetic level. The story related by Jim in the manuscript **My Ántonia**, in turn, represents a third narrative level. Hence, all the events and characters he presents, including himself during his childhood, adolescence, and adulthood, and such storytellers as Otto Fuchs, Russian Pavel, Ántonia, Lena Lingard, Frances Harling, and the Widow Steavens and their embedded narratives constitute the metadiegetic level. Operating on the extradiegetic level, the unnamed narrator of the "Introduction" is thus the only narrator who stands removed from Jim Burden; although the focus shifts to the Widow Steavens's perspective, for example, her story still remains embedded in Jim's narrative, and hence, is technically interpreted and written by him.

Jim is related to the narrative in three ways and on three levels: He is a character in someone else's narrative, he narrates his own story, and he functions as a principal character within that story. He is both a narrating subject and a narrated object, the subject of his énonciation, the object of his own énoncé, and the object of the "Introduction" narrator's énoncé.

Although there is an essential oneness of person of the narrator and the protagonist in **My Ántonia**, these two personae remain distinct. As a first-person autodiegetic narrator, Jim stands in a position that is retrospective to the events of the story. He is older, more knowledgeable and more experienced than the metadiegetic character Jim who is presented at various life stages. Because he is in a position that affords the opportunity for reflection, middle-aged Jim in his role as the intradiegetic narrator always knows more than the younger, more innocent, metadiegetic character Jim Burden, who is bound in his experiences and knowledge to the moment of any given event in which he participates or which he observes. Moreover, from his vantage point as the intradiegetic narrator, Jim is aware of the ultimate outcome of events and the fate of each of the metadiegetic characters. He, of course, remains unaware of the outcome of future occurrences involving characters on the intradiegetic and extradiegetic levels. However, in his role as narrator on the intradiegetic level, Jim can hypothesize about character motivation and the meaning behind certain actions and gestures, and he can situate those individuals and incidents within a larger context.

In the 1926 "Introduction" to My Ántonia, the intradiegetic narrator Jim describes his act of writing as simply an amusing pastime. During long trips, he explains, he simply jots down all that Ántonia's name recalls to him in a manner, for which he apologizes, lacking any form or artistic arrangement. Near the end of his manuscript, Jim, in his role as intradiegetic narrator, reflects that the remembrances he holds of Ántonia parade in his memory like the succession of "old woodcuts of one's first primer" (p. 353). Many readers have accepted these two explanations by Jim for what they consider to be the novel's basic formlessness. But as Jim's image of the succession of woodcuts suggests, there is an episodic design in his manuscript. Each narrative episode consists of a scenic depiction of an event in Jim's life as a metadiegetic character. Preceding and following each scene, there is usually a summary, describing in a general and iterative manner from the intradiegetic narrator Jim's perspective the background which provides a context for the highlighted occurrence which is portrayed through the metadiegetic character Jim's focalization. The links between episodes rely on the implicit chronological and seasonal order of the narrated events. The five major divisions of Jim's manuscript are joined together by temporal ellipses. The transition from the narration of one year's events in the first book to the events in the second book, for example, entails a significant leap forward in time: "I had been living with my grandfather for nearly three years when he decided to move to Black Hawk" (p. 143).

In his roles as a metadiegetic character and as an intradiegetic narrator, Jim plays an essential part in the temporal dimension of the novel. Metadiegetic character Jim's memories of occurrences depicted in previous books frequently function to inspire his thoughts, feelings, and actions in each of the subsequent books. When the middle-aged, metadiegetic character Jim visits Ántonia and her family in the fifth book, for example, he asks to sleep in the haymow with several of the boys in reminiscence of nights spent in the Shimerdas' hay shed. In turn, occurrences in later books also inspire memories of earlier events and people. While studying the Georgics in his lonely room in Lincoln, the metadiegetic character Jim discovers that although he "was in the very act of yearning toward the new forms that Cleric brought up before me, my mind plunged away from me, and I suddenly found myself thinking of the places and people of my own infinitesimal past" (p. 262).

As the writer of his memoirs, Jim's retrospective stance as well as his intradiegetic act of remembering affect the relations between the temporal order of the "actual" chronological succession of events in the story and the order of their arrangement in the narrative discourse. An examination of a brief, typical passage on the micronarrative level indicates that aside from the iterative manner of narration, there are seven chronological positions among the ten constituent elements. Each narrative segment in the following passage is signified by a letter and the chronological positions are numbered. In chronological order, these positions include: (1) the persecution of the Mormons; (2) the Mormon exodus to Utah; (3) the second Mormon exodus; (4) Otto Fuchs's chores before metadiegetic character Jim's arrival in Nebraska; (5) character Jim's first long pony ride; (6) character Jim's subsequent pony rides; and (7) intradiegetic narrator Jim's present.

(A5) On the afternoon of that same Sunday I took my first long ride on my pony, under Otto's direction./ (B6) After that Dude and I went twice a week to the post-office, six miles east of us, and I saved the men a good deal of time by riding on errands to our neighbours. When we had to borrow anything, or to send about word that there would be preaching at the sod schoolhouse, I was always the messenger./ (C4) Formerly, Fuchs attended to such things after working hours./

(D7) All the years that have passed have not dimmed my memory of that first glorious autumn./ (E6) The new country lay open before me: there were no fences in those days, and I could choose my own way over the grass uplands, trusting the pony to get me home again. Sometimes I followed the sunflower-bordered roads. Fuchs told me/ (F2) that the sunflowers were introduced into that country by the Mormons;/ (G1) that at the time of the persecution, when they left Missouri and struck out into the wilderness to find a place where they could worship God in their own way,/ (H2) the members of the first exploring party, crossing the plains to Utah, scattered sunflower seed as they went./ (I3) The next summer, when the long trains of wagons came through with all the women and children, they had the sunflower trail to follow./ (J7) I believe that botanists do not confirm Fuchs's story, but insist that the sunflower was native to those plains. Nevertheless, that legend has stuck in my mind, and sunflower-bordered roads always seem to me the roads to freedom. (pp. 28-9)

The sequential relationships between the two temporal dimensions are thus synthesized in the formula: A5-B6-C4-D7-E6-F2-G1-H2-I3-J7.

There is a hierarchy of interlockings, subordinations, and connections within the temporal structure of this passage. For example, since Jim's long pony rides by himself are contingent on his practice ride under Otto's direction, segment B is dependent on segment A. Segment C functions as an analepsis, that is, a retrospective explanation of how errands were run before Jim takes over the chore. Together, these three segments constitute a major analepsis, one of the memories that the adult, intradiegetic narrator mentions in segment D. Segments E through I compose another part of that same memory, that is, how the landscape appears to young, metadiegetic Jim during his pony rides. Within this second main analepsis, narrator Jim remembers segment E--Otto's explanation of how sunflowers came to line Nebraska's roads. Otto's story comprises segments F through I, the story of the Mormons' persecution and flight across the Nebraska plains to Utah. Even Otto's story is not arranged in a strictly chronological manner, however. Beginning with segment E, the Mormons introducing sunflowers to Nebraska, the story backtracks to segment G, their persecution in Missouri and their decision to move West. After this retrospective digression, the narrative returns to segment H, the Mormons planting sunflower seeds as they cross the plains. Since segment H supplements the information given in segment F, it is noted as $H2^1$ (prime). The dash linking H to I indicates a leap forward in time to the second group of Mormons following the sunflower trail. This second analepsis terminates with a return to the intradiegetic narrator's present in segment J, in which he expresses both the skepticism of botanists over this story and his own love of the legend. The temporal structure of this brief passage thus is rather more complicated than a linear sequence. Within the two major analepses, punctuated by returns to the narrator's present, are additional interlocked, subordinated analepses. The complete formula of this passage's hierarchical temporal structure appears thus:

$$[A5 \ (B6) \ (C4)] \ D7 \ [E6 \ (F2 \ (G1)) \ H2^1{-}{-}I3] \ J7$$

In a very general manner, without giving attention to the finely differentiated chronological succession of events, most passages on the micronarrative level of Jim's manuscript can be seen as having some if not all of five basic temporal positions: (1) the distant past; (2) the recent past before metadiegetic character Jim's arrival in Nebraska; (3) character Jim's remembered past as he grows older; (4) character Jim's present; and (5) intradiegetic narrator Jim's present. On the micronarrative level, attention to the finely differentiated chronological relations between segments is possible. Considerable simplification becomes necessary, however, when examining the main articulations of the novel's macronarrative structure. Thus, although nearly every scene and description contains a number of the five basic temporal positions, they are not as frequently evident on the macronarrative level.

The linear succession of the novel's main elements includes thirty segments spread over twenty-five temporal positions. The "Introduction" contains three segments--(A) the train ride, (B) Jim's act of writing, and (C) the delivery of the completed manuscript--each of whose temporal position corresponds to moments of the intradiegetic narrator Jim's present. Following the "Introduction," the major articulations of the text tend to adhere to a fairly straight-forward chronological ordering. Because the initial three segments all occur in the intradiegetic narrator Jim's present, the remainder of the novel must necessarily be bracketed as retrospective. Within this extended analepsis, there coalesce four major groupings of narrative segments, punctuated by returns to the intradiegetic narrator's present. These returns, particularly significant in their subject matter, include: The intradiegetic narrator Jim's retrospective thoughts on Mr. Shimerda's death and burial (K), his recollections of his intellectual and sexual awakening at college (V), and his fearful hesitation to visit Ántonia after a twenty-year lapse (BB).

The first grouping of segments begins with the ten-year-old, metadiegetic character Jim's trip to his grandparents' farm (D), and includes such episodes as meeting the Shimerdas (E), the rattlesnake killing (F), and the visit to dying Russian Pavel (G).

Pavel's act of storytelling (H) follows in this chronological sequence, but the story itself (I) functions as an analepsis that explains the two Russians' emigration to America. This grouping terminates with Mr. Shimerda's suicide and burial (J). Narrator Jim's
thoughts about the burial (K) signal a brief return to his present
moment on the intradiegetic level.

The second grouping completes the seasonal structure of Book I.
The first two segments, in chronological order, include the farmhand Jake's springtime fight with Ambrosch Shimerda (L) and the sum-
mertime reconciliation of the two families (M). Segment M, the reconciliation, is dependent on segment L, the fight, and therefore is
parenthetically subordinate to it. The dash following segment M
functions as an ellipsis, representing a two-year leap forward in
time to the Burdens' (and subsequently Ántonia's) move into Black
Hawk (N). Interspersed throughout the chronologically ordered segments of this grouping are several analepses, O, P, and Q. The
first, whose extent covers an unspecified period of time, is the
story of Lena Lingard's life tending cattle on her parents' farm
(O). Ántonia's story of the tramp's suicide the previous summer (P) represents a second analepsis of very limited extent. The
third analepsis is the story relating Blind d'Arnault's musical
brilliance as a child (Q). The extent of this analepsis is undetermined as is its reach into the past, and so it is catalogued into
the same chronological position as the two Russians' background
story. This analepsis concludes when Blind d'Arnault hears the
hired girls dancing to his music in an adjoining room (R). The
young people continue to dance throughout the spring, summer, and
autumn of that year, first in the Vannis' dance pavilion and then at
the Firemen's Hall. The beginning of Jim's sexual awakening also
occurs during this period of time with his erotic dreams about Lena
(S). These dreams serve as a subordinate segment to the preceding
one. This cluster of segments concludes with two chronologically
sequential passages, each of which illustrates Jim's growing sexual

awareness: His picnic with the hired girls (T) and Wick Cutter's attempted rape of Ántonia (U).

An ellipsis replacing an unspecified but brief amount of time bridges the conclusion of the second grouping of segments and the intradiegetic narrator's introduction to the third. That reflective overview of his first year-and-a-half of college life (V) precedes young metadiegetic Jim's romance with Lena (W). A dash, representing an ellipsis, indicates the passage of two years and links the end of Jim's romance and his return to Black Hawk after graduation from Harvard (X). The only major prolepsis (Y)--an account of Tiny Soderball's life for an unspecified number of years into the future--is followed by one last analepsis. The Widow Steavens relates to the metadiegetic character Jim the details of Ántonia's seduction, pregnancy, and the birth of her first daughter (Z)--events which reach two years into the past and extend for approximately one year. Jim and Ántonia's reunion (AA) and Jim's promise to return serve both to bring the narrative back to the metadiegetic character Jim's present and to conclude this cluster of segments.

An ellipsis of twenty years links the third and fourth groupings of segments. This last grouping is preceded by intradiegetic narrator Jim's expression of remorse at having failed to visit Ántonia and his hesitation to do so for fear of finding his childhood friend a broken, old woman (BB). As indicated by the hyphen, the final two segments are chronologically sequential. Both metadiegetic Jim's visit with Ántonia and her family (CC) and then his walk along the old, familiar farm road outside Black Hawk (DD) occupy temporal positions in intradiegetic narrator Jim's very recent past. Indeed, these concluding passages lead sequentially back to Jim's act of writing his memoirs as initially depicted in the "Introduction." The synthesized formula appears as follows:

A24 (B23) C25 [D2-E3-F4-G6-H7 (I1)-J8]

K23 [L9-(M10)--N11 (O5)-(P12)-(Q1) R13 (S13^1) (T14-U15)]--

V23 [W16--X18 (Y20) (Z17) AA19]--

BB23 [CC21-DD22]

The effect of the subordinate anachronies--several analepses and a prolepsis--within the four major clusters of narrative segments does not disrupt the basic chronological sequence of segments. The retrospective frame and the interspersed returns to the narrator's present emphasize the overall retrospective design and reflective quality of the novel. Such returns also suggest the important role that Jim's childhood, adolescence, and young adulthood play in his present life. Further, the several analepses that reach twenty-five to fifty years beyond Jim's childhood into the distant past reflect the significance that the historical past has for Jim as both a child and as an adult.

Throughout his manuscript, Jim's act of focalization and narration as intradiegetic narrator and as metadiegetic character remain distinct. Always subject to the code of internal focalization, the restrictive boundaries of his field of vision vary according to the shifts in focus between Jim as narrator and Jim as character. When the narrative focus is through the metadiegetic character's eyes, the vision is even more restricted than when it is through the intradiegetic narrator's eyes, for the character has access to considerably less information and experience than the narrator.

Throughout **My Ántonia**, the narrative perspective shifts between the focus of the young, metadiegetic character Jim at various stages of life and that of Jim as the middle-aged, intradiegetic narrator. The resulting patterns of shifts in perspective create both an array of gradations within the limited scope of the internal focalization and subtle blendings of the narrative discourse. Nearly all of the events and characters in Jim's memoirs are envisioned and depicted from these two perspectives, each marked by different attributes as well as by different levels of experience and knowledge.

This pattern of shifting narrative foci is most obvious in a number of major events throughout the first three books. For example, when returning home after a borrowing a spade from Russian Peter, ten-year-old Jim and fourteen-year-old Ántonia stop to explore the prairie-dog town. While examining a particularly large hole, Jim encounters his first great adventure. Sentences and clauses in which the narrator's énonciation is present are emphasized by the the bolder typeface:

I was walking backward, in a crouching position, when I heard Ántonia scream. She was standing opposite me and shouting something in Bohemian. I whirled round, and there, on one of the dry gravel beds, was the biggest snake I had ever seen. . . . When I turned, he was lying in long loose waves, like a letter "W." He twitched and began to coil slowly. **He was not merely a snake, I thought-- he was a circus monstrosity. His abominable muscularity, his loathsome fluid motion, somehow made me sick. He was as thick as my leg, looked as if millstones couldn't crush the disgusting vitality out of him.** He lifted his hideous little head, and rattled. **I didn't run because I didn't think of**

it--if my back had been against a stone wall, I couldn't have
felt more cornered. I saw his coils tighten--now he would
spring, spring his length, I remembered. I ran up and drove
at his head with my spade, struck him fairly across the neck,
and in a minute he was all about my feet in loops. I struck
him now from hate. Ántonia, barefooted as she was, ran up
behind me. Even after I had pounded his ugly head flat, his
body kept on coiling and winding, doubling and falling back
on itself. I walked away and turned my back. I felt seasick.
(pp. 45-6)

One senses a subtle interweaving of foci throughout the narrative of
this adventure. The initial sighting of the rattler and the metadiegetic characters' actions are presented from the perspective of
the participating youngster Jim. The description of the snake as he
coils to strike suggests a slightly increased distance between the
events transpiring under the gaze of the children and the narration
of them. This descriptive pause and the self-reflective moment--
that the snake "somehow made me sick"--hint at a shift in focus from
the young character to the older, intradiegetic narrator. The word
"somehow" here functions as an indicator of the narrator's énonciation. The focus then returns to the participating metadiegetic
youngster's perspective: "He lifted his hideous little head, and
rattled." Following this indication of the rattler's imminent attack, the focus again shifts briefly. Inserted retrospectively from
the adult narrator's more distant stance is the explanation of why
he did not run from the snake poised to attack. These explanatory
and self-reflective pauses suggest a storyteller's perspective
rather than that of a petrified boy, who, in the middle of an open
prairie feels too trapped to flee. Following this momentary shift,
the narrative focus is again through the eyes of the young, metadiegetic character as he hacks the snake to death. The focus remains

with young Jim in a reflective moment after he kills the snake: "I walked away and turned my back. I felt seasick." Unlike the previous admission of feeling sick, when the narrator's intradiegetic presence is marked by the indicator "somehow," this second admission is not. Rather, this moment of reflection is one in a series of actions performed by young Jim and depicted from his perspective.

The focus continues to shift almost imperceptibly during the ensuing conversation with Ántonia. The immediacy of the participating metadiegetic characters' presence is emphasized by the mimetic speech that imitates both the syntax and the sound of Ántonia's Bohemian-accented English: "'You is just like big mans,'" and "'this kawn-tree.'" The slang and aggravated tone of ten-year-old Jim is also evident. Again, the boldface print signals the presence of the intradiegetic narrator's énonciation:

Ántonia came after me, crying, "O Jimmy, he not bite you? Why you not run when I say?"

"What you jabber Bohunk for? You might have told me there was a snake behind me!" I said petulantly.

"I know I am just awful, Jim, I was so scared." She took my handkerchief from my pocket and tried to wipe my face with it, but I snatched it away from her. [1] **I suppose I looked as sick as I felt.**

"I never know you was so brave, Jim," she went on comfortingly. "You is just like big mans; you wait for him lift his head and then you go for him. Ain't you feel scared a bit? Now we take that snake home and show everybody. Nobody ain't seen in this kawn-tree so big snake like you kill."

[2] **She went on in this strain until I began to think that I had longed for this opportunity and had hailed it with joy.** Cautiously we went back to the snake. . . . (pp. 46-7)

The narrator's presence is interspersed throughout this dialogue. The narrative focus shifts the first time from the perspective of young Jim as the reflective, older narrator attempts to explain why Ántonia wipes Jim's face. The focus shifts a second time to the retrospectively positioned narrator for a brief, highly narratized summary of Ántonia's compliments and the youngster Jim's reaction. The narrator's presence here is also signaled by the exaggerated, ironic tone of the sentence. But the narrative focus is again located from the young character Jim's perspective when the two children begin their examination of the snake:

A faint fetid smell came from him, and a thread of green liquid oozed from his crushed head.

"Look, Tony, that's his poison," I said. . . .

We pulled him out straight and measured him by my riding-quirt; he was about five and a half feet long. He had twelve rattles, but they were broken off before they began to taper, so I insisted that he must once have had twenty-four. I explained to Ántonia how this meant that he was twenty-four years old, that he must have been there when white men first came, left on from buffalo and Indian times. As I turned him over, I began to feel proud of him, to have a kind of respect for his age and size. He seemed like the ancient, eldest Evil. Certainly his kind have left horrible unconscious memories in all warm-blooded life. When we dragged him down into the draw, Dude sprang off his tether and shivered all over--wouldn't let us come near him. (p. 47)

At the outset, the closeness between young metadiegetic Jim's narrative focus and the children's actions is emphasized by his mimetic speech. A series of actions follows this one instance of imitated speech, and the subsequent speech is all narratized and indirect, presented as additional actions undertaken by the young character Jim. As a result, the distance between the depicted occurrences and the narrative focus gradually widens. Although the narrative perspective is from young, metadiegetic Jim's eyes, there is not quite the same sense of character presentness and immediacy that is achieved by the mimetic speech in previous parts of the episode. The focus shifts only briefly to the adult, intradiegetic narrator's perspective for an explanation of why the pony shies away from the rattler's carcass, an explanatory note that precedes the actual occurrence. Dude's action, however, is presented from young Jim's perspective.

As the young, metadiegetic character Jim drags the snake back to the Burden farm, we can still sense a certain distance between the narrating perspective and the depicted action. Ántonia's exuberant cries are reported indirectly. In addition, her numerous exclamations are reduced to one mention in an iterative mode: "As she rode along slowly, her bare legs swinging against the pony's sides, she kept shouting back to me about how astonished everyone would be." Jim's adult, intradiegetic perspective becomes subtly evident once more. Following behind Ántonia, young Jim begins to feel the contagion of her excitement. It is not from the child's exulted state but from a retrospective stance that the narrator Jim states conditionally young Jim's feelings of invincibility: "The great land had never looked to me so big and free. If the red grass were full of rattlers, I was equal to them all. Nevertheless, I stole furtive glances behind me now and then to see that no avenging mate, older and bigger than my quarry, was racing up from the rear" (p. 48). Although the focus returns to young Jim as he hurries home, his feelings of courage and pride mixed with fear, there is a slight sense of distance that is suggested by the iterative expression "now and then." The children's conversation with the farmhand, Otto, as they proudly exhibit their kill, reestablishes the immediacy and presentness of the scene. The mimetic speech of the dialogue captures the accents, syntax, and idiolect of Jim's two metadiegetic companions:

"Where did you run onto that beauty, Jim?"

"Up at the dog-town," I answered laconically.

"Kill him yourself? How come you to have a weepon?"

. . . Otto shook the ashes out of his pipe and squatted down to count the rattles, "It was just luck you had a tool," he said cautiously. . . . "Your grandmother's snake-cane wouldn't more than tickle him. He could stand right up and talk to you, he could. Did he fight hard?

Ántonia broke in: "He fight something awful! He is all over Jimmy's boots. I scream for him to run, but he just hit and hit that snake like he was crazy." (pp. 48-9)

Both the child's metadiegetic and the adult's intradiegetic perspectives pace this episode, an adventure that tests young Jim's courage. The two narrative foci and the various forms of mimetic and narrated speech add to the dramatic flavor, and their interweaving creates a rhythmic effect that builds to a crescendo before it subsides. When the narrative focus rests with the young character Jim, the scene has a certain immediate presence. Although there is not that same intense immediacy when the focus shifts to the adult narrator's perspective, these shifts actually serve to intensify the scenes that precede and follow them. After young Jim's initial sighting of the big snake, a descriptive pause from the intradiegetic narrator's perspective heightens the adventure by depicting his foe in gigantic and grotesque terms. It is the more distanced focus of Jim again in his intradiegetic position as narrator that subsequently intensifies the drama by suggesting that the young metadiegetic character is trapped into doing battle with the hideous monstrosity. The kill itself is presented as a scene with all the immediacy and sharpness of young, metadiegetic Jim's narrative focus as he confronts and slays the rattler. The intensity of the narrative diminishes somewhat after the kill only to increase again as the children examine the snake. Young Jim attributes a certain epic stature to the rattler by describing him as "left on from buffalo and Indian times." It is the adult narrator, however, who exaggerates the snake beyond its physical dimensions to Biblical and abstract terms: "He seemed like the ancient, eldest Evil." Ántonia's exaggeration of Jim's struggle to kill the snake also contributes to young Jim's sense of heroism. The ballooned proportions of Jim's adventure shrink somewhat with Otto's wink as Ántonia relates her version of the battle: "After Ántonia rode on he said: 'Got him in the head first crack, didn't you? That was just as well" (p. 49). The final shift of the narrative focus to the narrator's perspective deflates the dimension of the episode further, returning it to normal size. From his retrospective stance, the narrator juxtaposes this first adventure to those experiences that followed later in his life:

Subsequent experiences with rattlesnakes taught me that my first encounter was fortunate in circumstance. My rattler was old, and had led too easy a life; there was not much fight in him. He had probably lived there for years . . . and he had forgot that the world doesn't owe rattlers a living. A snake of his size, in fighting trim, would be more than any boy could handle. (p. 49)

The adult, intradiegetic narrator does not allow the episode to be viewed even in these terms, however, and completely punctures with an ironic barb any sense of heroism and glory that might have remained:

> So in reality it was a mock adventure; the game was fixed for me by chance, as it probably was for many a dragon-slayer. I had been adequately armed by Russian Peter; the snake was old and lazy; and I had Ántonia beside me, to appreciate and admire. (pp. 49-50)

The young character Jim's visit to the dying Russian Pavel with Mr. Shimerda and Ántonia has a similar pattern of interweaving narrative foci. As with the snake-killing episode, the blending of the adult, intradiegetic narrator's perspective with that of the young, metadiegetic character Jim intensifies the dramatic aura in which the narrative is cast. As Jim and Ántonia ride in the wagon behind Mr. Shimerda and Russian Peter, the narrative focus is positioned from young Jim's perspective for a description of their bumpy ride. As the children lie burrowed into the straw for warmth, silently gazing at the stars, the presence of the adult narrator's voice becomes evident in the overview of the characters' thoughts, information that exceeds the ten-year-old Jim's purview. Moreover, the reference to Russian Peter's belief in the governance of fate by the stars proleptically portends the story the children are soon to hear about Pavel throwing the bride to the wolves by starlight:

> We lay still and did not talk. Up there the stars grew magnificently bright. Though we had come from such different parts of the world, in both of us there was some

dusky superstition that those shining groups have their influence upon what is and what is not to be. Perhaps Russian Peter, come from farther away than any of us, had brought from his land, too, some such belief. (p. 52)

This shift of narrative focus to the adult, intradiegetic narrator's perspective lends a universal and philosophical tone to what is otherwise depicted by the young, metadiegetic character Jim as a discrete occurrence. The focus shifts back to young Jim as the wagon approaches the house, its dying inhabitant, and the surrounding environment all seeming somewhat eerie to the child:

The little house on the hillside was so much the colour of the night that we could not see it as we came up the draw. The ruddy windows guided us--the light from the kitchen stove, for there was no lamp burning.

We entered slowly. . . . Pavel made a rasping sound when he breathed, and he kept moaning. We waited. . . . Each gust, as it bore down, rattled the panes, and swelled off like the others. They made me think of defeated armies, retreating; or of ghosts who were trying desperately to get in for shelter, and then went moaning on. Presently, in one of those sobbing intervals between the blasts, the coyotes tuned up with their whining howl. . . . This sound brought an answer from the bed--a long complaining cry--as if Pavel were having bad dreams or were waking to some old misery. (pp. 52-3)

The narrative focus shifts briefly to the adult narrator once again to foreshadow Pavel's tale. As Pavel recounts his long story to Mr. Shimerda, the narrative focus remains with young Jim, who is unable to comprehend the storyteller's whispered Russian. The horrific nature of Pavel's tale is further intensified by Ántonia, who is able to repeat only bits and pieces of the story to her friend: "'It's wolves, Jimmy,' Ántonia whispered. 'It's awful, what he says!' . . . On the way home . . . under the jolting and rattling Ántonia told me as much of the story as she could. What she did not tell me then, she told later; we talked of nothing else for days afterward" (pp. 54-6). The narrative focus moves gradually away from the immediacy of young Jim's perspective. A certain distance is suggested by Ántonia's speech, so highly narratized that no trace of her idiosyncratic speech remains. The distance between the narrative vision and the narrated events becomes even greater when the focus shifts to the adult, intradiegetic narrator, whose retrospective stance is indicated by the temporal expressions in the final sentence: "then," "later," "for days afterward." Pavel's story itself--about the circumstances leading to his and Peter's exile from their village in Russia--is embedded in Jim's manuscript, with no apparent storyteller. It is actually retold by Jim in his role as writer and narrator, based on Ántonia's translation of Pavel's confession to Mr. Shimerda. Jim's presence as the narrator of the story is evident only once in the embedded narrative: "The groom took her [the bride] up in his arms and carried her out to his sledge and tucked her under the blankets. He sprang in beside her, and Pavel and Peter (our Pavel and Peter!) took the front seat" (p. 56). Upon the completion of Pavel's story, the focus remains with the adult narrator who relates what happened to the two Russians: Pavel's death, Peter's bankruptcy and eventual relocation to a railway construction camp. The pattern of shifts in focus differs somewhat from that of the snake-killing episode and does not conclude with the adult, intradiegetic narrator's distanced, ironic overview. Instead, the narrative focus returns to young, metadiegetic Jim's perspective:

For Ántonia and me, the story of the wedding party was never at an end. We did not tell Pavel's secret to anyone, but guarded it jealously--as if the wolves of the Ukraine had gathered that night long ago, and the wedding party been sacrificed, to give us a painful and peculiar pleasure. At night before I went to sleep, I often found myself in a sledge drawn by three horses, dashing through a country that looked something like Nebraska and something like Virginia. (p. 61)

Although Ántonia's and Jim's shared secret and metadiegetic Jim's nighttime fantasy both suggest a certain intimacy, the iterative mood created by the expressions "at night" and "often" establishes a slight distance between young Jim's narrative perspective and his secrets and fantasy.

This pattern of subtle blending of the two foci is repeated in the narration of Mr. Shimerda's suicide and burial. At the outset of the episode, the narrative focus is located from the perspective of young, metadiegetic Jim as he awakens suddenly one January morning: "On the morning of the twenty-second I wakened with a start. Before I opened my eyes, I seemed to know that something had happened. I heard excited voices in the kitchen--grandmother's was so shrill that I knew she must be almost beside herself. I looked forward to any new crisis with delight" (p. 94). The adult, intradiegetic narrator's presence is subtly evident in the second sentence with its foreboding, proleptic hint at the recent occurrence of an as yet unknown event. It is this foreshadowing that some crisis is about to be made known to young, metadiegetic Jim that moves the narrative forward. The narrative focus remains with young Jim as the events of the previous evening are unfolded to him. He does not participate in the breakfast table conversation, but only listens as

Jake and Otto recount what they can surmise about Mr. Shimerda's suicide. The details of his death and Jake's suspicions of murder unfold through Grandmother's questioning and the farmhands' responses. It is not until the other members of the household depart for the Shimerdas', leaving Jim alone with Ambrosch, that any shift in the narrative focus occurs. Presented as a summary, young Jim's depiction of Ambrosch's pious devotion is more distanced than the previous scenes. The adult, intradiegetic narrator Jim's presence is apparent by the rather paternal tone and the iterative expression "several times" in the concluding sentence, which together suggest a retrospective overview:

> After Fuchs rode away, I was left with Ambrosch. I saw a side of him I had not seen before. He was deeply, even slavishly, devout. He did not say a word all morning, but sat with his rosary in his hands, praying, now silently, now aloud. He never looked away from his beads, nor lifted his hands except to cross himself. **Several times the poor boy fell asleep where he sat, wakened with a start, and began to pray again.** (p. 99)

For the remainder of the day, the narrative focus is with the young, metadiegetic character Jim as he performs some chores and, subsequently, when he shares the empty house with Mr. Shimerda's exhausted, restless spirit.

Following the afternoon during which young Jim reveals his intimate thoughts about Mr. Shimerda, the reader can sense a widening distance between the narrative focus and the narrated events as the household returns. Unlike the previous scene depicting young, metadiegetic Jim's thoughts and the morning scene with its mimetic speech, the evening scene is marked by considerable indirect and narrated speech. As Jake relates the events at the Shimerdas' to Jim, there are only occasional lapses in the narrated speech to include in mimetic speech a phrase characteristic of the farmhand (noted here by the underlining):

> Jake and I got supper, and while we were washing the dishes he told me in loud whispers about the state of things over at the Shimerdas'. Nobody could touch the body until the coroner came. If anybody did, something terrible would happen, apparently. The dead man was frozen through, "just as stiff as a dressed turkey you hang out to freeze," Jake said. The horses and oxen would not go into the barn until he was frozen so hard that there was no longer any smell of blood. . . .
>
> Ambrosch, Jake said, showed more human feeling than he would have supposed him capable of. . . . (pp. 102-3)

The narrator's presence is evident again when young, metadiegetic Jim protests against Jake's explanation of Purgatory: "'I don't believe it,' I said stoutly. 'I almost know it isn't true.' I did not, of course, say that I believed he had been in that very kitchen all afternoon, on his way back to his own country" (p. 103).

The focus shifts between Jim as metadiegetic character and Jim as intradiegetic narrator become more prominent in the concluding section of this episode--Mr. Shimerda's burial. Jim's arrival with his grandmother at the Shimerdas' house, the arrival of various other neighbors, and the beginning of the funeral are all depicted from the perspective of young Jim, who silently observes the events. When his grandfather prays at Mrs. Shimerda's request, the focus shifts briefly to the adult narrator, who seeks to confirm the powerful and memorable nature of the prayer: "Grandmother looked anxiously at grandfather. He took off his hat, and the other men did likewise. I thought his prayer remarkable, I still remember it. He began. . ." (p. 117). This shift in focus is repeated when the narrator verifies the evocative power of Otto Fuchs's hymn: "Whenever I have heard the hymn since, it has made me remember that white waste and the little group of people; and the bluish air, full of fine, eddying snow, like long veils flying. . ." (p. 118). At the conclusion of this episode, the narrative focus remains with the adult narrator, who looks backs nostalgically on Mr. Shimerda's grave:

> Years afterward, when the open-grazing days were over, and the red grass had been ploughed under and under until it had almost disappeared from the prairie; when all the fields were under fence, and the roads no longer ran about like wild things, but followed the surveyed section-lines, Mr. Shimerda's grave was still there, with a sagging wire fence around it, and an unpainted wooden cross. . . . I never came upon the place without emotion, and in all that country it was the spot most dear to me. I loved the dim superstition, the propitiatory intent, that had put the grave there. . . . (pp. 118-19)

For the middle-aged, intradiegetic narrator, this untended grave with its tall, red grass, standing just to the side of crossroads, is reminiscent of people, a place, and a spirit out of his unrecoverable past. As with previous episodes, this final distance between the narrating point of focalization and the narrated events offers a retrospective overview of the events experienced by and depicted through the eyes of the ten-year-old, metadiegetic character Jim Burden. Unlike the deflated and ironic conclusion of the snake-killing episode and the fantasy-laden ending young Jim experiences after Russian Pavel's story, however, this conclusion resounds with nostalgia.

The major articulations in the patterns of shifts in focus in the first book suggest a movement from the romantic vision of young, metadiegetic Jim to the older, intradiegetic narrator's vision that is alternately marked by romance, nostalgia, irony, and paternalism. In the second book that pattern is occasionally reversed as the narrative focus is initially located from the adult narrator's perspective, subsequently shifting gradually to the point-of-view of the teenaged, metadiegetic character Jim. Two episodes of Jim's first winter in Black Hawk are each preceded by a descriptive overview that is factual and philosophical in tone:

Winter comes down savagely over a little town on the prairie. The wind that sweeps in from the open country strips away all the leafy screens that hide one yard from another in summer, and the houses seem to draw closer together. The roofs, that looked so far away across the green tree-tops, now stare you in the face. . . . (p. 172)

The narrative focus remains with the retrospective, middle-aged, intradiegetic narrator throughout the general overview of winter's harshness and the dull, dreary life it creates in small prairie towns and then gradually blends into a more individualistic portrayal of the young, metadiegetic character Jim's activities. The distance between narrator and narrated events diminishes somewhat with the description of young Jim's typical daily activities. The adult narrator's poetic and philosophic tone, however, continues to pervade the passage, his narrative presence also being felt by the frequent iterative expressions:

In the morning, when I was fighting my way to school against the wind, I couldn't see anything but the road in front of me; but in the late afternoon, when I was coming home, the town looked bleak and desolate. The pale, cold light of the winter sunset did not beautify--it was like the light of truth itself. . . . It was as if we were being punished for loving the loveliness of summer. . . . Without knowing why, we used to linger on the sidewalk outside the church when the lamps were lighted early. The crude reds and greens and blues of that coloured glass held us there.

On winter nights, the lights in the Harlings' windows drew me like the painted glass. (pp. 173-74)

The focus gently and almost imperceptibly shifts to the young, metadiegetic character Jim as he describes the special Saturday evenings spent at the Harlings'. Mrs. Harling would play an opera on the piano, and Ántonia would make all the children taffy and tell them her stories. The narrative focus finally settles in young, metadiegetic Jim's field of vision on one particular evening as Ántonia entertains with a new story. Embedded in Jim's manuscript, the speech of Ántonia's narrative is mimetic, although her own speech is not as markedly idiosyncratic as in the first book. While Ántonia's represented speech does not reflect as intensely her accent and Bohemian syntax, the speech of the tramp within her story is highly imitative. Ántonia narrates:

After a while I see a man coming across the stubble, and when he got close, I see it was a tramp. His toes stuck out of his shoes, and he hadn't shaved for a long while,

and his eyes was awful red and wild, like he had some sick-
ness. He comes right up and begins to talk like he knows
me already. He says: "The ponds in this country is done
got so low a man couldn't drownd himself in one of 'em."
(p. 177)

Following the conclusion of Ántonia's tale about the tramp's suicidal jump into the threshing machine, the narrative focus shifts to
the adult, intradiegetic narrator's perspective. This temporal and
intellectual distancing allows Jim to characterize further Ántonia
and Mrs. Harling: "There was a basic harmony between Ántonia and
her mistress. They had strong, independent natures, both of them.
. . . Deep down in each of them there was a kind of hearty jovial-
ity, a relish of life, not over-delicate, but very invigorating. I
never tried to define it, but I was distinctly conscious of it" (p.
180).

This pattern of narrative shifts with its movement from the a-
dult narrator's analytic and philosophically marked overview to
young Jim's specific and particular experience recurs. A descriptive overview of winter and its effects on the long suffering
farmers and Black Hawk residents, narrated through the adult, intradiegetic narrator's perspective, precedes the Blind d'Arnault episode. A summary of the the young, metadiegetic character Jim's and
the Harlings' activities during the bleak month of March occurs
prior to the episode and appears to lessen somewhat the distance
between narrator and narrated events. The iterative mode of the
speech, however, still suggests the presence of a temporally distanced narrator. The narrative focus shifts to young Jim when he
attends pianist Blind d'Arnault's Boys' Home concert. As the mulat-
to entertains his audience, the narrative focus shifts away from
the perspective of the young listener. The embedded narrative that
recounts Blind d'Arnault's childhood discovery of the piano func-

tions as a paralepsis although it does not seem to disrupt the pre-dominating mode of focalization of the text as a whole. An alternation in the code of internal focalization that marks the first-person narration, the story presents information and details about Blind d'Arnault's childhood that would logically exceed even the adult, intradiegetic narrator's purview. Although the story is not explicitly attributed to any other storyteller, it is possible that young Jim could have heard parts of it from Mrs. Harling, who had known d'Arnault for years. Details from his early childhood, how-ever, would necessarily remain unknown to Mrs. Harling. The narra-tive code for the embedded narrative thus appears to shift to that of the authorial zero focalization. It is only through the author-ial narrator's omniscience and omnipresence of this code that the story of Blind d'Arnault could include the thoughts and feelings of the blind child--known as Samson--, his mother, and the plantation mistress, Nellie d'Arnault. At the conclusion of Blind d'Arnault's story, the narrative focus returns rather abruptly to the young, metadiegetic character Jim, who is listening to the loud, crashing waltz. The focus remains with young Jim for the rest of the concert and for his walk home with Ántonia, except for a few brief shifts to the adult, intradiegetic narrator for a description of Blind d'Ar-nault as an African god, a poetic mention of the country girls, and an explanation of the origin of d'Arnault's gold watch and topaz ring.

The narrative focus continues to shift between the young, meta-diegetic character Jim when he is at the university and the adult intradiegetic narrator throughout the third book. Adult Jim's pre-sence and retrospective stance are particularly evident in the first chapter of this book, which functions as a summary of Jim's two years in Lincoln. He emphasizes his temporal distance from the nar-rated events with such assertions as: "I shall always look back on that time of mental awakening as one of the happiest of my life" (p. 257),and "I remember vividly another evening, when something led us to talk of Dante's veneration for Virgil. . . . I can hear him now, speaking the lines of the poet Stratius, who spoke for Dante" (p. 261). The iterative mode of speech also reinforces the temporal distance between narrator and narrated events: "[Cleric], too, was in Lincoln all that summer. We played tennis, read, and took long walks together" (p. 257) and "Sometimes when [Cleric] came he was silent and moody. . . . Again, he would sit until nearly midnight, talking about Latin and English poetry. . ." (p. 260).

Unlike this introductory overview of Jim's college life in Lincoln, narrated from adult Jim's perspective, the narration of the two subsequent episodes in the third book--both of which concern his romance with Lena Lingard--entails shifts in the narrative focus. Each episode begins with an overview in which the adult, intradiegetic narrator's presence is evident. The principal part of each episode is then narrated from a perspective that alternates between the young participating character and the adult narrator. The episodes each close with the adult narrator's presence evident either by his philosophical tone or by a brief, retrospective summary of events. When Jim and Lena attend a performance of Camille by Dumas fils, the event is preceded by the adult narrator's summary of Lincoln's theatrical season. Throughout the depiction of their attendance at the play and their response to it, the narrative focus shifts constantly between the character Jim, who expresses his awe at all that transpires on stage, and the adult narrator. While the young and innocent, nineteen-year-old youth experiences total wonder and empathy for the distraught characters on stage, the more sophisticated, middle-aged narrator recognizes the mediocrity of the production:

> Our excitement began with the rise of the curtain, when the moody Varville, seated before the fire, interrogated Nanine. . . . This introduced the most brilliant, worldly, the most enchantingly gay scene I had ever looked upon. I

had never seen champagne bottles opened on the stage be-
fore--indeed, I had never seen them opened anywhere. The
memory of that supper makes me hungry now; the sight of it
then, when I had only a students' boarding-house dinner
behind me was delicate torment. I seem to remember gilded
chairs and tables, . . . linen of dazzling whiteness. . . .
The men were dressed more or less after the period in which
the play was written; the women were not. I saw no incon-
sistency. . . .

   Through the scene between Marguerite and the elder Duval,
Lena wept unceasingly, and I sat helpless to prevent the
closing of that chapter of idyllic love, dreading the return of the young man whose ineffable happiness was only to
be the measure of his fall.

   I suppose no woman could have been further in person, voice,
and temperament from Dumas' appealing heroine than the vete-
ran actress who first acquainted me with her. . . .
(pp. 274-76)

The young people's walk home is presented from the perspective of
the young character Jim. As he tramps along after leaving Lena and
smells the bitter sweetness of the blooming lilacs, he mourns the
death of Marguerite, the principal character in Camille. To close
the episode, the narrative focus shifts gently, and the adult narrator's presence again becomes evident with the nostalgic tone of
the concluding sentence: "Wherever and whenever that piece is put
on, it is April" (p. 278).
   The narration of events in books four and five does not follow
the patterns of focus shifts established in the three previous
books. Although the adult narrator's presence is occasionally suggested by a change in tone or rendered explicit by references to
himself as narrator, the narrative focus is situated predominantly

with the metadiegetic character Jim. Because of the character Jim's age in each of the final books--twenty-one in the fourth book and forty-one in the fifth book--and because of his increasing worldliness and sophistication, there are less pronounced differences in the breadth and depth of the vision and understanding of the character and that of the narrator. Temporal differences do remain, however. Thus, when twenty-one-year-old Jim visits Black Hawk the summer before entering law school, the intradiegetic narrator is still able to supplement what the metadiegetic character "knows" about the lives of the hired country girls. For example, after hearing what Frances Harling has to report about Ántonia, Lena, and Tiny Soderball, the focus shifts from young Jim to the middle-aged narrator who recounts Tiny's fortunes and adventures during the years subsequent to Jim's twenty-first summer: "How astonished we should have been, as we sat talking about her on Frances Harling's front porch, if we could have known what her future was really to be!" (p. 299).

In addition to the shift in focus to adult Jim for the narration of Tiny Soderball's story--the details of which were presumably obtained during one of his visits with Tiny and Lena--the other major focus shift in these final two books is to the Widow Steavens's perspective. Prior to his reunion with Ántonia, Jim spends the evening with Widow Steavens to learn the details of his friend's seduction. Because Jim has been away at school, he knows only what his grandmother had written and what Frances Harling has added. Having participated in the events herself, the Widow Steavens is able to depict them with considerable detail. Throughout her narrative, the Widow Steavens's presence as storyteller remains apparent with such indices as: "'If I remember rightly'" (p. 309); "'The next morning I got brother to drive me over. I can still walk, but my feet ain't what they used to be'" (p. 311); and "'Jimmy, I sat right down on that bank beside her and made lament'" (p. 313). The use of mimetic speech, although lacking any of the

Bohemian speakers' idiosyncracies, somewhat decreases the distance between Widow Steavens's retrospective narrative position and the events of her story.

In the fifth and final book, the temporal, spatial, intellectual, and experiential differences between Jim as metadiegetic character and Jim as intradiegetic narrator become even less distinct. Despite their closeness in age and the lack of obvious differences between character and narrator in this last book, however, the two retain separate, unique focalizations. Jim's visit with Ántonia after a twenty-year separation opens with the intradiegetic narrator's summary of his life events during the intervening years. As the narrator, Jim also seeks to explain his failure to visit her, blaming his own cowardice and dread at finding an aged and broken Ántonia. He also credits Lena with finally persuading him to visit Ántonia. Throughout the actual visit, the narrative focus is positioned from the perspective of the metadiegetic character Jim. The only shifts in focus to the narrator Jim are during a few reflective moments; for example, when Jim sees Ántonia for the first time in twenty years he writes:

> Ántonia came in and stood before me; a stalwart, brown
> woman, flat-chested, her curly brown hair a little griz-
> zled. It was a shock, of course. It always is, to meet
> people after long years, especially if they have lived as
> much and as hard as this woman had. We stood looking at
> each other. (p. 331)

Although the focus is primarily from the character Jim's perspective, the sense of immediacy of the narrated events is not uniform. The use of mimetic speech helps achieve a certain temporal closeness of events. Interspersed throughout the mimetic speeches, how-

ever, are numerous instances of indirect (underlined) and narratized (boldface type) speech which create degrees of distance
between the narrative focus and the narrated events:

> **While we were talking,** <u>Ántonia assured me that she could
> keep me for the night.</u> "We've plenty of room. Two of the
> boys sleep in the haymow til cold weather comes, but there's
> no need for it. . . ."
> <u>I told her I would like to sleep in the haymow with the
> boys.</u>
> "You can do just as you want to. . . ."
> I walked between the two older boys--straight, well-made
> fellows, with good heads and clear eyes. **They talked about
> their school and the new teacher, told me about the crops
> and the harvest, and how many steers they would feed that
> winter.** (pp. 344-45)

This passage begins with discourse that is highly narratized (boldface type), leaving no trace of the individual speakers' idiolect
and little indication of the exact subject of their conversation.
The distance decreases slightly in the second half of the first
sentence (marked by underlining) as the speech becomes indirect.
Although indirect speech is still somewhat distanced from the character's actual speech by its lack of the speaker's idiolect, it does
approximate the substance of what is said. The sense of distance is
further diminished when the speech becomes mimetic (no emphasis added), reflecting both the speaker's idiolect and what is said. The
gradations in distance are slight, but numerous enough in this example and throughout the novel to affect the overall structure. Not
only does the narrative focus shifting between the perspectives of
Jim as metadiegetic character and as middle-aged, intradiegetic

narrator create a hierarchically structured frame, the blending of different types of speech reinforces these retrospective, as well as occasionally prospective, movements.

This interweaving of perspectives through the shifts of narrative focus is evident not only in the depiction of scenes, but also in the presentation and development of most of the principal characters. For example, ten-year-old Jim sees his grandmother for the first time as he awakens in a tiny bedroom after his arrival in Nebraska. Through the eyes of the young boy, she is ". . . a tall woman, with wrinkled brown skin and black hair, . . . looking down at me; I knew that she must be my grandmother" (p. 8). A short while later, while bathing in the kitchen, Jim describes her a second time as she hurries to rescue her burning cakes: "While I scrubbed, my grandmother busied herself in the diningroom until I called anxiously, "Grandmother, I'm afraid the cakes are burning!" Then she came laughing, waving her apron before her as if she were shooing chickens" (p. 10). Seen from the spatially delimited perspective of a child who is watching his grandmother's movements, these initial impressions are followed immediately by another, more general description that begins by noting several of her physical characteristics: "She was a spare, tall woman, a little stooped, and she was apt to carry her head thrust forward in an attitude of attention, as if she were looking at something, or listening to something far away" (p. 10). Because the first sentence of the description removes his grandmother from the specific contexts in which she was previously depicted--the bedroom and the kitchen--we can sense a transition away from the young, metadiegetic character Jim's perspective to that of the adult, intradiegetic narrator. The subsequent sentence confirms in an explicit manner the adult narrator's presence:

As I grew older, I came to believe that it was only because

she was so often thinking of things that were far away.
She was quick-footed and energetic in all her movements.
Her voice was high and shrill, and she often spoke with an
anxious inflection, for she was exceedingly desirous that
everything should go with due order and decorum. Her laugh,
too, was high, and perhaps a little strident, but there was
a lively intelligence in it. She was then fifty-five years
old, a strong woman, of unusual endurance. (pp. 10-11)

The older, reflective narrator's presence is particularly evident
in the explanation offered for the anxious inflection of his grandmother's voice, the suggestion that "perhaps" her laugh was a little
strident, and the summation regarding her strength of character. In
addition, the adverb "then" functions as a temporal indication of
the narrator's retrospective stance. At the end of this more distantiated description, the narrative focus is once again through the
eyes of the young character Jim as he dresses and sets off to explore the adjoining cellar.

Similar to his first impressions of his grandmother, Jim's introduction to Mr. Shimerda begins with the narrative focus located
in the eyes of the young character Jim:

At that moment the father came out of the hold in the bank.
He wore no hat, and his thick, iron-grey hair was brushed
straight back from his forehead. . . . He was tall and slen-
der, and his thick shoulders stooped. He looked at grandmother's hand and bent over it. I noticed how white and well-
shaped his own hands were. They looked calm, somehow, and
skilled. His eyes were melancholy, and were set back deep
under his brow. His face was ruggedly formed, but it looked
like ashes--like something from which all the warmth and

light had died out. (p. 24)

It is from young, metadiegetic Jim's perspective that Mr. Shimerda's emergence from the cave, his greeting, and his physical appearance are depicted. The adult, intradiegetic narrator's presence becomes evident through the suggestion that the hands seemed calm and skilled and the eyes melancholy and by virtue of the simile used to describe the color and expression of the old man's face. Both similes with their reference to ashes, sterility, and death also portend Mr. Shimerda's imminent suicide. Since this event belongs to young Jim's future and to the adult narrator's past, only the latter can refer to it.

The perspectives of the young character Jim and the adult narrator Jim are also both evident in descriptions of the landscape and the seasonal changes. In the following description of his first Nebraska snowfall, for example, the adult narrator's presence is explicit at the outset with his assurance as to the accuracy of his memory:

The first snowfall came early in December. I remember how the world looked from our sitting-room as I dressed behind the stove that morning: the low sky was like a sheet of metal; the blond cornfields had faded out into ghostliness at last. . . .

Beyond the pond, on the slope that climbed to the cornfield, there was, faintly marked in the grass, a great circle where the Indians used to ride. Jake and Otto were sure that when they galloped round that ring the Indians tortured prisoners, bound to a stake in the centre. . . . Whenever one looked at this slope against the setting sun, the circle showed like a pattern in the grass; and this

morning, when the first light spray of snow lay over it, it
came out with wonderful distinctness, like strokes of
Chinese white on canvas. The old figure stirred me as it
had never done before and seemed a good omen for the winter.
(p. 62)

The narrative focus shifts to the young, metadiegetic character Jim
in order to depict the changed landscape of the farm from the perspective of a ten-year-old boy whose view is limited to what he can
see from behind the stove. The adult narrator's presence is subsequently suggested by the temporal adverb, "whenever," in the overview of the great Indian circle. The distance between narrator and
narrated events is diminished with the demonstrative adjective
"this morning" that specifies a return of the narrative focus to the
young character Jim. Another shift occurs when the simile with its
artistic reference points again to the presence of the adult narrator. The focus returns a final time to the young character Jim for
his concluding impression of the circle in the grass.

The presence of both the young, metadiegetic character's and the
middle-aged, intradiegetic narrator's perspectives in any scene or
description is apparent throughout My Ántonia. These two means of
narrative focus, supplemented by the extradiegetic and metadiegetic
voices, reflect the blending of past and present, an interplay whose
effect is felt by the young character Jim and the older narrator Jim
alike. The shifting focus, the distancing and foreshortening of
perspectives, the variations in types of speech, and speech idiosyncracies, in addition to the anachronies and iterative mode of the
temporal dimension, all contribute to the hierarchical structure of
this narrative situation. The relations between these constituent
elements, their alternations and the dissonant and complementary effects of their blending generate a tension that is central to the
novel's narrative structure. The structuralist method thus provides

a means for describing the unique gradations and narrative effects of My Ántonia; the phenomenological method enables a more in-depth examination of the artistic and thematic tensions and effects generated by the narrative situation.

A PHENOMENOLOGICAL READING

When Willa Cather described Ántonia Shimerda in terms of an exotic Sicilian apothecary jar set in the center of a table to be examined from all sides, she gave rise to the critical assumption that Ántonia is the focal point of the novel. Not only have many critics based their reading of the novel on what they considered to be the author's intentions, they have, in turn, frequently found fault with the "loose structure" of the text because Ántonia does not uniformly seem to be the focus of the work. Indeed, she is only one among several primary characters in the first two books in the novel and is completely absent from the third book, "Lena Lingard." Only books four and five appear to be wholly devoted to Ántonia. It is important to note, therefore, that Cather's anecdote also implicitly suggests the significance of the perceiving subject's vision of that centrally placed jar and, thus, in turn, of first-person narrator Jim Burden's perception of Ántonia. Hence, when narrator Jim Burden himself declares his intended subject matter to include all that "'I remember about Ántonia,'" he is announcing not only that he has written about Ántonia, but that he has more precisely written "'what I remember.'" Throughout the novel, Jim makes constant reference to his memory, thereby emphasizing the significance of his act of remembrance: "I can remember exactly how the country looked. . ." and "How well I remember her laugh." It is precisely such emphasis on his act of remembrance and subsequent interpretation of the scenes and characters fixed like a succession of woodcuts in his primer which suggest that Jim himself, both as character and narrator, is the focus of the novel. Moreover, when Jim introduces the third book, "Lena Lingard," he mentions that "I shall always look back on that time of mental awakening as one of the happiest in my life." If we consider that the focus of this third book is indeed Jim's intellectual and cultural awakening, then the scenes in the first two books can, when read from a phenomenological approach, also gain significance in relation to Jim, his growth, to his increasing sensory awareness, and to his discovery of the sexual and emotional aspects of his life. The characters and occurrences presented in the fourth and fifth books can thus be seen as they depict Jim's realization of what Ántonia has meant and still means to his life. We can grasp the richness of Jim's character development and thus the significance of his evolving vision of Ántonia by examining the various types of aspects that predominate in each of the five books successively and by exploring the contrasting and often dramatic tension that emerges from the constant juxtaposition of the two distinct centers of temporal orientation: That of Jim in his role as a character who ages from ten to forty during the course of the novel and that of Jim as a nostalgic narrator in his mid-forties.

The structure of **My Ántonia** consists of two major parts: The "Introduction" and first-person narrator-protagonist Jim Burden's manuscript. Also entitled "My Ántonia," Jim's collection of reminiscences is, in turn, divided into five books and covers a span of approximately thirty years. Framing Jim's manuscript, the "Introduction" presents two separate encounters between Jim and a childhood friend. During a train ride one hot summer day, Jim offers to show his manuscript to his friend as soon as it is finished, and, months later, Jim delivers the completed work to the friend's apartment. Thus, although the "Introduction" actually precedes the rest of the text, the occurrences are, in fact, depicted retrospectively after Jim's delivery of his opus.

In the "Introduction," the zero point of spatial orientation is located in the perspective of an explicitly presented, but unnamed, first-person narrator who, in the 1926 edition of the novel, is identified only as a childhood friend of both Jim and Ántonia. During this brief introduction to the second and considerably larger part of the text, all characters, objects, and occurrences are presented or exhibited as they are seen, experienced, and remembered by this unnamed narrator. It is from the somewhat distantiated point-of-view of this narrator, therefore, that Ántonia and particularly Jim are first presented.

A chance meeting during a train ride through Iowa provides the opportunity for a lengthy conversation between Jim and the unnamed narrator. For although the narrator suggests that they are "old friends" and that they both currently live in New York City, it is also specified that they rarely see each other: "He is legal counsel for one of the great Western railways and is often away from his office for weeks together. That is one reason why we seldom meet. Another is that I do not like his wife." This initial presentation of Jim allows us to glimpse several significant aspects of his personality as both a child growing up on the plains of Nebraska and as an adult living in New York. By mentioning Jim's career as an attorney for the railroad, the narrator is able to hint at the power Jim now wields over the country that awed him when he was a young child. But, the narrator insists, Jim has used his power to cultivate and develop the land he loves so passionately, not to expose and strip it of its magic. Indeed, the two friends agree that there is an aura of mystery that shrouds the initiates who grew up in that place and at that time of the emerging West: "We agreed that no one who had not grown up in a little prairie town could know anything about it. It was a kind of freemasonry, we said." There was thus a special, but elusive quality to a childhood spent on what was for a brief time the frontier dividing the Eastern and Western portions of the country, the refined culture of the cities and the rugged unknown of the wild. The narrator singles out Jim's romantic nature as one of the most predominent and longlasting aspects of his personality: "The romantic disposition which often made him seem very funny as a boy, has been one of the strongest elements in his success." This romantic quality, the narrator suggests, not only affected Jim's vision of life when he was young, but is still evident in his adult perspective, coloring his memories and his presentation of them. The narrator of the "Introduction" also stresses Jim's skill as a storyteller and the profound influence his memory of Ántonia appears to have on his present life. For although both of them reminisce about Ántonia as a symbol of "the country, the conditions, the whole adventure of our childhood," it is Jim who succeeds in imaginationally representing Ántonia for his traveling companion: "He made me see her again, feel her presence, revived all my old affection for her."

In addition to these portrayals of Jim and Ántonia, this more "objective" narrator sketches a highly schematic portrait of Jim Burden's wife. From the perspective of Jim's unnamed friend, Mrs. James Burden is depicted as an attractive and ambitious woman who does not share her husband's enthusiastic and romantic passion for the land and the past, reserving her energy instead for a group of what this narrator considers to be mediocre painters and poets. Based on this portrayal of Mrs. Burden, the unnamed narrator is able to allude to the sterility and unhappiness of Jim's marriage in contrast to the richness and happiness of his past: "She has her own fortune and lives her own life. For some reason, she wishes to remain Mrs. James Burden."

These sketches of Jim, Ántonia, and Mrs. Burden complement the characters and the world that Jim presents in his manuscript. In this initial portrayal through the seemingly more neutral perspective of the unnamed friend and narrator, Ántonia is certainly depicted as a significant and symbolic part of the past. Yet, the unnamed narrator's remembrance of Ántonia stands in contrast to Jim's, for it is Jim alone who is able to capture the power and vitality of Ántonia and the past as he vividly represents that world. The brief portrayal of Mrs. James Burden suggests a thematic contrast between the cold sterility and discontent of Jim's marriage and his present life and the warm friendship he shared with Ántonia in the past, a relationship he has recently managed to renew. Finally, the portrait of Jim provides insight into his personality and consequently his vision both as a child and as an adult of the world in which he grew up. By juxtaposing Jim's past and present, the introductory narrator also establishes the binary temporal structure that extends throughout Jim's manuscript, creating a cohesive narrative situation in the novel as a whole. This presentation of Jim's present moment as an adult necessarily colors the subsequent portrayal by Jim of his past childhood, adolescence, and adulthood. For although his perspective of life remains marked to some degree throughout his life by his romantic vision and sense of drama and passion, his depiction of those qualities as they come to appearance through the past occurrences and situations recounted in his manuscript contrast implicitly with his present life as seen by the narrator of the "Introduction." The "Introduction" and the unnamed first-person narrator thus function to emphasize the significance of multiple perspectives to the narrative situation of My Ántonia. Moreover, by presenting and scrutinizing Jim first as a character, the introductory narrator is able to stress the importance to the cohesion of the text of Jim's perspective both as a character discovering and experiencing the world around him and as a narrator retrospectively confronting and relating those experiences.

At the outset of Jim's manuscript, the zero point of spatial orientation shifts from the perspective of the unnamed traveling companion and narrator to Jim Burden's point-of-view. Hence, all characters, objects, and occurrences are depicted as they are seen, heard, felt, experienced, and remembered by Jim. The zero point of spatial orientation does not remain exclusively from Jim's point-of-view, however. During the course of his narrative, Jim presents a number of other storytellers who relate their own tales, thereby amplifying and enriching Jim's text. In each of these embedded, or boxed, narratives the center of spatial orientation shifts to the perspective of the presented character-narrator, be it Russian Pavel, Ántonia, Mrs. Harling, Otto Fuchs, or the Widow Steavens. Although each of these narratives is technically presented by Jim from his temporal position as narrator and filtered through his memory, the occurrences, characters, and objects are all presented and exhibited as they appear to the respective storyteller.

The embedded narratives serve a variety of functions within Jim's manuscript. When the zero point of spatial orientation shifts to Otto Fuchs one bitterly cold night, for example, the farmhand takes on the role of storyteller and recounts a favorite anecdote about his ocean voyage from Europe to America in order to provide an evening's entertainment for the snowbound Burdens. Similarly, several years later, when the young character Jim spends his evenings with the neighboring Harling family, Ántonia, working then as a hired girl, adopts the role of storyteller to amuse her young charges. On other occasions she has told Jim stories about her family's life in Bohemia. And on one winter evening at the Harlings', she thoughtfully probes the meaning of life as she relates the bloody tale of having witnessed a tramp's suicidal leap into the haymower the previous summer. In addition to providing a means of entertainment for young Jim and the other household listeners, these stories--both amusing and frightening--and the young character Jim's experience of listening to them convey the sense of familial warmth, comfort, and security he feels during his youth on the Nebraska plains.

The embedded stories do not function solely to convey what Jim in his temporal position as narrator remembers as the harmony of the past, however. The narratives recounted by Mrs. Harling and the Widow Steavens to twenty-year-old Jim, who is home for the summer following his college graduation, serve to acquaint him with all

that has happened to Ántonia during his absence. For her part, Mrs.
Harling is able only to sketch the major occurrences in Ántonia's
melodramatic seduction as she, in turn, heard them from other
sources. The Widow Steavens, Mrs. Harling tells Jim, can relate all
the particulars of Ántonia's story because she was the girl's con-
fidante throughout the course of the events: "'Why don't you go out
and see your grandfather's tenant, the Widow Steavens? She knows
more about it than anybody else. She helped Ántonia get ready to be
married, and she was there when Ántonia came back. She took care of
her when the baby was born. She could tell you everything" (p.
305). Thus, when the zero point of spatial orientation shifts to
the Widow Steavens's perspective, Ántonia's story is depicted in
considerable detail with many aspects coming to phenomenal appearance. What Mrs. Harling could only describe as helping "Ántonia get
ready to be married," the Widow Steavens can portray much more
fully. Because she watched Ántonia sew her linens, for example, the
Widow Steavens is able to depict the girl's merriment and happiness
as they are manifested through her gestures and behavior:

> She used to sit there at that machine by the window, pedal-
> ling the life out of it--she was so strong--and was always
> singing them queer Bohemian songs, like she was the happiest
> thing in the world.
>
> "Ántonia," I used to to say, "don't run that machine so
> fast. You won't hasten the day none that way."
>
> Then she'd laugh and slow down for a little, but she'd soon
> forget and begin to pedal and sing again. I never saw a girl
> work harder to go to housekeeping right and well-prepared.
> . . . We hemstitched all the tablecloths and pillow-cases,
> and some of the sheets. Old Mrs. Shimerda knit yards and yards
> of lace for her undercloths. (p. 308)

This "boxing" of narrators and acts of narration results in a highly complex narrative situation composed of numerous perspectives of the occurrences depicted in the presented world of the text. The "Introduction" functions as the "presentative text" for Jim in his role as a middle-aged character and writer and for Jim's manuscript. Jim, in turn, projects the states of affairs that describe the occurrences and relationships throughout his life in Nebraska, and his manuscript serves as the "presentative text" for the embedded stories narrated by such characters as Ántonia, Mrs. Harling, and the Widow Steavens. Although these narrators ostensibly relate their stories, it is Jim in his position as narrator, who functions as an invisible, copresented narrator and who projects the states of affairs which present them in their roles as characters and narrators. Similarly, in order to be an explicitly presented character in the "Introduction," the unnamed narrator and traveling companion and the respective act of narration are projected by another, but this time inconspicuous, "presentative text." Although all the narrative perspectives, with the exception of the unnamed friend's in the "Introduction," are ultimately mediated by Jim's vision in his position as narrator, the resulting narrative situation has a symphonic unity and cohesion. There emerges a certain harmony among these diverse narrators and their perspectives as they all, like Jim, recount stories about similar motifs--events from the past, either their own personal past or the communal, historical past--in their attempts to explain or enjoy or cultivate their present lives.

We can readily see the shift in the zero point of spatial orientation from the unnamed first-person narrator of the "Introduction" to the first-person narrator Jim Burden's perspective in his manuscript. Subsequently, we can also perceive the numerous shifts in the zero point of spatial orientation between Jim and such presented character-narrators as Otto, Ántonia, Mrs. Harling, and the Widow Steavens. A more subtle distinction in perspective is evi-

dent throughout Jim's narrative on the basis of the shifts in the
zero point of temporal orientation which, during the course of Jim's
manuscript, is located alternately in the present "now-moment" of
Jim as narrator of his memoirs and that of Jim in his role as a presented character. Because he is recounting his remembrances of his
past life growing up in Nebraska, Jim's point-of-view from his temporal position as narrator is necessarily retrospective. He
focuses his perspective on the occurrences, relationships, and associations of his past. Although the unnamed introductory narrator
notes that the romantic and passionate qualities of his youth are
still evident in his adult vision, language, and demeanor, the older
Jim in his temporal position as narrator also displays a degree of
self-consciousness as a writer and an analytic ability which are not
present when the zero point of temporal orientation is centered in
the perspective of the young character Jim. Although Jim in his
temporal position as narrator is bounded to an extent by having to
rely solely on his memory, he is nevertheless considerably more
knowledgeable with a greater accumulation of experience than the
young character Jim. As an older narrator, who has already experienced or witnessed the occurrences that he is recounting, Jim
knows in advance the outcome of events and the fate of the various
characters. In contrast to the temporally and emotionally more
distantiated narrator Jim, the character Jim is bounded by his
experience of the present "now-moment." Thus, for example, when
the immigrant hired girls--Ántonia, Tiny Soderball, and Lena Lin-
gard--are initially depicted from Jim's point-of-view in his temporal position as a fourteen-year-old, he cannot know what their
future lives will entail. When the zero point of temporal orientation shifts to the "now-moment" of Jim as narrator, however, he
is able to relate what has happened to the hired girls after they
they leave Black Hawk: "How astonished we should have been, as we
sat talking about her on Frances Harling's front porch, if we could
have known what her future was really to be! Of all the girls and

boys who grew up together in Black Hawk, Tiny Soderball was to lead the most adventurous life and to achieve the most solid worldly success" (p. 299). Jim's vision in his temporal position as the young character is in a sense, adumbrated by the prospective and anticipatory nature of his focus. In contrast to the middle-aged narrator who is looking back at events that he has already lived through and is remembering nostalgically, the young character Jim is experiencing events as they occur and also looking ahead with an air of expectancy to events that he has yet to experience.

Like the rest of the characters, objects, and occurrences which constitute a part of the presented world that Jim portrays, Jim himself--both as a first-person narrator retrospectively reminiscing about his past and as a character growing up and discovering life on the Nebraska prairie--is a schematically presented personage who comes to appearance through selected, readied aspects. Indeed, Cather was well aware of the importance to prose fiction of the judicious selection of aspects, citing Mérimée's remarkable essay on Gogol in her own study on the art of writing: "L'art de choisir parmi les innombrables traits que nous offre la nature est, après tout, bien plus difficile que celui de les observer avec attention et de les rendre avec exactitude."[25] By examining the aspects through which the objects, people, and occurrences come to appearance for Jim in his temporal position as a character and in his temporal position as narrator, we can grasp the distinction between his two, divergent and sometimes convergent perspectives. Moreover, our recognition of the uniqueness of Jim's vision of life as a character and as a narrator will enable us to apprehend Jim's growth, his discovery of the significance and the value of life, and his realization of the importance that Ántonia, the other hired girls, and, ultimately, his cherished memories of the past hold for him.[26]

When the zero point of temporal orientation is situated from young Jim's point-of-view, the newness and strangeness of events and situations are emphasized. As a young boy with virtually no experience in the world beyond the confines of his parents' Virginia farm, Jim sets out for his grandparents' farm in Nebraska. Everything seems different and somewhat exotic to Jim. On one leg of the trip he sees the train's conductor as the epitome of worldly sophistication. His worldliness and mysteriousness are exemplified by the many fraternal rings, pins, and buttons he wears: "Even his cuff-buttons were engraved with hieroglyphics and he was more inscribed than an Egyptian obelisk" (p. 4). Although Jim shies away from meeting Ántonia while on the train because she is a foreigner, his curiosity is pricked later that night when he hears the immigrant family speaking Bohemian, the first time he has ever heard a foreign language.

From the beginning, Jim thinks of his move to Nebraska as a Western adventure. He fuels that expectation by reading a story of the wild West, **The Adventures of Jesse James,** during his train trip with Jake Marpole. By the time they arrive in Black Hawk, young Jim is ready to equate the Nebraska frontier with the wild West depicted in his book. This notion, in turn, colors his first impression of his grandfather's hired man, Otto Fuchs, who meets the two travelers:

I looked up with interest at the new face in the lantern-light. He might have stepped out of the pages of "Jesse James." He wore a sombrero hat, with a wide leather band and a bright buckle, and the ends of his moustache were twisted up stiffly, like little horns. He looked lively and ferocious, I thought, as if he had a history. A long scar ran across one cheek and drew the corner of his mouth up in a sinister curl. The top of his left ear was gone, and his skin was brown as an Indian's. Surely this was the face of a desperado. (p. 6)

Only ten years old at the beginning of the first book, Jim's recent arrival in Nebraska allows him to experience and to explore a
new world.   The young character Jim describes the prairie with an
eye for detail that an initiate would overlook as too familiar and
ordinary. For young Jim, however, the prairie grass and the flat-
ness of the land with its distant horizon are totally unfamiliar.
He, in turn, conveys what is for him the strangeness of the prairie
with its oddly-colored grass by comparing it to the ocean, thereby
metaphorically defamiliarizing the scene: "As I looked about me I
felt that the grass was the country, as the water is the sea. The
red of the grass made all the great prairie the colour of wine-
stains, or of certain seaweeds when they are first washed up. And
there was so much motion in it; the whole country seemed, somehow,
to be running" (p. 15). Jim finds the countryside much different
from the familiar mountain range of Virginia. The vast openness
and slight undulation of the land give him the sense of being outside the world altogether, not just beyond his familiar Virginia.
He feels lost, erased from the face of the earth as if "the world
was left behind, that we had got over the edge of it, and were outside man's jurisdiction" (p. 7). The land is very important to Jim,
and in this natural world he gives free reign to his sensory perception. Not only does he perceive this world in a fresh and novel
way, he experiences it sensorially. In the following passage, for
example, he feels the earth's warm soil and, like the vegetables
around him, he bakes under the sun's strong rays. He presents aspects of his experience which exhibit phenomenal qualities perceptible to the reader. We, too, can visualize and feel his grandmother's garden and the warmth of the sun:

I sat down in the middle of the garden, where snakes could
scarcely approach unseen, and leaned my back against a

warm yellow pumpkin. . . . There in the sheltered draw-
bottom the wind did not blow very hard, but I could hear
it singing its humming tune up on the level, and I could
see the tall grasses wave. The earth was warm under me,
and warm as I crumbled it through my fingers. Queer little
red bugs came out and moved in slow squadrons around me.
Their backs were polished vermilion, with black spots. I
kept as still as I could. Nothing happened. I did not
expect anything to happen. I was something that lay under
the sun and felt it, like the pumpkins, and I did not want
to be anything more. (pp. 17-8)

This emphasis of focus on the exotic newness and strangeness of
his life in Nebraska, coupled with his sense of displacement, are
indicative of the romantic disposition of young Jim's character.
Acting as a filter, this disposition colors his vision. Jim also
views events in a disproportionate manner because he is situated so
close in time to those occurrences and because his bounded focus
denies him a complete understanding of what is happening around him.
Thus, events narrated in the first book frequently gain an epic
stature and are depicted from young Jim's perspective in language
that features heroic, Biblical, and exotic terms--a style that
further establishes his romantic nature.

Ordinary, everyday events fill the young character Jim with
wonder. As he listens to the evening Bible reading for the first
time, he is awed by the quality and intonation of his grandfather's
voice: "His voice was so sympathetic and he read so interestingly
that I wished he had chosen one of my favorite chapters in the Book
of Kings. I was awed by his intonation of the word 'Selah.' . . .
I had no idea what the word meant; perhaps [Grandfather] had not.
But, as he uttered it, it became oracular, the most sacred of words"
(p. 13). The young character Jim finds adventure everywhere. He

even visualizes the autumn landscape in Biblical as well as heroic terms:

> As far as we could see, the miles of copper-red grass
> were drenched in sunlight that was stronger and fiercer
> than at any other time of the day. . . . The whole
> prairie was like the bush that burned with fire and was
> not consumed. That hour always had the exultation of
> victory, of triumphant ending, like a hero's death--
> heroes who died young and gloriously. (p. 40)

Jim's sense of adventure extends to seeing Otto, Jake, and his grandfather as Arctic explorers during the winter months as they perform their daily chores (p. 65). Indeed, young Jim believes that the adventures of his first Nebraska winter outshine those experienced by the Swiss Family Robinson (p. 66) and Robinson Crusoe (p. 100), their lives being dull in comparison.

A visit with Ántonia to their neighbors Pavel and Peter is all the more exciting precisely because they are from Russia, they have unpronounceable last names, and they speak what is for Jim an incomprehensible, exotic language:

> . . . one of them was a wild-looking fellow and I was a
> little afraid of him. Russia seemed to me more remote
> than any other country--farther away than China, almost
> as far as the North Pole. Of all the strange, uprooted
> people among the first settlers, those two men were the
> strangest and the most aloof. Their last names were
> unpronounceable, so they were called Pavel and Peter.
> (p. 33)

A second visit with Ántonia and Mr. Shimerda to their Russian neighbors takes on the stature of an adventure because of the way in
which young Jim experiences and perceives sensorially the long wagon
ride and the actual visit:

> After the sun sank, a cold wind sprang up and moaned over
> the prairie. If this turn in the weather had come sooner,
> I should not have got away. We burrowed down in the straw
> and curled up close together, watching the angry red die
> out of the west and the stars begin to shine in the clear,
> windy sky. Peter kept sighing and groaning. (p. 52)

Jim's feeling of adventure and drama is heightened by his sensory
perception of the coldness of the wind as it penetrates his clothing. Coupled with the Russian man's anxious groans, the eerie moaning of the wind is the only noise that punctuates the children's silence as they huddle together in the back of the wagon. The young
boy's excitement is further intensified no doubt by the realization
that had the weather worsened any earlier, it would have prevented
his trip. Finally, young Jim's vision of first the angry coloration of the sky and subsequently the faraway brightness of the stars
enhances his anticipation of what is about to occur.

Upon their arrival at the darkened hut, the boy's experience is
exhibited predominantly through aspects of sound. Although young
Jim sees the sick Russian man lying on his bed and watches the fire-
light as it is reflected on the log roof overhead, these observations are secondary to the mysterious and frightening sounds he
hears as he and Ántonia wait in silence for the adults to begin
their conversation:

Pavel made a rasping sound when he breathed, and he kept
moaning. We waited. The wind shook the doors and windows
impatiently, then swept on again, singing through the big
spaces. Each gust, as it bore down, rattled the panes,
and swelled off like the others. They made me think of defeated armies, retreating; or of ghosts who were trying
desperately to get in for shelter, and then went moaning
on. Presently, in one of those sobbing intervals between
the blasts, the coyotes tuned up with their whining howl;
one, two, three, then all together--to tell us that winter
was coming. This sound brought an answer from the bed--a
long complaining cry--as if Pavel were having bad dreams
or were waking to some old misery. (p. 53)

The sounds play on young Jim's imagination, stirring up thoughts of
the supernatural. The ailing Pavel's response to the sound of the
coyotes suggests that the whining, howling, and moaning of this
night have succeeded in awakening him also to his past. The cries
uttered by the haunted man, in turn, draw the young character Jim's
attention away from the noises that had captured his attention. Observing Pavel, Jim is overwhelmed by the sick man's physical appearance and by the smell of liquor that permeates the room; the only
audible sound now is Pavel's occasional cough:

I could not take my eyes off the man in the bed. His
shirt was hanging open, and his emaciated chest, covered
with yellow bristle, rose and fell horribly. He began to
cough. Peter shuffled to his feet, caught up the teakettle
and mixed him some hot water and whiskey. The sharp smell

of spirits went through the room. . . . From our bench we could see what a hollow case his body was. His spine and shoulder-blades stood out like the bones under the hide of a dead steer in the fields. That sharp backbone must have hurt him when he lay on it. (pp. 54-5)

Not only does the young character Jim observe what transpires in this scene as the dying man unburdens his guilty conscience by recounting the crime of his more youthful days. The episode is exhibited from the temporal orientation of the ten-year-old boy as he sees, hears, and smells the phenomena around him. His sensorial perception of the characters, objects, and occurrences during the wagon ride and in the hut inspire his fearful reaction and enhance his sense of dramatic anticipation and adventure. The variety of different sensorial aspects, in turn, creates a patchwork or symphonic effect as the young boy Jim, with an admittedly romantic bent to his vision of life, cultivates his sense of drama with all possible types of sensory data.

The scenes depicting his interaction with Ántonia in the first book also convey the innocence of the ten-year-old boy who is exploring and discovering his own life and the life around him. His relationship with Ántonia is a part of his growing awareness of himself and the world and thus how he perceives it. Jim becomes aware of the comfort and vitality that Ántonia offers him with her friendship as they explore the wonders of the prairie world together, as the following incident with the grasshopper illustrates. It takes a child's intuitive and fresh perception to see the grasshopper's frailty in this manner, to understand its cold and lonely struggle, and to appreciate, almost envy, Ántonia's rescue of it:

While we were lying there against the warm bank, a little

insect of the palest, frailest green hopped painfully out
of the buffalo grass and tried to leap into a bunch of blue-
stem. He missed it, fell back, and sat with his head sunk
between his long legs, his antennae quivering, as if he were
waiting for something to come and finish him. Tony made a
warm nest for him in her hands; talked to him gaily and in-
dulgently in Bohemian. Presently he began to sing for us--
a thin, rusty little chirp. She held him close to her ear
and laughed, but a moment afterward I saw there were tears
in her eyes. . . .

When the bank on the other side of the draw began to
throw a narrow shelf of shadow, we knew we ought to be
starting homeward; the chill came on quickly when the sun
got low, and Ántonia's dress was thin. What were we to do
with the frail little creature we had lured back to life
by false pretences? I offered my pockets, but Tony shook
her head and carefully put the green insect in her hair,
tying her big handkerchief down loosely over her curls.
(pp. 39-40)

Ántonia's sheltering and care of the grasshopper points to her
subsequent nurturing and "protection" of Jim five years later as
portrayed in the second book, "The Hired Girls." In the first book,
Ántonia assumes the role of a playmate and companion with whom
young Jim can explore the new world in which they both find themselves and thus begin to discover his sense of self. In the second
book, however, as the adolescent character Jim continues to grow and
develop, he begins to discover his sexuality. Sensing Jim's sexual
awakening, Ántonia seeks to dissuade him from an involvement with
the Swedish Lena. Out of a maternal kind of love, she wants him "to
go away to school and make something of yourself." In apparent
contrast to her tender care of the grasshopper in her efforts to

bring it back to life, Ántonia's gruff actions with Jim nevertheless convey her desire to protect him and her wish to see him advance in life as well as her realization of his sexual awakening.
Thus, she rebuffs Jim's more than friendly kiss and tries to prevent his relationship with Lena:

"Lena Lingard lets me kiss her," I retorted, "and I'm not
half as fond of her as I am of you."
"Lena does?" Tony gasped. "If she's up to any of her non-
sense with you, I'll scratch her eyes out." (p. 224)

Subsequently, when Ántonia sees Lena romantically running her fingers through sixteen-year-old Jim's hair during a picnic and berry-
picking expedition, she again behaves toward Jim in a maternally
protective and affectionate manner:

[Lena] began to draw her fingers slowly through my hair.
Ántonia pushed her away. "You'll never get it out
like that," she said sharply. She gave my head a rough
touzling and finished me off with something like a box
on the ear. (p. 240)

Jim's awareness of his sexuality and thus the new aspect that is
developing in his vision and perception of the immigrant girls
living in Black Hawk is exhibited by the way he dances first with
Lena and then with Ántonia:

Lena moved without exertion, rather indolently, and

her hand often accented the rhythm softly on her part-
ner's shoulder. . . . The music seemed to put her into
a soft, waking dream, and her violet-coloured eyes
looked sleepily and confidingly at one from under her
long lashes. When she sighed, she exhaled a heavy per-
fume of sachet powder. To dance "Home, Sweet Home," with
Lena was like coming in with the tide. She danced every
dance like a waltz, and it was always the same waltz--the
waltz of coming home to something, of inevitable, fated
return. (pp. 222-23)

In depicting his dance with Lena from the temporal position of his
adolescence, Jim emphasizes the sensual aspects of his experience.
He portrays the softness and the languid sway of her physical movement. He exhibits the sense of intimacy he feels with Lena by
describing the confiding look he sees in her eyes. Jim perceives
that Lena also exudes sensuality through the scent of her breath and
by the enveloping rhythm of her familiar, undulating way of moving.

In contrast to the indolent sensuality of Lena's movement, the
adolescent character Jim perceives the vitality and vigor that Ántonia radiates when she dances. Like the adventures they used to
pursue as children out on the farm, the young character Jim feels a
sense of exhiliration as though he is discovering something new each
time he steps onto the dance floor with Ántonia:

When you spun out onto the floor with Tony, you didn't
return to anything. You set out every time upon a new
adventure. I liked to schottische with her; she had so
much spring and variety, and was always putting in new
steps and slides. She taught me to dance against and
around the hard-and-fast beat of the music. (p. 223)

Much as he might wish to the contrary, dancing with the vigorous and funloving Ántonia is not at all the sensual experience with the sexual undertones that young Jim perceives when he sways with Lena. This difference in his conscious perception of the two girls also becomes apparent on the subconscious level through the dreams the adolescent Jim has of each of them after he leaves the dance for the night. Although both sets of dreams are situated out in the country amidst haystacks, his dreams about Lena are laced with a symbolic eroticism:

> I was in a harvest-field full of shocks, and I was lying against one of them. Lena Lingard came across the stubble barefoot, in a short skirt, with a curved reaping hook in her hand, and she was flushed like the dawn, with a kind of luminous rosiness all about her. She sat down beside me, turned to me with a soft sigh and said, "Now they are all gone, and I can kiss you as much as I like." (pp. 225-26)

The young character Jim exhibits Lena's physical appearance as he perceives her walking toward him across the harvested field. In addition to the sexually suggestive symbol of the reaping hook, Lena's naked legs, the shortness of her dress, the flush on her skin, and the breathy seductiveness of her voice all bespeak the sexual manner in which young Jim experiences his dream of her. Although the adolescent Jim fervently wishes to have such dreams of Ántonia and although haystacks do figure in his dreams about her, they are not laden with the same sensuality. Rather, in his dreams, Ántonia comes to appearance through her boisterous games and activities: ". . . sometimes Tony and I were out in the country, sliding down strawstacks as we used to do; climbing up the yellow mountains over and over, and slipping down the smooth sides into soft piles of chaff" (p. 225).

When Jim is in high school, he frequently focuses his attention on the immigrant girls--Ántonia, Lena, Tiny, and the three Bohemian Marys--who hire out as domestic help to Black Hawk families. Throughout the second book, his adolescent vision of these young women is colored by the exotic and glamourous aura in which he casts them. Frances Harling points out his romanticising nature to him: "'I expect I know the country girls better than you do. You always put a kind of glamour over them. The trouble with you, Jim, is that you're romantic" (p. 229). Because he views the hired country girls, and particularly Ántonia, in such a romantic way, he has tremendous difficulty coping with the reality that occasionally intrudes. Thus, when Wick Cutter mistakenly beats up Jim in an attempt to rape Ántonia, Jim responds by refusing to see Ántonia. The young character Jim's ideal image of Ántonia has been shattered by Cutter's concrete and violent recognition of her sexuality, and so he "hate[s] her almost as much as . . . Cutter. She had let me in for all this disgustingness" (p. 250).

In the midst of this romantic and idealized portrayal of the hired girls from the temporal perspective of the young character Jim, the zero point of temporal orientation shifts to the point-of-view of the middle-aged narrator. Despite his ever-present romantic nature, the adult narrator is able to analyze somewhat more objectively his youthful fascination with the hired girls. In retrospect from his temporal position as narrator, Jim realizes that girls like Ántonia, Lena, and Tiny were more real to him than were the dull and lifeless town girls. From his more distantiated position, the adult Jim remembers sensing the lifelessness of the town girls' bodies as they danced, and he confesses that when they come to mind at all after so many years, he can only envision their refined, undifferentiated faces:

When one danced with them, their bodies never moved inside
their clothes; their muscles seemed to ask but one thing--
not to be disturbed. I remember those girls merely as
faces in the schoolroom, gay and rosy, or listless and
dull, cut off below the shoulders, like cherubs, by the
ink-smeared tops of the high desks that were surely put
there to make us round-shouldered and hollow-chested.
(p. 199)

In contrast to the refined, but lifeless and unmemorable town girls,
the hired girls still appear in the narrator Jim's memories as
unique individuals, as real people, full of life and vigor:

I can remember a score of these country girls who were in
service in Black Hawk during the few years I lived there,
and I can remember something unusual and engaging about each
of them. Physically they were a race apart, and out-of-door
work had given them a vigour which, when they got over their
first shyness in coming to town, developed into a positive
carriage and freedom of movement, and made them conspicuous
among Black Hawk women. (p. 198)

In the third book of his memoirs, Jim portrays the time of his
intellectual and cultural awakening. It is during this time of his
life while a student at the University of Nebraska that Jim in his
temporal position as a character begins to understand the significance he attaches to his past and how much he values all of his
memories of that time. When the young character Jim reads Virgil's

Georgics under the tutelage of his professor, Gaston Cleric, he comprehends the full meaning the hired girls have for him. After Lena Lingard's first visit to his room in Lincoln, Jim reflects that: "Lena had brought them all back to me. It came over me, as it had never done before, the relation between girls like those and the poetry of Virgil. If there were no girls like them in the world, there would be no poetry" (p. 270). In this moment of reflection following his reading of the *Georgics* and Lena's brief visit, the hired girls achieve an heroic and, in a sense, immortal stature in nineteen-year-old Jim's eyes.

Jim's years as a student in Lincoln include more than his realization of the significance that the past holds for him; it is here that he has his first love affair. Jim's romance with Lena is conducted and depicted from the young man's temporal position in a lighthearted style, for the most part devoid of any heavyhanded sentimentality. When Jim's romance with Lena ends, however, he does present their farewell scene in dramatic terms reminiscent of the mediocre production of *Camille* which they see together: "At last she sent me away with her soft, slow, renunciatory kiss. . . . She always kissed one as if she were sadly and wisely sending one away forever" (p. 293). The melodramatic tone of this tender parting is undercut somewhat by Jim's own admission that the kiss of eternal renunciation is repeated many times before his actual departure: "We said many good-byes before I left Lincoln, but she never tried to hinder me or hold me back. 'You are going, but you haven't gone yet, have you?' she used to say" (pp. 293-94).

In his temporal position as a young character Jim seems to try to divert attention from his own romantic nature during his affair with Lena by poking fun at Lena's neighbor, the proud and aging concert violinist, Ordinsky, for his overly protective and chivalrous behavior toward Lena. Jim captures Ordinsky's pomposity by including in dialogue a few of the French phrases with which the violinist tends to sprinkle his conversation. After a misunderstanding about

Jim's intentions toward Lena, for example, Ordinsky gravely offers his apology: "'Miss Lingard . . . is an absolutely trustful heart. She has not learned the hard lessons of life. As for you and me, noblesse oblige" (p. 287). About the "coarse barbarians" and wretched state of culture in Lincoln, Ordinsky concludes to Jim: "'You see how it is . . . where there is no chivalry, there is no amour-propre'" (p. 288). Jim also parodies Ordinsky's extreme romantic character by relating his behavior over a newspaper article in terms of a duel. Incensed over what he considers the low level of musical taste in the city, Ordinsky writes an article attacking the populace for its mediocrity. He asks Jim to act as his second by delivering the challenge to the newspaper editor. Jim recounts: "If the editor refused to print it, I was to tell him that he would be answerable to Ordinsky 'in person'" (pp. 287-88). Fully prepared to defend his honor and his principles, Ordinsky declares that he is willing to lose all his pupils rather than back down. Moreover, he confides to Lena, he is forever grateful to Jim for standing by him while he was "under fire" (p. 288).

Following his subsequent graduation from Harvard, Jim returns to Black Hawk for his summer vacation. While at home, he decides that he must renew his friendship with Ántonia. Since he last saw her at the time of Wick Cutter's attempted rape, Ántonia has been seduced by a ne'er-do-well railroad conductor and has born her child out-of-wedlock. Having learned of Ántonia's fate, Jim initially expresses his bitter disappointment and tries to shut her out of his mind. She has fallen from the idealized and heroic position to which the young character Jim had romantically elevated all of the hired girls, and he believes that he cannot "forgive her for becoming an object of pity, while Lena Lingard, for whom people had always foretold trouble, was now the leading dressmaker of Lincoln, much respected in Black Hawk" (p. 298).

Jim's reconciliation with Ántonia begins in an indirect manner. He sees an enlarged, gilt-framed portrait of Ántonia's daughter on display at the local photographer's studio. This portrait, in turn, inspires his wish to see Ántonia again. Prior to seeing her in her fallen state, however, Jim stops by the Widow Steavens's to hear a tender, detailed version of Ántonia's seduction. The events of the story, as the Widow Steavens relates them, have a certain dramatic flavor: Ántonia plods home in the deepening snow, having tended cows for the day, and gives birth in complete silence; the Widow Steavens, who attends the birth, defends Ántonia and her baby against the veiled threats uttered by a sullen Ambrosch. By seeing first the enlarged portrait and then by having the events of Ántonia's life, her humility and strength of character lovingly re-counted in a story, Jim in his temporal position as character is able to elevate her once again to an almost mythic stature.

After hearing the Widow Steavens's story, the young character Jim ventures to the Shimerda farm to see Ántonia. As they reminisce over the childhood they shared growing up together and discuss their future plans, Jim relates to Ántonia that he associates her with nearly all aspects of his life and with his discovery of himself. Indeed, he sees her as an archetypal woman. The image of Ántonia's protective maternity, playing with and caressing the grasshopper, stands magnified behind Jim when, from his temporal position as a character, he tells Ántonia of her importance to his life:

"Do you know, Ántonia, since I've been away, I think of you more often than of anyone else in this part of the world. I'd have liked to have had you for a sweet-heart, or a wife, or my mother or my sister--anything that a woman can be to a man. The idea of you is a part of my mind; you influence my likes and dislikes, all my tastes, hundreds of times when I don't realize it. You really are a part of me. (p. 321)

As their afternoon together ends, and Jim and Ántonia walk across the field, the young character Jim's romanticizing nature is again evident. He dramatically pauses to compare the two of them to the sun and the moon, the two orbs they can see briefly stationed on the horizon:

> . . . the sun dropped and lay like a great golden globe
> in the low west. While it hung there, the moon rose in
> the east, as big as a cart-wheel, a pale silver and
> streaked with rose color, thin as a bubble or a ghost-
> moon. For five, or perhaps ten minutes, the two lumi-
> naries confronted each other across the level land, rest-
> ing on opposite edges of the world. (pp. 321-22)

It is not Ántonia and the other hired girls alone who achieve heroic stature for the teen-aged Jim. He also sees historical events on an epic level when he entertains the hired girls during a picnic one afternoon, casting a romantic aura over the story of Coronado's quest northward in search of the Seven Gold Cities. Although the young character Jim is unable to answer any questions about the expedition, he is able to tell the hired girls that Coronado "died in the wilderness of a broken heart" (p. 244). In his temporal position as a student at the unversity, Jim also remembers the people of his youth--Jake, Otto, and Russian Peter among others--in heroic terms: "They stood out strengthened and simplified now, like the image of the plough against the sun. . . . They were so much alive in me that I scarcely stopped to wonder whether they were alive anywhere else, or how" (p. 262).

For Jim in his temporal position as both character and narrator, it is his own heroically proportioned image of the people from his

past that lives for him, not the people themselves of whose where-
abouts he often knows nothing. They are for him like the plow left
standing in front of the sinking sun, an image that the character
Jim describes in striking terms:

> Just as the lower edge of the red disk rested on the
> high fields against the horizon, a great black figure
> suddenly appeared on the face of the sun. . . . Mag-
> nified across the distance by the horizontal light, it
> stood out against the sun . . . black against the mol-
> ten red. There it was, heroic in size, a picture writ-
> ing on the sun. (p. 245)

The romantic disposition evident in young Jim's perspective and
language also marks the middle-aged Jim's vision in his temporal
position as narrator. As both a young character and as a narrator, he casts life in heroic, mythic, and exotic terms. Yet there
is a significant difference between the two visions of life. In
his temporal position as a young man with a prospective, anticipatory vision, Jim usually observes or participates in the events
as they occur, although sometimes the larger-than-life proportions
of events seem due to the very distance between Jim and the event
as he listens to someone else's narrative. In his temporal position as a middle-aged writer of his memoirs, however, Jim's stance
is strictly retrospective. Some distinction between the older,
reflective narrator Jim and the younger character Jim continues to
exist throughout the narrative despite the character's increasing
self-awareness and the diminution in time that separates the two
temporal perspectives toward the end of the narrative. No matter
how recent the occurrences, the narrator Jim must still confront his
remembrances and then incorporate what we perceive as his roman-

ticized portrayal of them into his manuscript. In his temporal position as narrator, Jim does not focus on the newness of different types of experiences, nor does he see them as adventures. Rather, he looks nostalgically back at what has become familiar and beloved--the country, the time, the people, and the adventure of his childhood and youth. His passionate love for the West is deeply rooted in the boyhood he spent growing up on the prairie, and it is only in this way, he feels, that one can possess the intimate knowledge of the land, nature, and the life endured and cherished by the inhabitants.

Jim's retrospective gaze and act of writing often function to distantiate the events and the people of his past, affording him the opportunity to philosophize about their true significance and to situate them within a larger world context. But this does not diminish the importance of the past occurrences in the eyes of the older, more experienced narrator Jim. Indeed, in some instances, the temporal distantiation between the middle-aged narrator and the narrated events serves to aggrandize and romanticize the past to heroic dimensions. Ultimately, in the fifth book, by sharing the experience of Ántonia's family life, the character Jim, now in his forties, is able to probe the sensorial depth of his memories and virtually unite his past to his present. By hearing his past, he is able to achieve a sense of a completed self, a self whose present and past are inextricably joined: "I had only to close my eyes to hear the rumbling of the wagons in the dark, to be overcome by the obliterating strangeness. The feelings of that night were so near that I could reach out and touch them with my hand. I had the sense of coming home to myself and of having found out what a little circle man's experience is" (pp. 371-72).

This reliving of a moment from the past is experienced through the temporal perspective of the younger character Jim with no shift in the center of temporal orientation to the older, retrospective narrator Jim. On frequent other occasions throughout his manuscript, however, the center of temporal orientation does shift to Jim in his role as narrator for explicit assurances as to the accuracy of the recounted memories: "All the years that have passed have not dimmed my memory of that first glorious summer"; "I remember how the world looked from our sittingroom window as I dressed behind the stove that morning." These explicit statements of remembrance point to the binary temporal structure within Jim's narrative. In addition, they emphasize the two senses of time in the narrative structure: The apparently static present-moment of the older Jim, "the author of the memoirs," in opposition to the constantly displaced temporal moment and the unfolding of occurrences within the younger character Jim's experience of his past. Finally, these shifts in the center of temporal orientation are significant because they focus the reader's attention on the retrospective and, as a result, nostalgic nature of the narrative. By directly pointing to his act of remembrance, Jim emphasizes his own importance as both narrator and thematic focus of the novel.

In the "Introduction," Jim announces that his story lacks form and order: "'I didn't take time to arrange it; I simply wrote down pretty much all that her name recalls to me. I suppose it hasn't any form.'" When we read the text as the story of Jim's own growth and self-discovery, however, the form and structure of the narrative become more readily apparent. Indeed, Jim's act of narration is much like the musicianship of Blind d'Arnault, whose piano playing Jim listens to as an adolescent in Black Hawk: "No matter how many wrong notes he struck, he never lost the intention of a passage, he brought the substance across by irregular and astonishing means. . . . As piano-playing, it was perhaps abominable, but as music it was something real, vitalized by a sense of rhythm that was stronger than his other physical senses. . ." (p. 189). The coherence of the underlying narrative structure is not always evident, and the reader may be misled by deceptive suggestions and digressions; but, by means of his "untrained" writing, Jim manages to tell a story that has a powerful rhythm that reverberates between the two temporal perspectives and visions. Despite his digressions, Jim always returns to the true intention of the work. By revealing all that Ántonia means to him, Jim is, of course, revealing himself as he comes to know himself and his world.

Ántonia's name and all that that name recalls has, by virtue of Jim's romantic nature in his temporal positions as both character and narrator, become mythic in stature. At the conclusion of the second book--which marks also the conclusion of his childhood and adolescent experience with Ántonia--Jim describes the plow silhouetted against the sun: "Magnified across the distance by the horizontal light, it stood out against the sun, was exactly contained within the circle of the disk, the handles, the tongue, the share . . . there it was, heroic in size, a picture writing on the sun" (p. 245). Just as the sun magnifies the plow, making each of its aspects larger than life, so Jim magnifies aspects of Ántonia and the other people from his past in his imagination and in his memoirs. And just as the image of the silhouetted plow is momentarily frozen before the sun sinks, so a series of images of Ántonia and his past is frozen like woodcuts from his primer in Jim's mind. The sinking of the sun causes the plow to diminish to its ordinary size, and similarly, the mythical Ántonia of Jim's imagination returns to her normal proportions when he sees her twenty years later. Ántonia is a physically changed and aging woman; however, Jim recognizes that, "She was there, in the full vigour of her personality, battered but not diminished, looking at me, speaking to me in the husky breathy voice I remembered so well" (pp. 331-32). Unlike the plow, Ántonia has an inner vitality and a spiritual essence, which enable her constantly to renew Jim's remembered image of her. It is this image of Ántonia and of the past which, in turn, enfuse Jim's own life and his art with meaning.

6:
CONCLUSION

First-person narration is a technique of prose fiction that is particularly well-suited to **Bildungsromanen,** confessions, and memoirs, creating the illusion of intimacy between the reader, the narrator, and the presented world. As I have attempted to demonstrate through examinations of Genette's method and selected elements of Ingarden's theory, however, the first-person narrative situation as such defies strict classification as an indicator of autobiography and historical reality. The function of a first-person narrator is not to verify the authenticity of the world presented in a given literary work, nor does it guarantee the autobiographical nature of a text. Indeed, both Genette and Ingarden argue specifically that the life and times of the author remain distinct from the world presented in a literary work. Moreover, the actual author of a text stands at all times ontically removed from the projected "author" of the confession or memoirs--that is, the first-person character-narrator. Genette and Ingarden both recognize first-person narration as a technique of fiction whose effect on the literary work is much more complex and inclusive than a mere pronominal categorization of a text as being "first-person" would allow.

In **Figures** III, Genette outlines a method that directs our exploration of the structural hierarchy of a text's diegesis (story) and discourse, including its temporal dimensions, the interrelationships of narrative voices, and the effect of gradations in the narrator's focalization and speech. With its strict emphasis on enumerating the elements of the text and their variations, Genette's method provides a means of describing the literary work itself, the story and its mediation and presentation by the narrative discourse. Although the invariant core of the story must technically pre-exist its narration through a particular discourse, the story and the discourse are nevertheless inextricably linked. The story and discourse together create meaning; alone they are meaningless.

Like the structuralist method, the phenomenological method provides a means for illuminating the complexity of the first-person narrative situation. Ingarden's focus on the unfolding layered structure of the literary work of art allows us to examine the first-person narrative situations in L'Immoraliste and My Ántonia on the basis of the nested structure which results from the shifting zero point of spatial orientation and the "presentative text." In addition, the continuous relocation of the zero point of temporal orientation enables us to distinguish the particular narrative perspectives of the first-person character-narrator as he relates the story of his earlier life. The uniqueness of these two temporally distinct points-of-view is enhanced by virtue of the schematized aspects through which the objects, characters, and occurrences of the world that the narrator visualizes and projects come to appearance. Together the layers of schematized aspects and presented objects allow the reader to apprehend the peculiarly distinctive and complex binary structure that typically extends throughout the first-person narrative situation and gives rise to the thematic focus and meaning of the text.

Both Genette and Ingarden focus on the text itself and on its component parts in their examinations of first-person narration. Yet, the methods that they propose and the illuminations of L'Immoraliste and My Ántonia that result are each marked by fairly significant differences. The structuralist reading of L'Immoraliste enables us to identify the two narrative foci, that of the character Michel and that of the narrator Michel. By tracing the shifts in the different types of speech and in the focus from the character's perspective to the narrator's, we are able to describe the increasingly complex blending and binding of the two points-of-view, the narrator's more distanced stance and the character's seemingly unmediated view. Ultimately, by extending the potential of Genette's concepts of focalization and imitated, indirect, and narrated speech considerably further than he originally proposed, we are able to see the major articulations of Michel's character development. In addition, our examination of the sequential order of events and narrative segments in the discourse in comparison to their chronological order in the diegesis reveals the significant role Michel plays as narrator and confesser of his story. Michel's presence as narrator is not as evident on the macronarrative level of the text; however, a typical passage from the micronarrative level reveals the frequent presence of his énonciation. I have intentionally pushed Genette's concept of the interrelationships between the diegesis and the discourse beyond its theoretical outline in an attempt to see how what Genette has identified as the temporal, voice (aspectual), and modal dimensions affect and shape the first-person narrative situation of L'Immoraliste.

Although the structuralist reading of Gide's novel provides a description of the narrator, his narrating act, and his relationship to the story he relates, this method allows us to perceive neither the complexities of the double structure that extends throughout the narrative nor the richness of Michel's development as both a character and a narrator. By examining L'Immoraliste as a layered structure, we can perceive Michel's vision both from his temporal position as a character just discovering the world, himself, and his philosophy of individualism and from his temporal position as a narrator, constantly trying to explain and justify his actions in an effort to win freedom from the deadening monotony of his present life. Michel's perspectives as first a younger character and then as an older narrator are each stamped by the manner in which he perceives the world around him, that is, how the people, objects, and occurrences of that world come to appearance for him. Michel's egocentric perspective of life and his desire to exist strictly according to his own will, in turn, emerge from the very structuring of the sentences with their peculiar expansive and dramatic word ordering. The universality of Michel's dilemma ultimately becomes apparent by virtue of the juxtaposition of Michel's confession and his perspective to the introductory portion of the letter and the unnamed friend's point-of-view. During our "pre-aesthetic investigation" of L'Immoraliste, we are able to discern the artistic elements composing the narrative situation. We are consequently able to appreciate the resulting symmetry of Michel's visions in his temporal positions as both character and narrator as he fails to develop beyond his original egocentricity. We can also apprehend the complementarity of Michel's individualism and his companion's more universal perspective. Ingarden's method thus enables us not only to describe the significance of the first-person narrator and his act of narration; it also allows us to examine the artistically effective elements throughout the narrative situation from which, in turn, emerge the work's artistic and thematic values.

Like Gide's L'Immoraliste, Willa Cather's My Ántonia portrays the "coming of age" and self-discovery of the first-person character-narrator. In contrast to Michel's intense struggle to escape his parochial and repressive past, Jim Burden celebrates his personal past and the communal past, embracing it in his memories. As in the structuralist reading of L'Immoraliste, Genette's method reveals the importance of the character-narrator, particularly on the micronarrative level of the temporal dimension. Moreover, we can describe the major articulations of the narrative situation, how the two foci of Jim as narrator and as character interweave with the various types of speech throughout the text.

It is with Ingarden's method, however, that we are able to grasp the extraordinary richness of Jim's vision from his temporal position as a character exhilirated and entranced by the adventure of life and as a nostalgic narrator retrospectively trying to reclaim the elusive, romanticized past. By examining the artistic significance of Jim's perspective from his temporal position as narrator and as character and by exploring the changes in the way he sees, experiences, and remembers the world on the prairie--that is, how the objects, people, and occurrences of that world come to appearance for him--we can ultimately apprehend the novel's circular cohesiveness. Moreover, by noting the shifts in the zero point of spatial orientation and the resultant nested structure within the narrative situation, we can see the aesthetic beauty of a veritable symphony of perspectives as they further embroider Jim's already richly woven tapestry. Thus, my derivation of Ingarden's method illuminates the thematic signficance that the past and his memories of that time hold for the narrator Jim Burden; but it also aids the reader in recognizing the artistically effective elements of the text, and subsequently, the novel's artistic and aesthetic values.

Both Genette and Ingarden advocate liberating the first-person narrative technique from its confining and ambiguous association with autobiography and historical authenticity. Further, both consider first-person narration to be an artistic technique of fiction, one that cannot be wholly defined on the basis of a limiting and restrictive code. Both the structuralist and phenomenological methods thus prove to be valuable tools in that they direct readers' attention to the text itself. Although both Genette and Ingarden describe the components of the first-person narrative situation as it extends throughout the literary work, affecting various dimensions or layers, Ingarden alone examines the artistic effectiveness of those textual elements which, in turn, generate the artistic, aesthetic, and thematic values that emerge from the reader's concretization of the work. Although Genette recognizes the importance of discourse-generated artistic values, his critical method does not include an explicit model either to illuminate or to evaluate artistic effectiveness or thematic structure. Genette's model thus proves useful for **describing** the components of a narrative situation; however, his structuralist orientation tends to lead the reader to emphasize a reduction of the text's narrative situation to a "literary lowest common denominator." Descriptions of the temporal, aspectual, and modal dimensions of a text's macronarrative structure accomplish little more than the sketching of a rough blueprint of a building after its construction; such a picture generates a rather schematic outline of the plot. Even examinations on the micronarrative level are not envisioned to penetrate beyond an enumeration of the component parts and the interrelationship of those parallel elements in the story and the discourse.

This philosophical tendency toward reductionism prevails throughout Genette's approach. Although Genette has proposed a model that may be theoretically workable, it is a model that in practice lacks the ability to expand beyond its rather rigid, tripartite structure. The three levels of extra-, intra-, and metadiegetic narrative voices may well prove extensive enough to account for the narrative situations of such texts as **Manon Lescaut** (Genette's example) and L'Immoraliste; however, the three voices are not adequate to describe the more complex narrative situations of Genette's other example A la **recherche du temps perdu** or My Ántonia. Granted, Genette's terms allow for an easy identification of narrative levels, but the terms also leave us hanging in critical mid-air in our attempts to label and thereby identify the narrating acts and narratives of the various metadiegetic characters who become narrators in Cather's text. Although Ingarden does not label each level for easy identification, neither does his method eventually curtail the expansiveness of the very narrative situation it is being used to describe.

Finally, as a critical reader, I am left feeling vaguely uncomfortable with Genette's constant effort to establish hierarchical relationships between first the story and the discourse and, then, on the discourse level, between each of the component parts of the temporal, modal, and aspectual dimensions. Genette and his critical proponents have explained this hierarchical ordering on the basis of the model's grounding in Saussurian linguistic structuralism.[1] Yet, examination of Saussure's concept of the signifié and the signifiant reveals that the signe is composed of two mutually interdependent parts that are not hierarchically related. As a critical model, this tendency to establish hierarchies can prove dangerously naive, encouraging readers to superimpose structural gradations and valuations and thereby unintentionally to construct new and misleading meanings where none is called for by the text. Ingarden, too, speaks to the technique of embedded narrative voices and perspectives. But, in his method, he seeks to demonstrate how artistic and thematic values can emerge from the effects and functions of the nested narratives and from the shifts between the various, different centers of spatial and temporal orientation, that is, narrators whose uniqueness and distinctive peculiarities are determined by the aspects that exhibit phenomenally and existentially their personalities and their evolving perspectives.

By recognizing and seeking to illuminate the artistry inherent in first-person narrative technique, Ingarden provides us with a means of understanding and appreciating a certain mode of artistic perception and presentation. Ingarden realizes, as did the Russian Formalist Viktor Shklovskij early in the twentieth century, that:

> . . . art exists that one may recover the sensation of life; it exists to make one feel things, to make the stone **stony.** The purpose of art is to impart the sensation of things as they are perceived and not as they are known. The technique of art is to make objects "unfamiliar," to make forms diffi- cult, to increase the difficulty and length of perception because the process of perception is an aesthetic end in itself and must be prolonged. **Art is a way of experiencing the artfulness of an object; the object is not important.**[2]

My derivation of Ingarden's phenomenological model illustrates how first-person narration occupies our attention and how it can occa- sionally prolong our perception of it precisely because it is a highly visible technique. By laying bare the narrative process and narrating act, the first-person narrative situation redirects the reader's focus away from an exclusive concentration on the unme- diated presented world and to an observation and appreciation of the very mode of vision and presentation. Our recognition of the pecu- liarities and uniqueness of first-person narration as a technique of art and as a particular perspective through which the presented world of the text comes to appearance thus imparts to us a new and vital perception of life and of our own humanity.

ONE: A CRITICAL ASSESSMENT

1. André Gide recorded Oscar Wilde's remarks many years after their 1898 conversation, publishing them in his Oeuvres complètes, III (Paris: Nouvelle Revue Française, 1932-39), p. 499.

2. André Gide recorded Marcel Proust's response to the latter's reading of Corydon on 14 May 1921. The comments are reprinted in the Journal d'André Gide included in the Oeuvres complètes d'André Gide, X (Paris: Nouvelle Revue Française, 1932-39), p. 515.

3. Such is the conclusion arrived at by David R. Ellison in The Reading of Proust (Baltimore: The Johns Hopkins University Press, 1984), p. 139 and pp. 133-185, passim. Ellison credits his interpretation in part to Philippe Lejeune, Le Pacte autobiographique (Paris: Seuil, 1975).

4. Michal Glowinski, "On the First-Person Novel," New Literary History 9 (1977), 110-11.

5. Glowinski, "On the First-Person Novel," 110-11.

6. Georges May, Le Dilemme du roman au XVIIIe siècle: étude sur les rapports du roman et de la critique (1715-1761) (New Haven: Yale University Press, 1963), pp. 22-3.

7. Clara Reeve, Progress of Romance (1785), ed. Esther M. McGill (New York: Facsimile Text Society, 1930), I, p. 111.

8. Ian Watt, The Rise of the Novel: Studies in Defoe, Richardson, and Fielding (Berkeley: University of California Press, 1957), p. 13. For excellent discussions of realism as artistic technique in the novel, see Erich Auerbach, Mimesis: The Representation of Reality in Western Literature, trans. Willard R. Trask (Princeton: Princeton University Press, 1953); Roland Barthes, "L'Effet du réel," Communications 11 (1968), 84-9; and Marshall Brown, "The Logic of Realism: A Hegelian Approach," PMLA 96 (1981), 224-41. For discussions of the effect of mimesis on aesthetics and on the novel as a genre, please see Hans Blumenberg, "The Concept of Reality and the Possibility of the Novel," and Herbert Dieckmann, "The Transformation of the Concept of Imitation in Eighteenth-Century French Esthetics"; both articles are in New Perspectives in German Literary Criticism: A Collection of Essays, eds., Richard Amacher and Victor Lange (Princeton: Princeton University Press, 1979).

9. Abbé Prévost, Manon Lescaut, intro. M.-H. Deloffre (Paris: Librairie Générale Française [Le Livre de poche], 1972), pp. 1-2.

10. Claudio Guillén, "Toward a Definition of the Picaresque," in Actes du IIIe Congrès de l'Association de Littérature Comparée 21-26 VIII 1961 ('s-Gravenhae Netherlands, 1962), pp. 258-59.

11. Michal Glowinski, "On the First-Person Novel," 111-12.

12. Philippe Lejeune, L'Autobiographie en France (Paris: Librairie Armand Colin, 1971), p. 62.

13. Lejeune, L'Autobiographie en France p. 24. For further discussion of le pacte autobiographique, see Lejeune's more recent Le Pacte autobiographique (Paris: Seuil, 1975) in which he elaborates on the necessary identification by name of author,

narrator, and protagonist as a means of determining whether a given text is intended by its author to be autobiographical. It is partly as a result of this later work that David R. Ellison reads A la recherche du temps perdu as vacillating between autobiography and fiction. Other discussions of autobiography, its substance and form and its relation to fiction, can be found in Jacques Borel, "Problèmes de l'autobiographie," in Positions et oppositions sur le roman contemporain, Actes du colloque de Strasbourg (Paris: Klincksieck, 1971), pp. 79-90; James Olney, Metaphors of Self: The Meaning of Autobiography (Princeton: Princeton University Press, 1972); Roy Pascal, Truth and Design in Autobiography (Cambridge: Harvard University Press, 1960); William C. Spengemann, The Forms of Autobiography: Episodes in the History of a Literary Genre (New Haven: Yale University Press, 1980); Jean Starobinski, "Le Style de l'autobiographie," Poétique 3 (1970), 83-98; and Michel Zeraffa, Personne et personnage, le romanesque des années 1920 aux années 1950 (Paris: Klincksieck, 1969).

14. Käte Hamburger, The Logic of Literature, trans. Marilynn Rose (Bloomington: Indiana University Press, 1973), p. 313.

15. Hamburger, The Logic of Literature, pp. 73-4.

16. Hamburger, The Logic of Literature, p. 20.

17. Roman Ingarden, The Literary Work of Art, trans. and intro. George G. Grabowicz (Evanston: Northwestern University Press, 1973). In his preface Ingarden responds directly to Hamburger's critique of his theory.

18. Alexandr Sergeyevitch Pushkin, "The Captain's Daughter," trans. Gillon R. Aitkin, in The Complete Prose Tales of Alexandr Sergeyevitch Pushkin (New York: W. W. Norton and Company, Inc., 1966), p. 363.

19. Margaret Atwood, Surfacing (New York: Fawsett Popular Library, 1972), p. 17.

20. Barbara Herrnstein Smith, On the Margins of Discourse: The Relation of Literature to Language (Chicago: The University of

Chicago Press, 1978), p. 26.

21. Smith, On the Margins of Discourse, p. 29.

22. Smith, On the Margins of Discourse, p. 24.

23. Plato, The Republic, Book III, chapters 6 and 7.

24. Aristotle, The Poetics, chapters 4 and 14. For an interpretation of Aristotle's writings concerning this point, see Katherine E. Gilbert, "Aesthetic Imitation and Imitators in Aristotle," The Philosophical Review 45 (1936), 558-73.

25. Gustave Flaubert, Letter to Amélie Bosquet, 20 August 1866, published in Correspondance, V (Paris: Louis Conard, 1926), pp. 226-28.

26. Friedrich Spielhagen, Beitrage zur Theorie und Technik des Romans (Leipzig: Verlag Staackmann, 1883). John R. Frey provides an overview of the German objectivity-subjectivity controversy led by Spielhagen in "Author-Intrusion in the Narrative: German Theory and Some Modern Examples," The Germanic Review 43 (1948), 274-89. For further discussion of this narrative controversy, see Norman R. Friedman's chapter on narrative point-of-view in Form and Meaning in Fiction (Athens: The University of Georgia Press, 1975); Françoise van Rossum-Guyon, "Point de vue ou perspective narrative: théories et concepts critiques," Poétique 1 (1970), 474-97; and particularly, Wayne C. Booth, The Rhetoric of Fiction (Chicago: University of Chicago Press, 1961), pp. 10-149.

27. Gustave Flaubert, Madame Bovary (Paris: Garnier-Flammarion, 1966), pp. 269-70.

28. Allen Tate, The Fathers, intro. Arthur Mizener (Chicago: The Swallow Press, Inc., 1938), p. 13.

29. Henry James, The Art of Fiction and Other Essays, intro. Morris Roberts (New York: Oxford University Press, 1948), p. 25. René Wellek surveys Henry James's roles as literary critic and theoretician in "Henry James's Literary Theory and Criticism," American Literature 30 (1958), 293-321.

30. Henry James, The Art of the Novel, intro. R. P. Blackmur

(New York: Charles Scribner's Sons, 1907), pp. 320-21.

31. Ford Madox Ford, The English Novel: From the Earliest Days to the Death of Joseph Conrad (Philadelphia: J. B. Lippincott, Co., 1929), pp. 121, 122, and 138-39.

32. Joseph Warren Beach, The Twentieth Century Novel: Studies in Technique (New York: Appleton-Century-Croft, 1932), p. 468.

33. Beach, The Twentieth Century Novel, p. 469.

34. A. A. Mendilow, Time and the Novel (New York: Humanities Press, 1972), p. 102.

35. Mendilow, Time and the Novel, pp. 100-10, passim.

36. Oskar Walzel, Das Wortkunstwerk: Mittel seiner Erforschung (Leipzig, 1926; Heidelberg: Quelle und Meyer, 1966) and Käte Friedemann, Die Rolle des Erzählers in der Epik (Darmstadt: Wissenschaftliche Buchgesellschaft, 1965) both argue emphatically for artistic value of the explicit narrator in literature. Friedemann, in particular, asserts that the "objectivity" Spielhagen demanded was merely the formal absence of the author or narrator from the literary work.

37. Percy Lubbock, The Craft of Fiction (1921; rpt. New York: The Viking Press, 1957), p. 251.

38. Kandinsky's reaction to Monet's "Haystacks" can be found in Point and Line to Plane, trans. Howard Dearstyne and Hilla Rebay, ed. Hilla Rebay (1947; rpt. New York: Dover Publications, Inc., 1979). See also Wasily Kandinsky's seminal essay concerning the interrelationship of the arts, Concerning the Spiritual in Art, trans. and intro. M. T. H. Sadler (1914; rpt. New York: Dover Publications, Inc., 1977).

39. The Russian Formalist, Viktor Shklovskij, in O teorii prozy (Moskva: Krug, 1925) wrote of the importance of technique (or discourse) to aesthetic perception of a literary work of art. Some of the essays have been translated, including "Art as Technique," in Russian Formalist Criticism: Four Essays, trans. and intro. Lee T. Lemon and Marion J. Reis (Lincoln: University of Nebraska Press,

1965) and "The Connection Between Devices of Syuzhet Construction and General Stylistic Devices (1919)," in Russian Formalism: A Collection of Articles and Texts in Translation, eds. Stephen Bann and John E. Bowit (Edinburgh: Scottish Academic Press, 1973).

40. For examples see Wayne C. Booth, The Rhetoric of Fiction; Booth, "Distance et point de vue: essai de classification," Poétique 1 (1970), 511-24; Michel Butor, "L'Usage des pronoms personnels dans le roman," Les Temps Modernes 16 (1961), 936-48; Norman R. Friedman, "Point of View in Fiction: The Development of a Critical Concept"; Friedman, Form and Meaning in Fiction; Wolfgang Kayser, "Qui raconte le roman?" Poétique 1 (1970), 498-510; Andrew Lytle, "Impressionism, the Ego, and the First Person," Daedelus 92 (1963), 281-96; Jean Pouillon, "Les Règles du je," Les Temps Modernes 12 (1957), 1591-98; Bertil Romberg, Studies in the Narrative Technique of the First-Person Novel (Stockholm: Almqvist and Wiksell, 1962); Françoise van Rossum-Guyon, "Point de vue ou perspective narrative: théories et concepts critiques."

41. Friedman, "Point of View in Fiction: The Development of a Critical Concept," 1169-79, passim.

42. Romberg, Studies in the Narrative Technique of the First-Person Novel, p. 4.

43. Booth, The Rhetoric of Fiction, p. 150.

44. Gérard Genette, Narrative Discourse: An Essay in Method, trans. Jane E. Lewin (Ithaca: Cornell University Press, 1980), p. 188.

45. Franz K. Stanzel, Narrative Situations in the Novel: Tom Jones, Moby-Dick, The Ambassadors, Ulysses, trans. James P. Pusack (Bloomington: Indiana University Press, 1971), p. 50.

46. Stanzel, "Second Thoughts on Narrative Situations in the Novel: Towards a 'Grammar of Fiction'," Novel: A Forum on Fiction 11 (1978), 249.

47. Stanzel, Narrative Situations in the Novel, pp. 68-9.

48. Franz K. Stanzel, "Teller-Characters and Reflector-

Characters in Narrative Theory," **Poetics Today** 2 (1981), p. 6. This article is excerpted mainly from chapter six of Stanzel's **Theorie des Erzählens** (Gottingen: Vandenhoeck & Ruprecht, 1979), in which he reconsiders his seminal 1955 study of narrative situations.

49. In an attempt to familiarize American critics with Stanzel's unfortunately not very well known (but very useful) approach, Dorrit Cohn offers a point-by-point comparison of it with Genette's method as presented in **Figures III**, in "The Encirclement of Narrative," **Poetics Today** 2 (1981), 157-82. For Cohn's own recent work on narratology, see: **Transparent Minds: Narrative Modes for Presenting Consciousness in Fiction** (Princeton: Princeton University Press, 1978).

50. Franz K. Stanzel, "Teller-Characters and Reflector-Characters in Narrative Theory," 5.

51. Jean Rousset, **Narcisse romancier: essai sur la première personne dans le roman** (Paris: J. Corti, 1973), p. 112.

52. Rousset, **Narcisse romancier**, p. 91.

53. Rousset, **Narcisse romancier**, p. 91.

54. Rousset, **Narcisse romancier**, p. 128.

55. André Gide, **La Porte étroite** (Paris: Mercure de France, 1909), pp. 32-33.

56. Willa Cather, **My Ántonia** (Boston: Houghton Mifflin Company [Sentry Edition] 1918), pp. 306-18.

57. For examples, see Mendilow, **Time and the Novel**; Robert Scholes and Robert Kellogg, **The Nature of Narrative** (New York: Oxford University Press, 1966), pp. 240-82; Friedrich Spielhagen, **Beitrage zur Theorie und Technik des Romans** (Leipzig: Verlag Staackman, 1883). One of Spielhagen's chapters that particularly concerns first-person narration has been reprinted as "Der Ich-Roman," in **Zur Poetik des Romans**, ed. Victor Klotz (Darmstadt, 1965).

58. Hans Meyerhoff, **Time in Literature** (Berkeley: University of California Press, 1955), p. 21. Lubomir Dolézel provides an analy-

sis of physical time, psychological time, and sign time based on Meyerhoff's study in "A Scheme of Narrative Time," in **Semiotics of Art: Prague School Contributions**, eds. Ladislav Matejka and Irwin R. Titunik (Cambridge: The MIT Press, 1976), pp. 209-17. For further study on the importance of time in narrative, particularly as it "proves restrictive" to first-person narration, see Margaret Church, **Time and Reality: Studies in Contemporary Fiction** (Chapel Hill: The University of North Carolina Press, 1949); Mendilow, **Time and the Novel;** and Georges Poulet, **Etudes sur le temps humain** (Paris: Plon, 1972)--the English translation published by The Johns Hopkins University Press concludes with an appendix on American literature.

59.   For discussions on narrator unreliability see Booth, **The Rhetoric of Fiction**, pp. 339-74; A. A. Mendilow, **Time and the Novel**, pp. 106-12; Scholes and Kellogg, **The Nature of Narrative**, pp. 263-65; and most recently, Tamar Yacobi, "Fictional Reliability as a Communicative Problem," **Poetics Today** 2 (1981), 111-26.

60.   Gide, **La Porte étroite**, pp. 73-4.

61.   Gide, **La Porte étroite**, p. 54.

62.   Scholes and Kellogg, **The Nature of Narrative**, pp. 240-82.

63.   These examples are taken from Cather, **My Ántonia**, p. 83 and Gide, **La Porte étroite**, p. 47.

64.   Gide, **La Porte étroite**, p. 97.

65.   Both examples are taken from Cather, **My Ántonia**, pp. 28 and 83.

66.   Tate, **The Fathers**, pp. 14-5.

67.   Gide, **La Porte étroite**, pp. 61-2.

68.   For a discussion of "verbs of inner action" versus "verbs of outer action," see Käte Hamburger, **The Logic of Literature**, pp. 82-3; and Paul Hernadi, "Dual Perspectives: Free Indirect Discourse and Related Techniques," **Comparative Literature** 24 (1972), 32-43. Scholes and Kellogg, **The Nature of Narrative**, pp. 258-60; Norman R. Friedman, "Point of View in Fiction: The Development of a Criti-

cal Concept," describe the intellectual limitations of the first-person narrator.

69. For additional examples, see Mendilow, Time and the Novel and James, The Art of the Novel.

70. Lawrence Sterne, The Life and Opinions of Tristram Shandy, Gentleman (New York: New American Library [A Signet Classic] 1962), p. 40.

71. Denis Diderot, Jacques le fataliste, in Oeuvres Romanesques, ed. H. Bénac (Paris: Garnier Classiques, 1962), pp. 504-5.

72. Diderot, Jacques le fataliste, pp. 610-11.

73. Diderot, Jacques le fataliste, p. 717.

74. Otto Ludwig, "Formen der Erzählung," Gesammelte Schriften (Leipzig: Grunnow, 1891), IV, p. 202.

75. Lubbock, The Craft of Fiction, p. 267.

76. See Lubbock, The Craft of Fiction and Phyllis Bentley, Some Observations on the Art of Narrative (New York: The MacMillan Company, 1947).

77. Lubbock, The Craft of Fiction, p. 262.

78. Stanzel, "Second Thoughts on Narrative Situations in the Novel: Towards a 'Grammar of Fiction'," p. 255. See also Stanzel's Theorie des Erzählens (Gottingen: Vandenhoeck & Ruprecht, 1979) and Boris Uspensky, A Poetics of Composition: The Structure of the Artistic Text and Typology of a Compositional Form, trans. Valentina Zavarin and Susan Wittig (Berkeley: University of California Press, 1973).

79. For a succinct survey of different theories of character, see Seymour Chatman, Story and Discourse: Narrative Structure in Fiction and Film (Ithaca: Cornell University Press, 1978), pp. 111-37.

TWO: A STRUCTURALIST APPROACH

1. Tzvetan Todorov, Qu'est-ce que le structuralisme? 2. Poétique (Paris: Editions du Seuil, 1968), p. 64.

2. In Temps et roman (Paris: Editions Gallimard, 1946), Jean Pouillon outlines three basic categories of narrative situation: La vision avec, la vision par derrière, and la vision du dehors. He defines la vision as the psychological or intellectual position of the narrator in relation to the characters' psyche and to the events of the story, the manner in which the narrator perceives those elements, and the way in which he or she presents them. In each of these situations, the narrator can be an explicit or an implicit element of the story (the presented world), narrating either in the first- or the third-person.

Pouillon rejects the traditional Anglo-American classification of simply first- and third-person point-of-view, seeing it as merely a pronominal categorization that cannot adequately describe the internal and external structures that emerge from the use of a particular narrative perspective. In "Les Règles du 'je'," Les Temps Modernes 12 (1957), 1591-98, Pouillon points out the danger of describing a novel as first-person or third-person and of thereby attributing to it a set of qualities strictly on the basis of the narrator's use of "I." For a discussion of a structuralist method of examining first-person perspective, see also Pouillon's article, "Présentation: un essai de définition," Les Temps Modernes 22 (1966), 469-90.

3. Todorov's and Genette's studies of narrative perspective are, to a great extent, mutually illuminating and contain numerous references to each other's work. In 1966, both Todorov and Genette published in Communications 8 significant studies offering structuralist approaches to the examination of narrative perspective.

See Todorov's "Les Catégories du récit littéraire," and Genette's "Frontières du récit." The following year, Todorov published several essays on narrative perspective and particularly on first-person narration in **Littérature et signification** (Paris: Larousse, 1967). Genette subsequently presented an abbreviated version of his study of narrative discourse (published in 1972 as **Figures III**); see "Time and Narrative in **A la recherche du temps perdu**," in **Aspects of Narrative: Selected Papers from the English Institute**, ed. J. Hillis Miller (New York: Columbia University Press, 1971). In **Qu'est-ce que le structuralisme? 2. Poétique**, Todorov directs the reader to Genette's discussion of time, aspect, and mood in the latter's preliminary presentations of **Figures III** (Paris: Editions du Seuil, 1972).

4. Gérard Genette, **Figures III** (Paris: Editions du Seuil, 1972). In English translation, **Narrative Discourse: An Essay in Method**, trans. Jane E. Lewin (Ithaca: Cornell University Press, 1980).

5. Ferdinand de Saussure presents his concept of the sign in **Course in General Linguistics**, eds. Charles Bally and Albert Sechehaye, trans. and intro. Wade Baskin (New York: McGraw-Hill Book Company, 1966). For a discussion of how the structuralist linguistic model serves as a foundation for descriptive and generative theories of narrative analysis, see Philip Pettit, **The Concept of Structuralism: A Critical Analysis** (Berkeley: University of California Press, 1977) and Jonathan Culler, **Structuralist Poetics: Structuralism, Linguistics and the Study of Literature** (Ithaca: Cornell University Press, 1975). More recently Culler has begun to examine the relationship of what Genette terms the diegesis and the discourse to the Russian Formalist concept of **fabula** and **sjuzhet** in "Fabula and Sjuzhet in the Analysis of Narrative: Some American Discussions," **Poetics Today** 1 (1980), 27-37. Viktor Shklovskij first discussed the formal concepts of **fabula** and **sjuzhet** in O **teorii prozy** (Moskva: Krug, 1925; facsimile edition Ann Arbor:

University Microfilms International, 1980). Shklovskij's important essay on these concepts has since been translated and reprinted as "The Connection between devices of **Syuzhet** Construction and General Stylistic Devices (1919)," in Stephen Bann and John E. Bowit, eds., **Russian Formalism: A Collection of Articles and Texts in Translation** (Edinburgh: Scottish Academic Press, 1973). For a translation of Shklovskij's study of **sjuzhet** in **Tristram Shandy**, see **Russian Formalist Criticism: Four Essays**, trans. and intro. Lee T. Lemon and Marion J. Reis (Lincoln: University of Nebraska Press, 1965). For Vladimir Propp's contribution to the examination of **fabula** and **sjuzhet**, see **Morphology of the Folktale**, ed. and intro. Svatava Pirkova-Jakobson, trans. Laurence Scott (Bloomington: Indiana University Press, 1953).

6. For Emile Benveniste's discussion of subjectivity in language, see his essay, "De la subjectivité dans le langage," in **Problèmes de linguistique générale**, I (Paris: Editions Gallimard, 1966), pp. 258-66.

7. Tzvetan Todorov, **Poétique de la prose** (Paris: Editions du Seuil, 1971), p. 25.

8. For discussions of modalizing locutions as indices of the narrator's énonciation, see also Leo Spitzer, "Zum Stil Marcel Prousts," in **Stilstudien** (Munich: Hueber, 1928); Marcel Muller, **Les Voix narratives dans 'A la recherche du temps perdu'** (Geneva: Droz, 1965); and Boris Uspensky, A **Poetics of Composition.**

9. Todorov, **Poétique**, p. 46.

10. Benveniste, **Problèmes de linguistique générale**, II, p. 82.

11. Benveniste, **Problèmes de linguistique générale**, II, p. 82.

12. Benveniste, **Problèmes de linguistique générale**, II, p. 83.

13. Benveniste, **Problèmes de linguistique générale**, II, p. 83.

14. Todorov, **Littérature et signification**, p. 83.

15. Willa Cather, My **Ántonia** (Boston: Houghton Mifflin Company [Sentry Edition], 1918), pp. 86 and 87.

16. Cather, My **Ántonia**, pp. 6-7 and 17.

17. Todorov, Littérature et signification, p. 85.

18. Todorov, Littérature et signification, p. 85.

19. Todorov, Littérature et signification, p. 85.

20. Todorov, Poétique, p. 65. See also Todorov's discussion of simple and complex transformations in Poétique de la prose. His concept of simple and complex transformations illustrates on the syntactic and semantic levels the degree to which the traces of the narrator and the narrating act vary depending on the mode of discourse.

21. Todorov, Poétique, p. 65.

22. Todorov, Poétique, p. 66.

23. Todorov, Poétique, p. 66.

THREE: A PHENOMENOLOGICAL APPROACH

1. Wolfgang Kayser, "Wer erzählt den Roman?" in Die Vortragsreise: Studien zur Literatur (Bern: A. Francke, 1958), p. 90. Kayser's Das Sprachliche Kunstwerk: Eine Einfuhrung in die Literaturwissenschaft (Bern: A. Francke, 1948) is also a very helpful study of narrative perspective and the narrator's role in the presented world of the text.

2. Roman Ingarden, The Literary Work of Art, trans. and intro. George G. Grabowicz (Evanston: Northwestern University Press, 1973). Although Grabowicz translates Ingarden's term as "represented object," I use the expression "presented object" in most instances to distinguish clearly my discussion from the literary work's potential representational function, a distinction that is drawn in Chapter One. For further analysis of Ingarden's method, see Mikel Dufrenne, The Phenomenology of Aesthetic Experience, trans. Edward S. Casey, Albert A. Anderson, Willis Domingo, Leon Jacobson (Evanston: Northwestern University Press, 1973); Rudolf E. Kuenzli, "The Intersubjective Structure of the Reading

Process: A Communication Oriented Theory of Literature," Diacritics 10 (1980), 47-56; Robert R. Magiola, **Phenomenology** and **Literature** (West Lafayette, In.: Purdue University Press, 1977); and Félix Martinez-Bonati, **Fictive Discourse and the Structures of Literature: A Phenomenological Approach**, trans. Philip W. Silver (Ithaca: Cornell University Press, 1981).

3. Ingarden, **The Literary Work of Art**, p. 199.

4. Willa Cather, **The Professor's House** (1925; rpt. New York: Random House, Inc., 1973 [A Vintage Book]), p. 180.

5. For further discussion of the mode of presentation of objects, see Eugene H. Falk, **The Poetics of Roman Ingarden** (Chapel Hill: The University of North Carolina Press, 1981), particularly pp. 71-7.

6. Cather, **The Professor's House**, pp. 182-83.

7. Cather, **The Professor's House**, p. 239.

8. Cather, **The Professor's House**, p. 240.

9. Cather, **The Professor's House**, p. 240.

10. Ingarden, **The Literary Work of Art**, p. 204.

11. For an excellent and concise presentation of Ingarden's concept of the **presentative text**, see Falk, **The Poetics of Roman Ingarden**, pp. 69-71.

12. Ingarden, **The Literary Work of Art**, p. 207. In Grabowicz's translation, this citation reads "a dramatic **representation**"; however, in keeping with Ingarden's intended meaning for this passage, I use the term "presentation."

13. Ingarden, **The Literary Work of Art**, p. 198.

14. Paul Armstrong uses this concept of "points of indeterminacy" in his original study of selected works by Henry James in **The Phenomenology of Henry James** (Chapel Hill: The University of North Carolina Press, 1983). See also Wolfgang Iser for his albeit rather loose adaptation of Ingarden's "points of indeterminacy" or "gaps" as part of the theoretical foundation for his reader-response criticism in **The Act of Reading: A Theory of Aesthetic Reading**

(Baltimore: The Johns Hopkins University Press, 1978) and The Implied Reader: Patterns of Communication in Prose Fiction from Bunyan to Beckett (Baltimore: The Johns Hopkins University Press, 1974).

15. Willa Cather, My Ántonia (Boston: Houghton Mifflin Company [Sentry Edition], 1918), pp. 10-11.

16. Ingarden, The Literary Work of Art, p. 223.

17. Ingarden, The Literary Work of Art, p. 223.

18. Ingarden, The Literary Work of Art, p. 240.

19. Ingarden, The Literary Work of Art, p. 241.

20. Ingarden, The Literary Work of Art, p. 241.

21. Ingarden, The Literary Work of Art, p. 242.

22. Ingarden, The Literary Work of Art, p. 258.

23. For a very helpful discussion of "schematized apsects," see Falk, The Poetics of Roman Ingarden, pp. 89-111.

24. Ingarden, The Literary Work of Art, p. 266.

25. Ingarden, The Literary Work of Art, p. 279.

FOUR: L'IMMORALISTE: Mask of Innocence

1. André Gide, L'Immoraliste (Paris: Mercure de France [Folio Edition], 1902), p. 7. All future references will be to this edition and will be cited in the text.

2. Gide's undated letter was published in Gide's Oeuvres complètes, IV (Paris: Nouvelle Revue Française, 1932-39), pp. 616-17. The text of the letter has been widely reprinted in critical studies on Gide and his work. See, for example, Kenneth I. Perry, The Religious Symbolism of André Gide (The Hague: Mouton and Company, N.V., 1969).

3. See, for example, Jean Delay's La Jeunesse d'André Gide (Paris: Librairie Gallimard, 1956-57); in English translation: The Youth of André Gide, trans. June Guicharnaud (Chicago: The Univer-

sity of Chicago Press, 1963).

4. For examples, see Albert J. Guérard, André Gide, 2nd Ed., (Cambridge: Harvard University Press, 1969); Justin O'Brien, "Gide's Fictional Technique," Yale French Studies 7 (1951), 81-90 and O'Brien's Portrait of André Gide: A Critical Biography (New York: Alfred A. Knopf, 1953); and Martin Turnell's chapter on Gide in The Art of French Fiction (New York: New Directions Publishing Corporation, 1959).

5. Germaine Brée, André Gide: L'Insaisissable protée (Paris: Société d'Edition "Les Belles Lettres," 1953), p. 164.

6. Thomas Cordle, "Gide and the Novel of the Egoist," Yale French Studies 7 (1951), p. 92.

7. See, for example, Henri Peyre's chapter on Gide in French Novelists of Today (New York: Oxford University Press, 1955).

8. André Gide's unpublished letter to Arthur Fontaine, 8 July 1902 was originally quoted in full by Yvonne Davet in her Introduction to L'Immoraliste (Lausanne: La Guilde du livre, 1951), p. 16. Justin O'Brien also cites the letter in English in Portrait of André Gide, pp. 175-76.

9. Cordle, "Gide and the Novel of the Egoist"; Delay, La Jeunesse d'André Gide; Mischa Harry Fayer, Gide, Freedom, and Dostoevsky (Burlington, Vt.: The Lane Press, 1946); Ralph Freedman, The Lyrical Novel: Studies in Hermann Hesse, André Gide, and Virginia Woolf (Princeton: Princeton University Press, 1963); Guérard, André Gide; Peyre, French Novelists of Today; Laurence M. Porter, "Autobiography versus Confessional Novel: Gide's L'Immoraliste and Si le grain ne meurt," Symposium 30 (1976), 144-58; Vinio Rossi, André Gide: The Evolution of an Aesthetic (New Brunswick: Rutgers University Press, 1967).

10. Georges Kassaï suggests that the structure of the text in L'Immoraliste is a fairly simple binary one in "Forme de phrase et forme de récit dans L'Immoraliste," Les Lettres nouvelles 3 (1973), 148-71. Martin Turnell reads each of Gide's three récits as deal-

ing primarily with marriage and, thus, sees L'Immoraliste as the story of a failed marriage in The Art of French Fiction. Robert O'Reilly describes the novel as having a simple ternary structure consisting of the hero's maturation and decline, the Marceline-Ménalque opposition, and their effect on Michel in "Ritual, Myth, and Symbol in Gide's L'Immoraliste," Symposium 28 (1974), 346-55.

11. Gide, L'Immoraliste, p. 186.

12. Cordle, "Gide and the Novel of the Egoist," pp. 92-3.

13. Germaine Brée, "Form and Content in Gide," The French Review 30 (1957), 424-25. See also Laurence M. Porter, "The Generativity Crisis of Gide's L'Immoraliste," French Forum 2 (1977), 65-6.

14. André Gide, Journal d'André Gide, I (Paris: La Pléiade, 1939), p. 41.

15. Kassaï, "Forme de phrase et forme de récit dans L'Immoraliste," p. 167.

FIVE: MY ANTONIA: Listening to the Past

1. Elizabeth Shepley Sergeant reported Cather's comment in Willa Cather: A Memoir (Philadelphia: J. B. Lippincott Company, 1953), p. 139.

2. Edith Lewis, Willa Cather Living: A Personal Record (New York: Alfred A. Knopf, 1953). Lewis mentions that, for the time, the structure and subject matter of My Ántonia were "revolutionary" because it was not a Western novel and it did not involve a love story. John H. Randall discusses the advice offered Cather by Sarah Orne Jewett in The Landscape and the Looking Glass: Willa Cather's Search for Value (Boston: Houghton Mifflin Company, 1960), pp. 60-61.

3. This particular review was written by T. K. Whipple and entitled simply "Willa Cather." It was originally published in the New York Evening Post, December 8, 1923 and is reprinted in James

Schroeder, ed., **Willa Cather and Her Critics** (Ithaca: Cornell University Press, 1967), pp. 35-40.

4. Maxwell Geismar, "Willa Cather: Lady in the Wilderness," in **The Last of the Provincials** (Boston: Houghton Mifflin Company, 1947; rpt. in James Schroeder, ed., **Willa Cather and Her Critics**), p. 180.

5. Bernice Slote, "Willa Cather: The Secret Web," in John J. Murphy, ed., **Five Essays on Willa Cather; The Merrimack Symposium** (North Andover, Ma.: Merrimack College, 1974), p. 9.

6. E. K. Brown, **Willa Cather: A Critical Biography** (New York: Alfred A. Knopf, Inc., 1953), p. 152.

7. For examples, see Yvonne Handy, **L'Oeuvre de Willa Cather** (Rennes: Imprimeries Oberthur, 1940); Don D. Walker, "The Western Humanism of Willa Cather," **Western American Literature** 1 (1966), 75-90; Eudora Welty, "The House of Willa Cather," in Bernice Slote and Virginia Faulkner, eds., **The Art of Willa Cather** (Lincoln: University of Nebraska Press, 1974); and James Woodress, "Willa Cather: American Experience and European Tradition," in Bernice Slote and Virginia Faulkner, eds., **The Art of Willa Cather**.

8. H. L. Mencken, "My Ántonia," **Smart Set** (February 1919; rpt. in James Schroeder, ed., **Willa Cather and Her Critics**, p. 9.

9. Carl van Doren, "Willa Cather," **Contemporary American Novelists: 1900-1920** (New York, 1922; rpt. in James Schroeder, ed., **Willa Cather and Her Critics**), p. 17.

10. René Rapin, **Willa Cather** (New York: R. M. McBride and Company, 1930). See also Handy, **L'Oeuvre de Willa Cather**, p. 191.

11. David Daiches, **Willa Cather: A Critical Introduction** (Ithaca: Cornell University Press, 1951), p. 45.

12. Brown, **Willa Cather: A Critical Biography**, p. 154.

13. For examples, see Lois Feger, "The Dark Dimension of Willa Cather's My Ántonia," **English Journal** 59 (1970), 774-79; John H. Randall, III, **The Landscape and the Looking Glass**, pp. 106-43; John H. Randall, III, "Willa Cather and the Pastoral Tradition," in John

J. Murphy, ed., Five Essays on Willa Cather, p. 77; Robert E. Scholes, "Hope and Memory in My Ántonia," Shenandoah 14 (1962), p. 25; and Wallace Stegner, "Willa Cather: My Ántonia," in Wallace Stegner, ed., The American Novel from James Fenimore Cooper to William Faulkner (New York: Basic Books, Inc., 1965).

14. See, for example, Sister Peter Damian Charles, O.P., "My Ántonia: A Dark Dimension," Western American Literature 2 (1967), 91-108.

15. David Stouck, "Perspective as Structure and Theme in My Ántonia," Texas Studies of Literature and Language 12 (1970), p. 286.

16. Brown, Willa Cather: A Critical Biography, pp. 152-56; and Curtis Whittington, Jr., "The 'Burden' of Narration: Democratic Perspective and First-Person Point of View in the American Novel," Southern Humanities Review 2 (1968), 236-39.

17. See James E. Miller, Jr., "My Ántonia: A Frontier Drama of Time," American Quarterly 10 (1958), 477; and William J. Stuckey, "My Ántonia: A Rose for Miss Cather," Studies in the Novel 4 (1972), 473-83.

18. For discussions of Jim's retreat to his romanticized memories, see Blanche H. Gelfant, "The Forgotten Reaping-Hook: Sex in My Ántonia," American Literature 43 (1971), 60-82; Terence Martin, "The Drama of Memory in My Ántonia," PMLA 84 (1969), particularly pp. 307-11; John J. Murphy, "Willa Cather: The Widening Gyre," in John J. Murphy, ed., Five Essays for Willa Cather, particularly pp. 56-7; and Whittington, "The 'Burden' of Narration: Democratic Perspective and First-Person Point of View in the American Novel," p. 243.

19. A number of critics have made this assumption including Lillian D. Bloom and Edward A. Bloom, "The Poetics of Willa Cather," in John J. Murphy, ed., Five Essays for Willa Cather, p. 113; David Daiches, Willa Cather: A Critical Introduction, p. 44; Philip L. Gerber, Willa Cather (Boston: G. K. Hall and Company, 1975), pp.

25-89; Handy, L'Oeuvre de Willa Cather, p. 193; Stegner, "Willa Cather: My Ántonia," p. 147; and Woodress, "Willa Cather: American Experience and European Tradition," p. 48.

20. Brown, Willa Cather: A Critical Biography, p. 152.

21. This comment was made by Eudora Welty during the concluding seminar panel discussion at the 1973 conference on Willa Cather held at the University of Nebraska-Lincoln. The proceedings were record- ed and published in Bernice Slote and Virginia Faulkner, eds., The Art of Willa Cather, p. 232.

22. Throughout my study of My Ántonia, I will be referring to the 1926 edition with the revised "Introduction" (Boston: Houghton Mifflin Company, 1918 [Sentry Edition]). All references will be cited in the text.

23. Carl van Doren, "Willa Cather," p. 18.

24. Brown, Willa Cather: A Critical Biography raises this question when he examines the two different versions of the "Intro- duction" in the 1918 and 1926 editions. See pp. 153-54.

25. Willa Cather cites Mérimée's discussion of the technique of selection in On Writing: Critical Studies on Writing as Art (New York: Alfred A. Knopf, Inc., 1949), pp. 36-7. Mérimée's remarkable observations show that he anticipated Ingarden's theory of schema- tized aspects by half a century.

26. Richard Giannone examines some of the senses that are de- picted in My Ántonia with an emphasis on sounds in "Willa Cather and the Human Voice," in John J. Murphy, ed., Five Essays for Willa Cather; see particularly pp. 21-48.

SIX: CONCLUSION

1. Mieke Bal, "Narration et focalisation," Poétique 29 (1977), 107-127; Seymour Chatman, Story and Discourse: Narrative Structure in Fiction and Film (Ithaca: Cornell University Press, 1978); and

Dorrit Cohn, "The Encirclement of Narrative," **Poetics Today** 2 (1981), 157–82, all discuss Genette's tendency to envision the narrative structure of any given text in hierarchical terms. For other analyses of Genette's method and variations thereof, see particularly Mieke Bal, **Narratologie. Essais sur la signification narrative dans quatre romans modernes** (Paris: Klincksieck, 1977); and Shlomith Rimmon, "A Comprehensive Theory of Narrative: Genette's **Figures** III and the Structuralist Study of Fiction," PTL 1 (1976), 33–62.

2. Viktor Shklovskij, "Art as Technique," in **Russian Formalist Criticism: Four Essays,** trans. and intro. Lee T. Lemon and Marion J. Reis (Lincoln: University of Nebraska Press. 1965), p. 12. For additional theoretical discussions of modes of aesthetic perception and experience, see Roman Ingarden, **The Cognition of the Literary Work of Art,** trans. Ruth Ann Crowley and Kenneth R. Olson (Evanston: Northwestern University Press, 1973); and Francis Sparshott, **The Theory of the Arts** (Princeton: Princeton University Press, 1982).